COLUMBIA RIVER

SHEET No.1

Scale $\frac{1}{40000}$

Triangulation by R.D.Cutts and J.J.Gilbert Assistants in..........1852 and 1873-'74
Topography by C.Rockwell Assist. between   1868 and 1889
Hydrography of the Entrance from a survey by the Corps of Engineers, U.S.A. in ..1889-'90
That inside of the line from Pt.Ellice to Tansy Pt. and off shore soundings
by E.Cordell and C.Rockwell Assistants in...1868 and 1889
Astronomical observations by G.Davidson and R.D.Cutts Assists. in........1851 and 1852
Magnetic observations by G.Davidson Assist. in 1851 and W.Eimbeck Sub-Asst. and
Lieut.Comdr.H.E.Nichols,U.S.N.,Assistant.............................in 1873 and 1881
Verification of Hydrography by Comdr. C.M.Thomas U.S.N.Inspector of Hydrography

Published Oct.1890 T.C.MENDENHALL Superintendent.
Verified B.A.Colonna Assistant in charge of Office
(Date of first Publication 1870.)

LIGHT HOUSE

Name	Latitude	Longitude West from Greenwich Observatory In arc	Longitude West from Greenwich Observatory In time	Character	Height above Level of Sea	Distance visible in Naut. Miles	Fog Signals
Cape Disappointment Lt.Ho..........	46°16' 29"	124° 03' 11"	8ʰ16ᵐ12ˢ7	*Fixed White*	232 ft.	21¾	
Point Adams Lt.Ho.........................	46 11 32	123 58 37	8 15 54.5	*Fixed Red*	99 „	11¼	

BUOYS

Red Buoy to be left in entering on Starboard hand
Black   „   „   „   „   „   Port   „
Black and White perpendicular stripes_Channel Buoy
C.N. or S. signifies Can, Nun or Spar

ABBREVIATIONS

hrd. for hard   sft. for soft

Cover: "Early Morning View of Tongue Point from Astoria Waterfront," 1883 watercolor. Columbia River Maritime Museum Collection.

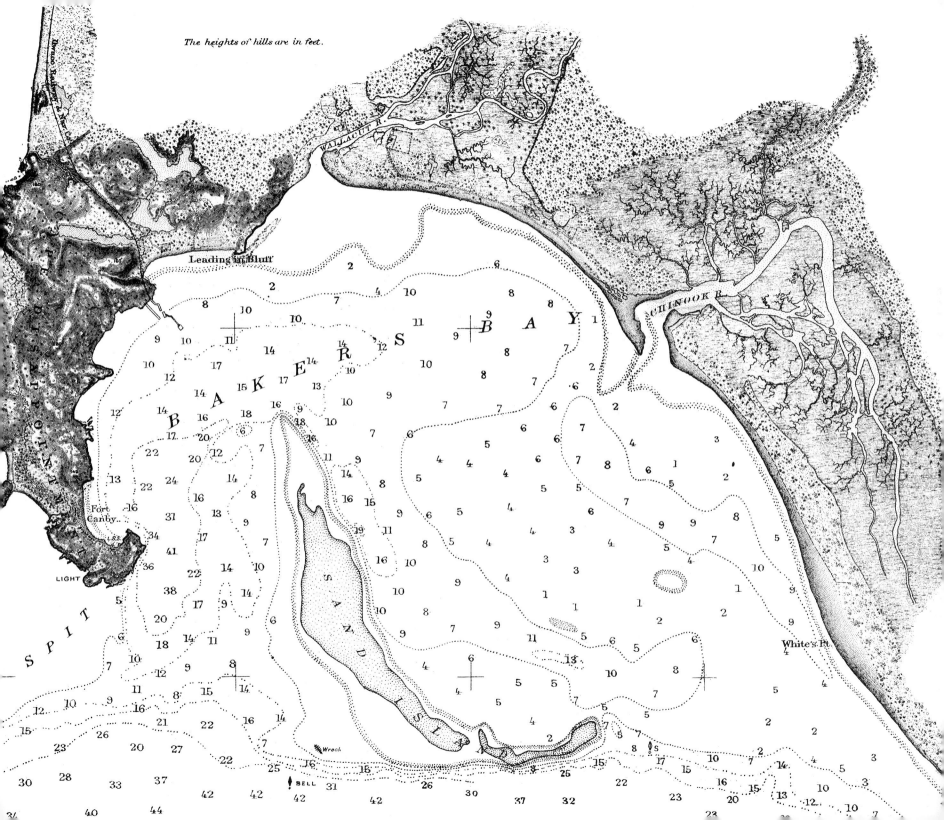

Three masted sailing ship overtaken by sternwheeler on Columbia River, with Coffin Rock in background. The 1892 watercolor is titled "Scene on the Columbia River." Collection of Mr. and Mrs. Lloyd O. Graves.

CLEVELAND ROCKWELL

SCIENTIST AND ARTIST, 1837 - 1907

BY

FRANZ STENZEL, M.D.

Portland, Oregon 1972

Errata: p. 9, Chapter title should have Colombia, S.A.

p. 83, In Lenders, Glenbow-Alberta Institute, is of course, located at Calgary, Canada.

p. 108, "Fishing with Dynamite" should be credited to the collection of Capt. David S. Edwards, USN (Ret.), as on p. 127.

FOREWORD

A SURPRISING NUMBER of painters through its history, have come to Oregon and the Oregon Country and we have a familiarity with their names and some part of their work. But among them all, Cleveland Rockwell has been a mystery man. Now, at last, fame and a recognition of his skill have been partially restored to this forgotten man.

Over twenty years ago I first saw Rockwell's work depicted in two oils of the Columbia Bar done for the famous pilot, Captain George Flavel of Astoria. Unhappily, these paintings are not available for exhibition. During the same period I had the good fortune to see the paintings and sketches of the perceptive collectors Lloyd and Eleanor Graves. Years later I saw the outstanding Rockwell group patiently and skillfully assembled by Doctor and Mrs. Franz Stenzel. It was very apparent that Captain Rockwell, a once esteemed marine scientist and painter of the American ocean and estuarine scene, deserved a show all to himself and a biography.

Dr. Stenzel kindly took time from his busy schedule to compile the Rockwell biography concerning his absorbing life in the United States Coast and Geodectic Survey and his productive life in several American communities from Maine to California and north.

Residents along the Pacific Coast and the Oregon and Columbia River shores in particular will find the Rockwell scientific and artistic combination produced pictures absorbing in every detail. This is a record of exceptional value in an era especially sensitive to an ever changing natural scene.

We are especially grateful to Dr. Stenzel and Mrs. Stenzel and to all the generous contributors who made possible the reconstruction of this elusive and complex story. Because of their cooperation the life of this master painter has been re-established and permanently secured.

THOMAS VAUGHAN
Oregon Historical Society

ACKNOWLEDGEMENTS

THANKS TO ALL of the people who contributed their paintings to this exhibit and especially Mr. and Mrs. Lloyd O. Graves, who also loaned seven sketchbooks which added interest to the exhibition and supplied background of the artist.

Also to Yale University Library and Miss Judith A. Schiff, Chief Research Archivist; Rensselaer Polytechnic Institute and Mr. K. H. Bauer, Institute Archivist; the Division of Military History of the Smithsonian Institution and Curator and Acting Director, Mr. Edgar M. Howell; The Western Reserve Historical Society and the Director Mr. Meredith B. Colket, Chief Librarian, Kermit Pike and General Reference Supervisor Mrs. Virginia R. Hawley; San Francisco National Cemetery at The Presidio and Superintendent Roland E. Lex; The Sutro Library, San Francisco, and Librarian Mr. Richard H. Dillon; The Bancroft Library, University of California, and the Director Mr. James Hart and Head, Public Services, Mr. John Barr Tompkins; the Henry E. Huntington Library and Art Gallery, Librarian Mr. Robert O. Dougan and Head of Department of Reader Services, Miss Mary Isabel Fry; the California Academy of Sciences and Librarian Mr. Ray Brian; the National Archives and Records Service, Chief Industrial and Social Branch Civil Archives Division, Mr. Jerome Finster, and Director of Social and Economic Records Division, Miss Jane F. Smith; The Library of Congress, Chief of Reference Department, Manuscript Division, Mr. Roy P. Basler; the Glenbow-Alberta Institute, Executive Vice-President, Mr. J. A. Hammond; The Episcopal Diocese of California, Custodian of Records, Mrs. Helen Maretta; Trinity Church of New Haven, Connecticut, Parish House Clerk, E. L. Bergmann; The Connecticut Historical Society, Director Mr. Thompson R. Harlow; Mr. Michael Harrison of Fair Oaks, California and Dr. Joseph Baird, San Francisco Art Historian; the New-York Historical Society, Director Mr. James J. Heslin; Tennessee State Library and Archives, Assistant Reference Librarian Mrs. Ellen D. Ross.

Despite continuing effort, no person was located who personally knew Cleveland Rockwell. Three had a passing acquaintance but could give no detailed information. Several persons did give facts.

Mr. and Mrs. Lloyd O. Graves of Seattle, Washington, interviewed Col. Patrick H. Mullay, USA (Retired), Cleveland Rockwell's son-in-law and husband of Gertrude Rockwell, then deceased, in 1945. The Graves were also friends and visitors to the home of Cornelia Rockwell Kearney in San Francisco in the 1940s.

Other persons acquainted with one or both of the two Rockwell daughters include a nephew of Colonel Mullay, Mr. William F. Mullay of Los Angeles. He wrote several letters and gave a personal interview. Mrs. R. D. Delehanty, now living in New Mexico, had known Cornelia since 1927 and subsequently until her death. She knew Gertrude Rockwell, as well, in San Francisco. Another friend of the Rockwell daughters was Mrs. S. S. Woodin of San Francisco. Finally, Capt. David S. Edwards, USN (Retired) of Bolinas, California, whose grandmother married William S. Edwards, graduate of Princeton (then called University of South Jersey) in 1853. He joined the Coast Survey and died in 1882. Subsequently his wife married Assistant Louis A. Sengteller of the Coast Survey, who worked several seasons with Cleveland Rockwell. These sources have supplied what is known of Rockwell as a person.

Mr. Thomas Vaughan, Director of the Oregon Historical Society, who proposed this study and exhibition and all of the staff members have been most helpful. Special thanks to Miss Priscilla Knuth for her perceptive editing of this biography. And to the Louis and Maud Hill Family Foundation and to the Western Imprints, OHS.

Then I must particularly acknowledge the many hours of work which Mrs. Philip (Marianne) Feldman, Research Librarian, expended before I accepted the assignment to write the book.

I would like to try to express my gratitude to my wife, Kathryn, for her patient helpfulness. Not only did she do all of the typing but cheerfully checked runs of several publications for Rockwell paintings and articles and other tedious and thankless tasks. So, Kathryn, my thanks — and love.

FRANZ STENZEL, M.D.
Portland, Oregon

CONTENTS

THE SCIENTIST

THE ARTIST

"Mt. Hood from near Fisher's landing" in 1894. The pen and ink drawing was one of the three scenes engraved on the Battleship *Oregon* punchbowls. Collection of Dr. and Mrs. Franz Stenzel.

CLEVELAND ROCKWELL

1837 - 1907

Cleveland Rockwell. 1901.

FAMILY; EDUCATION; EARLY U.S. COAST SURVEY CAREER

DOUBLY GIFTED Cleveland Salter Rockwell, eminently successful as both scientist and artist, was born in Youngstown, Ohio on November 24, 1837.[1] From Michelangelo down to the present time there are examples of persons with such a double endowment, yet in any generation they are scarce indeed.

Cleveland Rockwell's birth in northeastern Ohio does not indicate his long line of Puritan Yankee forebears. Reputedly he was "the eighth generation by direct descent from Governor Bradford" of the Plymouth Massachusetts Colony.[2] The research required to establish this connection back into the 1600s has been both successful and interesting, for the industrious, ingenious, conscientious, God-fearing and independent traits associated with the New England Yankee come through in the examination of the family. Much in the background throws light on their activities and character and in turn, leads to a better understanding of the tradition of which Cleveland Rockwell was a part.

His father, Edward Rockwell, was born in Colebrook, Connecticut, June 30, 1801. He entered Yale College as a freshman in 1817 and received his Bachelor of Arts degree in 1821. He had his Master of Arts from Yale College in 1824, "read law" in New Haven under Seth P. Staples and Judge Hitchcock, and was admitted to the Connecticut bar in 1825. A year or two later he moved to Youngstown, Trumble County, Ohio, to practice his profession.[3] He was a pioneer in the then recently opened portion of Ohio known as the Western Reserve.

The Western Reserve, historically unique, came about through English crown grant of a charter to the Colony of Connecticut in 1664. Due to limited knowledge of American geography, the grant included not only present-day Connecticut but extended vaguely westward to the Pacific Ocean — and it became one of the mishmash of conflicting claims, grants and patents which had to be adjudicated when the colonies became the independent United States. The State of Connecticut relinquished its claim to over three million acres west of its present border, but retained rights to the land bordering Lake Erie — hence, the Western Reserve. But this, too, was impractical to protect and administer: the region lay between the 41st parallel and two minutes north of the 42nd, and extended from the Pennsylvania border 120 miles to a short distance west of Sandusky, Ohio.

One part, of a half-million acres, was called the Fire Lands, since it was portioned out to Connecticut citizens who lost their property, mostly by fire, during the Revolutionary War. It took thirty years to settle the claims, make treaties with the Indians, allot the lands and draw up the deeds. By that time many of the original claimants were dead or too old to travel. Gradually their descendants took up the claims and settled the Fire Lands; the names of towns often indicate the area in Connecticut from which they came.

The remainder of the Western Reserve was purchased by the Connecticut Land Company, whose general agent was

Seascape," Clatsop beach, 1901 watercolor. Collection of Dr. D. W. E. Baird.

Moses Cleavland. Cleveland Rockwell was his namesake (the spelling is altered, as is that of the city of Cleveland which Moses Cleavland laid out in 1796), for there were family ties to the Rockwells. Genealogical sources mention at least two family members who had an interest in Western Reserve lands, which became part of Ohio Territory in 1800.[4]

In 1828 Edward Rockwell returned to New Haven, Connecticut, where he married Matilda du Plessis Salter. The marriage was performed by the Rev. Harry Croswell, Rector of Trinity Church, on April 29, 1828.[5] The couple returned to Ohio where Edward continued to practice law until 1834. At that point he became interested in "mercantile affairs" and in the manufacture of iron. The 1830 census indicates that the family was living in Youngstown, and as mentioned, his son Cleveland was born there in 1837.

Apparently Edward Rockwell moved from Youngstown to Cleveland about 1852, when he was first listed in that city's directory. He maintained an office in the Merchants Bank Building through 1855. He must have felt quite at home: there was a Rockwell Street, and there is now a Rockwell School.[6] His wife Matilda had two sisters living in Cleveland. One, Mary Salter, had married Edward Rockwell's Yale classmate, Dr. Charles C. Cooke. Another sister, Rebecca Salter, married Zalmon Fitch. The sisters are reported as "cultivated young women and fine musicians." Mrs. Rockwell was described as a superior instructor on the pianoforte.[7]

Edward Rockwell became associated with the Cleveland and Pittsburgh Railroad in 1855. The 9th Annual Report of the directors' meeting in Cleveland, January, 1857, lists Edward Rockwell as secretary and treasurer. Zalmon Fitch of Cleveland, Edward's brother-in-law, appears on the board of directors, of which a Charles Rockwell, of New York City, was president.[8]

Matilda, Edward's wife, had died in 1846. They had been married 18 years and had five children.[9] In addition to Cleveland Rockwell there were two sisters. One, Sara, was married to John M. Isaacs of Cuyahoga, Ohio and later lived in New York City. His other sister, Matilda, married George Kent and lived in New York City.[10] Edward Rockwell continued his legal work as an official of the Cleveland and Pittsburgh Railroad. Directories indicate that he lived in Wedell House and Huntington House hotels from 1852 to 1869.

When Edward Rockwell resigned his position as secretary and treasurer of the Cleveland and Pittsburgh Railroad in 1866, he was 65 and in ill health.[11] He accepted a responsible position in a large commercial house in New York City — perhaps his son-in-law's firm of Kent and Company. Ill health soon forced him to retire. He spent several years in foreign travel and returned with increased feebleness to Winsted, Connecticut, where he died at his sister's home February 25, 1874.

One step further back in Cleveland Rockwell's paternal ancestry was his grandfather, Alpha Rockwell of Winsted, Connecticut. As the first white male child born in Colebrook, Connecticut, September 21, 1767, therefore named Alpha, he was the fifth son of Captain Samuel Rockwell. Alpha's brother Martin made several trips on horseback to the Western Reserve in connection with Rockwell family lands. Alpha and his wife, who had six children, moved from Colebrook to Winsted in 1801. He was an Episcopal deacon and also engaged in the manufacture of iron with his brothers. He died May 31, 1818 of consumption.

Captain Samuel Rockwell, Cleveland Rockwell's great-grandfather and Alpha's father, was the son of William Rockwell, emigrant ancestor from England living in Dorchester, Massachusetts in 1630. William Rockwell moved to Windsor, Connecticut in 1637, and died in 1672. His son, Captain Samuel Rockwell, lived in East Windsor in 1672. He married Hepzibah Pratt. Samuel Rockwell & Sons, the firm he founded in Colebrook, manufactured pig and bar iron to supply the armory at Springfield, Massachusetts. Only iron of the highest quality and purity was suitable for the manufacture of firearms. The business was carried on for over 50 years by members of the Rockwell family.

The foundry was moved to less populated Winsted because the work was the source of smoke and noxious odors, as well as contamination of a small river, and neighbors objected — a 17th century example of pollution and community environmental control!

After the death of Captain Samuel Rockwell and his son Timothy, the name was altered to Solomon Rockwell & Sons. The partners, until 1810, were Solomon, Alpha, Reuben and Martin Rockwell.[12]

Before turning from Cleveland Rockwell's paternal to his maternal ancestry, a brief medical note seems in order. The ratio of children born to those who survived in the sixteen and seventeen hundreds is appalling. Since bacteria were not recognized as the cause of disease, the prevailing concept was "spontaneous generation of disease" caused by changes in the "humors," by the night air, and other such speculative causes. Scientific knowledge came painfully and slowly. Most modern concepts evolved much later, some applications of the germ theory were pasteurization of milk introduced in 1860, and vaccination for smallpox in 1796, both bitterly resisted for many decades. Infant diarrhea raged every summer. Pneumonia, smallpox, diphtheria, tetanus, typhoid and other infectious fevers all spread unchecked with no scientific method of prevention or treatment. There were no vitamins,

no antibiotics, no refrigeration. Purification of drinking water was unknown.

Tuberculosis was the most insidious in the families we are considering. They came from England and it is a medical fact that bovine tuberculosis was endemic in Great Britain until modern times when testing and eliminating infected cattle was carried out and milk was sterilized. In the 17th and 18th centuries, the infection rate of humans in some areas approached that of the bovine population. There was no understanding that tuberculosis or consumption, as it was called, was transmitted by bacteria sprayed into the air or on food by a coughing victim. People closed their windows tightly against the night air and its "vapors" which they believed caused diseases. Meanwhile, an infected elderly aunt or grandmother living with the family unknowingly infected the children placed in her care. Consumption was considered stylish. It glazed the cheeks of its victims with a pink glow. This flush of disease on the faces of children and delicate young women inspired poets of that day to write sonnets. It is not surprising that the average duration of life was under 40 years!

Returning now to Cleveland Rockwell's ancestry, on the maternal side his grandmother, Rhoda Ensign, wife of Deacon Alpha Rockwell, was the daughter of John Ensign of Litchfield, Connecticut. (He was the son of Mary Sedgwick Ensign, who died March 26, 1824, at age 76.) Rhoda was born in April 1775, in Canaan, Litchfield County, Connecticut, married Alpha Rockwell in May, 1790 and her date of death was February 25, 1817.

Cleveland Rockwell's great-grandmother was Rhoda Lee, daughter of the Rev. Jonathan and Elizabeth Metcalf Lee. Rhoda Lee was born February 13, 1753, married John Ensign on November 14, 1771, and died April 2, 1812 in Salisbury,

Litchfield, Connecticut. Rhoda Lee Ensign "was a direct descendant of William Bradford, the second governor of the Plymouth Colony."[13]

From another source the final connection with the Bradford family is established. The oldest granddaughter of Governor Bradford and his wife Alice Southworth was Alice Bradford, a daughter of Major William Bradford by his first wife, Alice Richards.

Alice Bradford married the Rev. William Adams, the second minister of Dedham, Massachusetts, on March 29, 1680. They had three children including Elizabeth, whose daughter Mary married the Rev. Thomas Clap on November 23, 1727, later president of Yale College.

The third daughter of William and Alice Adams was Abiel, born December 15, 1685. About 1707 she married the Rev. Joseph Metcalf, minister of Falmouth, Massachusetts, born in Dedham in 1682, graduated (Yale) 1703 and died May 24, 1723.

Joseph and Abiel Metcalf's daughter Elizabeth married the Rev. Jonathan Lee, minister of Salisbury, Connecticut. Elizabeth and Jonathan Lee had eight children of whom the fourth, Rhoda Lee, married John Ensign, and the latter couple's daughter, Rhoda Ensign, married Deacon Alpha Rockwell.[14]

It follows that Edward Rockwell was eighth and Cleveland Rockwell was ninth in descent from Governor Bradford — or by the more usual method of counting Governor Bradford's son as the first, Cleveland Rockwell was eighth.

Concerning Cleveland Rockwell's youth in Youngstown, Ohio, there is no record. He had two sisters, Sara and Matilda, already mentioned, a brother Edward who died in his youth and another brother whose name is not known. There were family friends and acquaintances from Connecticut living in the village of Youngstown. Nearby was his maternal aunt Rebecca and his uncle, Zalmon Fitch. His other maternal aunt, Mary, was married to Dr. Charles C. Cooke. His playmates included the cousins from these two families.

His later references indicate his long established familiarity with a fishpole. It is a reasonable assumption that he learned early in life to use a gun and hunt in that frontier area.

Knowing the Yankee background of the family, there would have been love and discipline at home. The children would be taught respect for parents and elders, honesty, dependability, promptness, respect for each other's rights and both love and fear of God.

Their mother, Rhoda Rockwell, taught piano to the young ladies of the village. The money she earned helped out at home. Edward Rockwell's law practice was not thriving. "Dr. Cooke and Mr. Rockwell were graduates of Yale, and had taken degrees in medicine and law. The doctor found patients, but the peaceful citizens of the village furnished few, if any, clients for the lawyer. So after a few years, the school girls of Youngstown had a superior instructor on the pianoforte in Mrs. Rockwell."[15]

The family was too engrossed in living to note a shortage of material things. For Cleveland, his childhood was happy until the age of nine when his mother died.

There is scant record of the next decade. It is established that his father transferred his base of operations to Cleveland. His aunt Rebecca and uncle Zalmon Fitch also moved to that town and young Cleveland may have lived with them. As already noted, his father lived in a hotel after his wife died and seems not to have maintained a home in Cleveland. Cleveland's sisters may have attended Grove Hall in New Haven where his mother and her two sisters had been educated. They both were married when quite young. His remaining brother died.

The years between age 9 and 16 were enjoyable for Cleveland. He became attached to his new surroundings. On several occasions in his adult life he referred to his home in Cleveland. In asking for leave from the Coast Survey, he wrote, "Cleveland is my home."

It has been reported in two brief published biographies that he was educated at the "Polytechnic School at Troy," New York.[16] By 1854, when Rockwell was 17 years of age, a preparatory school for Rensselaer Polytechnic Institute had been formed and was known as The Institute Training School or Troy Academy. The school which Rockwell attended must have been that or the Renssalaer Polytechnic Institute, since there were no other polytechnic institutions then in Troy. The records of the preparatory school have been lost and his name does not occur on those printed lists which survive of students of either school. The state of the early records does not permit any final negative conclusion.

In 1856 "C.S. Rockwell" of Cleveland, Ohio, is listed as a sophomore in the "Circular and Catalogue of the University of the City of New York, March 1856."[17] No catalogue for the year of 1855 is available and he is not listed in 1857. It is not certain, therefore, whether he attended the University of New York for two years or whether he had a year of college work at Rensselaer Polytechnic before coming to New York. There is no record of his having been graduated.

On July 1, 1856, Rockwell was appointed to the Coast Survey. His title was Aid and his salary was $15 a month plus room and board. The United States Coast Survey is one of the oldest scientific bureaus of the Federal Government. It was proposed by President Jefferson and on February 10, 1807, "An Act to Provide for Surveying the Coasts of the United States," was passed by Congress. Jefferson appointed a distinguished scientist, Ferdinand R. Hassler, to head the survey. He was an engineer who had an outstanding career in his native Switzerland and had become teacher of mathematics at West Point.

Little was done for the next two decades. Instruments of sufficient accuracy to make such a survey had to be obtained in Europe. The War of 1812 came about while Hassler was in Europe buying supplies, and he did not return to the United States until 1815. Congress repealed the 1807 act and it was not until 1832 that Congressional action, including a new appropriation, permitted work to resume. The work which began along the eastern seaboard became increasingly more complicated. The complete triangulation survey of the entire Atlantic Coast required the use of vessels to complete the hydrographic surveys for marine charts. The charts involved copper-plate engraving and in turn, printing presses.

The length of the coastline had been greatly increased by the Louisiana Purchase, the addition of Florida and Texas, and the conquest of California. Superintendent Hassler's work was technically above reproach. His problem was one of personality. His prejudices and uncompromising opinions led to some difficulties. He had little regard for American trained scientists, and engaged mostly assistants with European training. Superintendent Hassler died in 1843. The new superintendent of the Coast Survey was Alexander Dallas Bache, Philadelphia-born from a family of distinguished scientists and a graduate of the United States Military Academy, where he was retained as Assistant Professor of Engineering. Subsequently, he became Professor of Natural Philosophy and Chemistry at the University of Pennsylvania. Here he remained until 1843 when he took over the superintendency of the Coast Survey.

Under his direction, the survey flourished and expanded its operation, demonstrating its practical value. His work was aided by Congress and encouraged by scientific societies and their leaders. At the same time, Bache was ex-officio Superintendent of Weights and Measures, served on the Lighthouse Board and was one of the incorporators of the Smithsonian Institution in 1846. During the Civil War he served as Vice-President of the United States Sanitary Commission, forerunner of the American Red Cross, and lent the resources of the Coast Survey to the defenses of Philadelphia and Washington, D.C. His engaging personality and friendly manner served him well. He was head of the Coast Survey for twenty-four years. He died February 17, 1867 in Newport, Rhode Island, following a stroke which occurred three years earlier.

The work of the Coast Survey was divided into sections covering the entire coast of the United States. The plan of activity was that one assistant, and occasionally two, was in charge of each party. Frequently there was an assistant and a sub-assistant with a varying number of workmen, usually three or four, and a foreman. The trained staff advanced through the ranks of aid, sub-assistant and assistant. There were one or more assistants working in each section. The overall direction was by the superintendent in Washington, D.C. A sub-office for the West Coast was maintained in San Francisco.[18]

Each assistant received an assignment for the ensuing season. Often it took thirty days to assemble the necessary papers and project the season's work. A foreman and crew had to be hired and a vessel, belonging to the survey or privately owned, had to be engaged and to arrive on the scene. The season's work might be delayed or hampered by high water due to spring runoff, dense fog, and on land,

abrupt changes in elevation, swampy or sometimes extremely high, rocky terrain, dense forests through which a path had to be cut so the surveying instrument could sight the next point, unfriendly Indians, numerous bears and hordes of mosquitoes. Particularly on the West Coast, work was done in surveying *terra incognita*. Some places were so remote that it was difficult to get food supplies; in the summer and fall the smoke of forest fires was so irritating to the mens' eyes that work was, at times, impossible. Sometimes the men had only what they could carry in their packs. A rollup tent, a couple of blankets and two or three changes of socks and underwear was their usual pack.

The field work of the survey began in the spring — just when, depended upon preparation and the weather conditions. Longer projects were carried through until the close of the season for field work. This was often in October. From the time field work was closed, the crews were discharged, instruments and equipment were stored and boats were put up for the winter. Then the assistants, sub-assistants and aids were engaged in translating their results from field work onto charts. Once this was completed in pencil, the charts were inked. Sometimes in the course of a given year an individual party might work in two or three locations. To avoid being repetitious, the office work and inking of charts will not be alluded to frequently. It should be understood, however, that this was the objective of field work and that it went on every season after field work ended. The final charts were sent on to the superintendent's office in Washington, D.C.

In following the career of Cleveland Rockwell, it becomes obvious that the Coast Survey was composed of a hardy and dedicated group of men. Mr. Rockwell's first assignment was working on a section of New York Harbor. He was working under Assistant H.L. Whiting surveying Ward and Randall's islands, the North and South Brother, and Rickers Island in the East River. Aid Rockwell's work was singled out for commendation by Assistant Whiting and Superintendent Bache recorded Whiting's comment in the Annual Report covering the year 1857: " 'The sheet containing the islands, surveyed by Mr. Rockwell, is also a fine specimen of work.' "[19]

That Rockwell quickly established his ability and reliability is evidenced in the same report, since "Assistant Whiting left his own party in charge of Mr. Rockwell, in the middle of October, and engaged in a resurvey of Provincetown Harbor."[20]

In 1858 Rockwell worked on a survey of Charleston Harbor and part of the coast of South Carolina in the party of Assistant John Seib. Rockwell is again mentioned. "Assistant Seib, in his report, refers especially to the efficient and acceptable services rendered by Mr. Rockwell who accompanied his party as Aid."[21]

In 1859 the party, under John Seib, made a shoreline survey from St. Helena Sound, South Carolina toward the mouth of the Savannah River, Georgia. Rockwell had the opportunity of working directly under Superintendent A.D. Bache, who commented: "At the end of April I visited the party of Assistant Seib, in passing southward on a tour of inspection. The work then in progress, and since completed, is intricate in character and was not favored by more than

an average of fair weather for field duty. The large return in results is mainly due to the constant energy of the chief of the party, and to the able support given by Mr. Rockwell."[22]

It was not the usual thing for newly appointed aids to be mentioned by name in the Annual Report, let alone to be singled out for such favorable comment. These men were all serious scientists and their commendation was based on an appreciation of Rockwell's ability and dedication to his work. The commendations suggest both his adequate preparation for the work and his natural aptitude for the applied science involved.

Further evidence of Cleveland Rockwell's reputation came in 1859 when Assistant John Seib, with whom he had worked, suddenly died on December 23rd. Aid Rockwell, who had been working with him, was assigned to complete the plane table sheets of the Port Royal, Savannah River area surveyed in 1859. Rockwell was placed in charge of the party in the field January 23, 1860 and completed the work on May 22. The report states that "Mr. Rockwell's knowledge of the ground enabled him to push on the work, and, with the advantage of weather favorable upon the whole for field operations, to make a large return of material." The party, under Rockwell, had completed surveying 190 miles of coastline between January and June 1, 1860.[23]

CHAPTER I: NOTES

1. Certified death record of Cleveland Rockwell, No. 92, Vital Statistics Section, City of Portland.
2. The statement in Harvey K. Hines, *An Illustrated History of the State of Oregon* (Chicago, 1893), p. 598, was based on a personal interview.
3. The information regarding Edward Rockwell comes from Judith A. Schiff, Chief Research Archivist, Manuscripts and Archives, Yale University Library, who cited his listing in *The Annual Catalogues of Yale College*, 1813-35, the *Catalogue of Graduates, 1701-1924,* and the *Obituary Record of Graduates of Yale College Deceased from June, 1870, to June, 1880.* The last cited gives family information and names Edward Rockwell's parents.
4. The condensed version of Western Reserve comes from *Encyclopedia of American History,* edited by Richard B. Morris and Henry S. Commager (New York, 1965). Two maps and supplementary information on the Rockwell family were supplied by Mrs. Virginia R. Hawley, General Reference Supervisor, The Western Reserve Historical Society, Cleveland, Ohio.
5. *New Haven Vital Records,* p. 511. Information supplied by Connecticut Historical Society, Hartford, Conn.
6. Directory listings come from Mrs. Virginia R. Hawley, previously cited.
7. *Memorial to the Pioneer Women of the Western Reserve,* edited by Mrs. Gertrude Van Rensselaer Wickham (Cleveland, Ohio, 1896), Part III, p. 387.
8. Letter from Western Reserve Historical Society, *op. cit.* The situation suggests a slight case of nepotism, though the president's relationship to his secretary-treasurer and his board member has not been established.
9. *Obituary Record of Graduates of Yale College, op. cit.,* p. 124.
10. *Records of the Descendants of James Ensign and his Wife Sarah Elson, 1634-1939-1960,* compiled and published by Martha Eunice Ensign Nelson (Salt Lake City), p. 206. Copy in Sutro Library, San Francisco, Calif.
11. *Annals of Cleveland,* 1866, p. 635, from Western Reserve Historical Society, *op. cit.*
12. *The Rockwell Family in One Line of Descent,* by Francis Williams Rockwell (Pittsfield, Mass., 1924), pp. 54, 59, 60, 61, 65, 66, 201. Copy at Sutro Library, San Francisco, Calif.
13. Rhoda Lee Ensign's relationship with Governor Bradford and the details of the Ensign and Lee families are from *Records of the Descendants of James Ensign and his Wife Sarah Elson, op. cit.,* pp. 51, 249, 105, 206.
14. "Descendants of Alice Bradford," by Rev. William Allen, in *New England Historical and Genealogical Register* (Boston, Mass.), Vol. IX, (1855), pp. 127-28.
15. *Memorial to the Pioneer Women. . .Western Reserve,* p. 387.
16. H. K. Hines, *History of Oregon, op. cit.,* p. 598; Joseph Gaston, *The Centennial History of Oregon, 1811-1912* (Chicago, Illinois, 1912), Vol. III, p. 368.
17. Information on Rockwell's listing as a student at the University of the City of New York comes from Miss Helen Cleverdon, Archivist, at New York University, University Heights Library.
18. The fiscal year ran from November to November through 1872, and activities for that period were reported in the Superintendent of the Coast Survey's Annual Report to the Secretary of the Treasury, the department to which the Coast Survey belonged. In 1873 the fiscal year was changed to end with June, and the balance of each year from June to December is reported in the superintendent's report for the following year.
19. *Report of the Superintendent of the Coast Survey...during...1857, Sen. Ex. Doc. No. 33,* 35 Cong., 1 Sess. (Washington, 1858), p. 50. (These reports will be referred to hereafter as *Annual Report,* with the year.)
20. *Ibid.*
21. *Annual Report, 1858,* p. 75.
22. *Annual Report, 1859,* pp. 66-67.
23. *Annual Report, 1860,* p. 59.

CIVIL WAR EXPERIENCE; MAGDALENA RIVER SURVEY, COLUMBIA

THE TENSIONS between the North and the South had been mounting. No compromise or search for a middle ground had spanned the breach despite numerous and repeated attempts at all levels of government. Abraham Lincoln's election in November, 1860 was a victory for the North. Before the year was over, South Carolina had seceded from the Union. In January and February of 1861, six other states followed and, with later additions, formed the Confederate States of America.

The impending possibility of hostilities brought an awareness to both sides regarding the military significance of the activities of the Coast Survey. There was nothing of partisan substance published in the Annual Reports until after the outbreak of open war. The work of the Survey continued in all sections of both the East and West coasts.

The military importance of the charts of the North and South Carolina, Georgia and Florida coasts was not lost on the superintendent of the Survey. In the several years before the onset of the war some of the best assistants, in terms of ability and experience, were assigned to that region of the Atlantic Coast. These included Assistant John Seib, Assistant H. L. Whiting and Sub-Assistant F. W. Dorr. The Superintendent of the Survey himself, Alexander Dallas Bache, made an "inspection tour" of the seacoast from North Carolina to Georgia, as noted, in 1859.

Although Rockwell had other assignments on a portion of New York Harbor and resurvey of a section of Boston Harbor, his principal assignment from 1858 through 1861 was the South Carolina and Georgia coast. Each year he returned to the Port Royal and Savannah area, and he completed the 1860 season's work after John Seib died. It was in October, 1860 that he was ordered back to Port Royal-Savannah to finish the charts. He was delayed by the completion of the Boston Harbor charts and was not free to leave for his assignment until December. At that time, the Treasury announced that funds were not available and cancelled the project. It was another way of saying that the Rebel forces were so entrenched along the shore in the Port Royal and Savannah River region as to make the survey impossible.

Even though the field work was not entirely complete, Rockwell spent much of his time, between December, 1860 and May, 1861, preparing and inking the plane table sheet for the Port Royal-Savannah River work which had been surveyed previously. That particular chart suddenly gained an added military significance on April 12, 1861: Fort Sumter was fired on and the Civil War began.

Northern military strategy included among its principal objectives the starving of the South by a blockade of the coastline, shoring up the defenses of Washington and environs, and sending an army to seize the Rebel capital at Richmond, Virginia. The Coast Survey now openly alluded to its activities in providing charts of vital portions of the south Atlantic coastline which proved to be useful in the blockade. Also, the military significance of its operations ashore in making maps for both offensive and defensive military operations was acknowledged as the policy of the organization.

Writing of Coast Survey activities in 1861, Superintendent Bache stated policy in dispatching field parties for duties on the lower sections of the Atlantic seaboard and the Gulf of Mexico:

... though the temper of the public mind was then stirred, there was nothing on which to reckon hazard in sending the parties and vessels to continue work on the parts of the coast on which they had been respectively engaged .... In two instances only were vessels seized and held ... In several others, instruments, which had been either stored with responsible persons at the close of the previous working season, or had been in actual use during the early part of this year [1861] were forcibly taken by lawless persons in arms, and acting under assumed authority.[1]

In that same Annual Report, Bache outlined the new policy which was to continue for the duration of the war. "The Topographical surveys made by assistants of the Coast Survey, in cooperation with the accomplished officers of topographical engineers," he wrote, "have supplied rapidly, maps essential to the operations of the Army. Especially has this been the case in the neighborhood of the capital, where the immediate completion of the map of the District of Columbia, and of its approaches, was called for by the military authorities ..."[2]

Completion of the Port Royal and Savannah River entrances proceeded in the latter part of 1861, since the United States forces had occupied Port Royal Sound and vicinity. Four parties were sent out under the general direction of Assistant C. O. Boutelle. Rockwell was in charge of one of these parties.[3]

Superintendent Bache details Rockwell's activity: "Mr. Cleveland Rockwell arrived on the first of December in the steamer *Bienville* . . . [He] was directed to take up for military purposes the topography of the inside shore of Port Royal Island and that of adjacent islands. This service he steadily prosecuted, under orders of Brigadier General I. I. Stevens ... and his zeal and activity were warmly commended in a communication addressed to me by that Commander."[4]

Earlier in 1861 Rockwell, acting under Assistant H. L. Whiting, did a minute topographical survey of the parts of Fairfax County, Virginia, adjacent to the Potomac River, between Little Falls and Mount Vernon. The survey for the defense of Washington, D.C. was made at the request of Lt. Gen. Winfield Scott, General-in-Chief:

... by authority of the Treasury Department, arrangements were made for this work at the beginning of June by the assignment of the most experienced field assistant, H. L. Whiting, esq., for the general supervision of two working parties. The charge of one of the plane tables was given to Sub-Assistant F. W. Dorr, and that of the other to Mr. Cleveland Rockwell .... The working sheets were laid out to include all the detailed features of ground then occupied by the army under Brigadier General Irvin McDowell, and those immediately to the north and west of his line of pickets, as far as practicable, in the direction of Fairfax Court-house, and as high up the Potomac as the bridge which now occupied the site of a former "chain" bridge.

By the 5th of July, Rockwell had "extended the topography of the middle section as far west as Fall's Church, then the headquarters of General [Daniel] Tyler, to the immediate vicinity of Vienna, and generally to limits beyond the outposts." Though Rockwell was interrupted in his survey by a hostile approach on June 24, by the middle of July, he had connected his survey with the topography done by Sub-Assistant Dorr. Tracings were furnished to General McDowell, Brigadier General Tyler and Col. Samuel P. Heintzelman. Photographic copies were supplied to the corps of engineers and placed at the disposal of the officers.[5] On the "critical nature of the field duty performed by Messrs. Dorr and Rockwell, at times between two extensive lines of military outposts," Superintendent Bache quoted Assistant Whiting's remarks:

"The circumstances and conditions of the service have required the constant exercise of watchfulness and prudence, and that, I am happy to say, has been most judiciously displayed."

Mr. Whiting visited the working parties frequently and gave close and attentive supervision to all the details of the survey. His report on its completion concludes as follows: "In closing, I am gratified to report that the general results of our work have been successful. The detailed survey shows all the important topographical features of the country which it embraces: the main roads, by-roads, and bridle-paths; the woods, open grounds, and streams; houses, out-buildings, and fences; with as close a sketch of contour as the hidden character of the country would allow — producing in all a map by which any practicable military movement might be studied and planned with perfect reliability."[6]

In October the same parties, in charge of Messrs. Dorr and Rockwell, aided by Mr. J. W. Donn, extended the survey northward and westward from Fall's Church and the Chain bridge.

The survey in the region of Washington, just mentioned, occurred prior to and continued following the first Battle of Bull Run, which began on July 21, 1861. General Scott ordered General McDowell, with a force of 30,000, to advance from his position southwest of Washington against the Confederate forces in a march toward Richmond. The seemingly successful attack was brought to a halt by the firm stand and advance of Confederate reinforcements commanded by Gen. Thomas J. Jackson. His determined stand, which earned him the appelation "Stonewall," turned an apparent southern rout into a victory. McDowell's men began an orderly retreat which soon became a confused, panicky stampede toward Washington.

The outcome of the Battle of Bull Run roused the North to the peril of the capital. The more thorough plan for the defenses of Washington, Philadelphia and other northern cities was a result. General McDowell was replaced by Gen. George B. McClellan. When Scott retired a few months later in November, McClellan became General-in-Chief.[7]

The usefulness of Rockwell's Port Royal survey, even though it was incomplete, is assessed in the report of C.O. Boutelle, who watched the battle between Union vessels and shore batteries for Port Royal Bay from aboard the Coast Survey steamer *Vixen*. He wrote Bache on November 8, 1861:

... We are in possession of this noble harbor and the flag of the Union again floats over two places in South Carolina.... Today I have been with General Sherman on a reconnaissance up ... the inland passage which leads from Port Royal Sound to the Savannah River. He does us the honor to say that a large share of the credit of the success here is due to the Coast Survey .... [Samuel F.] DuPont desires me to present his regards to you, and say that he will ... express his appreciation of our services ... [8]

In 1862 Rockwell completed the topography of the section of Port Royal Sound which had been interrupted by the presence of Rebel troops, and then was ordered to resume his work in that region on the topography between the Beaufort and Coosaw rivers. The latter part of May he was ordered to report to Stono Inlet. The locations mentioned are on the South Carolina coast, a few miles south of Charleston Harbor and north of St. Helena Sound. From Savannah north to Charleston the coastline is extremely complicated, with many inlets and inland passages where Rebel ships might hide and await their opportunity to run the Union blockade. With charts produced by the Coast Survey, the blockade's effectiveness increased. Chances of capture were estimated at one in ten in 1861, and increased to one in three in 1864 after the Union navy set up bases along the southern coast. One of the most important of these bases was at Port Royal Sound, in the segment of coast which Rockwell's party surveyed between Savannah and St. Helena Sound. Rockwell's activities for the summer of 1862 are not described in the Annual Report, but in September he began the topography of Frenchman's Bay and Winter Harbor, Maine.[9] Field work was closed on November 18, 1862.

At the beginning of 1863 Rockwell was under the orders of Major-General J. G. Foster, acting at special call for military purposes. Sub-Assistant P. F. C. West and Rockwell were assigned on the triangulation of the Neuse River in North Carolina. West erected signals for triangulations, while Rockwell surveyed a base line at the forks of the Neuse and Trent rivers. Triangulation followed the course of the Neuse to about 12 miles below Newbern. Begun in February, the project was completed by the middle of May.[10]

Major-General Foster commented on the work in a letter to Superintendent Bache, dated June 1, 1863 at Newbern, North Carolina:

Mr. Fairfield has just given me a copy of his triangulation work on the Neuse river, which puts me in mind to thank you for the assistance which you have rendered me in sending him, Mr. West, and Mr. Rockwell here. Their labors have aided very much in obtaining a correct knowledge of the country for military purposes.

Mr. West's work, from Newport barracks to Morehead City, has been especially valuable. Hardly less so is the mapped reconnaissance of Mr. Rockwell on the north side of the Neuse. Mr. Rockwell's work about Little Washington, and on the route from Newbern to that place, was excellent, and of great military value.[11]

Rockwell's work of that time was conducted in a cloak and dagger atmosphere, and the Coast Survey Annual Report gives the following hair-raising summary of 26-year-old Rockwell's adventures. He found himself in the company of leading Union generals, who requested his services:

Besides the regular work of the survey accomplished this season... the circumstances of the military service in North Carolina at the opening of the present year led to a very effective co-operation by Assistant P.

F. C. West and ... Cleveland Rockwell with the forces under command of Major General Foster. Mr. Rockwell reached Newbern on the 2d of February, just after the departure of the general. On being advised by Brigadier General Prince of the need of a topographical survey of the approaches to the city, that work was immediately commenced, and was for a short time steadily prosecuted. Frequent calls, however, were made in the following two months for Mr. Rockwell's services in reconnaissance, and for the compilation of such maps as rapid tours would afford. On the 16th of March he was ordered to make a thorough reconnaissance of the roads and of the country generally on the northern side of the Neuse. For this purpose the 85th regiment New York volunteers, Colonel Belknap, was assigned as escort. Mr. Rockwell was engaged in this service until the 1st of April, and brought back with him material for a reliable map of the district within a circuit of ten to twelve miles. Some time after, when General Foster was still at Washington [North Carolina], on the Tar river, and during the siege of that place, Mr. Rockwell accompanied General Prince to the Tar river at his request, to reconnoitre the battery of the enemy at Hill's Point. The garrison of Washington was relieved soon after by a force led by General Foster in person. Under his direction Mr. Rockwell accompanied the detachment and completed the map of the road between the besieged town and Newbern. At Washington he sketched the ground held by the enemy, their batteries and field-works, and also the lines of defence erected to repel the attack, and the country adjoining, and furnished copies of the map to General Foster and General Prince.

Early in May ... Rockwell was sent on a reconnaissance with four companies of cavalry, with direction to pass through Pollockville, Young's Cross-roads, Pelatier's Mills, and by White Oak river, to return by way of Newport barracks. Lieutenant Colonel Lewis, of the 3d regiment New York cavalry, was in command of the escort. One of the enemy's mounted videttes [a sentry] was captured at Young's Cross-roads. On learning soon after that a company of rebel cavalry had passed down the same road, the purpose of the expedition was changed to a pursuit. The enemy was taken by surprise at Pelatier's Mills ... Rockwell rode in the cavalry charge, the result of which was the capture of thirteen prisoners with their arms, and thirty-five horses with their accoutrements. Though the rapidity of the march on the enemy's camp did not admit gathering local information, Mr. Rockwell noted that the command had passed over the more elevated part of a great swampy track between the Trent and White Oak rivers, and that the railroad to Beaufort could be approached from the southward for a stretch of about twenty-seven miles, only by a few swampy roads branching from the main road which runs along White Oak river. Mr. Rockwell had previously added to his map of the upper side of the Neuse by attending the command of General Spinola in a movement towards Washington before it was relieved.[12]

On June 1, 1863, Cleveland Rockwell was promoted to Sub-Assistant after six years' service in the Coast Survey.[13]

Anticipating the movement of Rebel forces into Pennsylvania, Coast Survey Superintendent Bache offered his services in June to the governor of Pennsylvania and the mayor of Philadelphia. Learning of the offer, Major General N. J. T. Dana, in charge of defenses for Philadelphia and environs, responded: "We have no engineer, and your aid would be invaluable if you are still able to . . . come at once, with such of your corps as you can bring."

Assistant George Davidson was placed in charge. A reconnaissance of Philadelphia and environs indicated the feasible lines of defense. Fort Dana was begun under the direction of Davidson, employing 60 men from the city gas works.

Assistance from many sources was utilized. In addition to a dozen others on the Survey staff, including P. F. C. West, H. L. Whiting, C. O. Boutelle and Cleveland Rockwell, civilian engineers, college professors, private business concerns and civil volunteers came forward. The North Pennsylvania, the Atlantic Railroad and interconnecting lines offered available plans and surveys, as well as material help.

The emergency shoring up of Philadelphia's defenses was made necessary by Confederate General Robert E. Lee's attempt to invade the North. Early in June, the army of northern Virginia began to move up the Shenandoah Valley. It crossed the Potomac River into Pennsylvania on June 17. An aroused North quickly raised 100,000 volunteers in response to President Lincoln's call on June 15. The towns of Carlisle and York, Pennsylvania, fell on June 27 and 28. On the 29th, Confederate forces were only 10 miles from Harrisburg, about 75 miles from the populated limits of Philadelphia.

The three-day Battle of Gettysburg, July 1 to July 3, cost the Rebels almost 4,000 killed and about 24,000 wounded. Lee and the Confederate armies retreated across the Potomac. The casualties were nearly as great for the Union forces, but the defeat of the southern forces tipped the scales militarily and diplomatically in favor of the North.

Before the Philadelphia emergency Rockwell had been assigned to Maine. He was recalled and reported on July 1, to begin a plane table survey near Philadelphia. He became ill but recovered in a few days. Rejoining the survey group, he was sent to work under Assistant Whiting, and completed topographical reconnaissance of several localities west of the Schuylkill. By August 18, he had completed his assignments in the Philadelphia area.[14]

He went back to his Maine assignment, arriving at Winter Harbor on September 9, 1863. Working from the deck of the schooner *Caswell*, he completed his survey east of Frenchman's Bay in October after running ten miles of shoreline.[15]

In November, Rockwell began a survey of Sewall's Point, in Virginia, at the request of Major-General Benjamin F. Butler, who had just been made Commander of Fortress Monroe. Sewell's point was adjacent to the fort which was to be used as a depot for Rebel prisoners. Rockwell completed the assignment within a month.[16]

His next assignment was in Tennessee. The day after his arrival in Knoxville, on December 12, Cleveland Rockwell was commissioned Captain of Engineers, Topographical Corps, Army of the Ohio, for the duration of the war.[17]. It is surprising that his commission as an army officer was so long delayed. He had been operating behind enemy lines

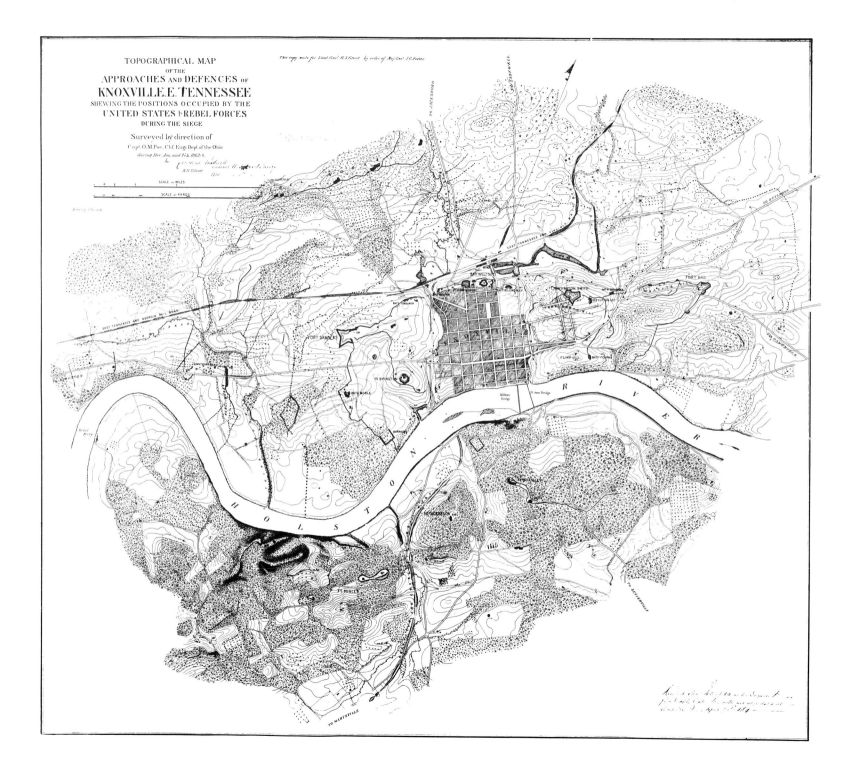

for a part of the last three years. He needed the rank to command some of the men assigned as his escort and other soldiers he encountered in his work. More importantly, if captured, he would now be a prisoner of war; as a civilian, his capture might well have resulted in his being shot as a spy.

Superintendent Bache's 1864 report details Captain Rockwell's involvement with the Knoxville survey:

Major General [Robert S.] Foster having requested the detail of two officers of the Coast Survey for service with his command in East Tennessee, Sub-Assistant [and Captain] Rockwell and Mr. R. H. Talcott were directed to report at Cincinnati in the latter part of November, 1863. After a toilsome journey by way of the Cumberland Gap, the party reached Knoxville with their instruments on the 11th of December. Next day, under the immediate orders of Captain O. M. Poe, then chief engineer in the department of the Ohio, a plane-table survey was begun of all the grounds of approach towards Knoxville. A base line of about fifteen hundred metres was measured, and signals were set up and determined in position by means of the plane table. The area to be included lay on both sides of the Holston river, Mr. Rockwell took the north side, and his survey was made to include the city of Knoxville and the heavy fortifications, with the contour of the ground which they commanded. Mr. Talcott surveyed the southern approaches, which are more hilly, and quite thickly wooded. One peculiarity of the region under notice is the numerous "sink holes" through which the smaller streams disappear suddenly, to the surprise of the topographer.

The map of the survey around Knoxville comprises about thirteen square miles.[18]

It was mid-March, 1864, before Captain Rockwell completed his work at Knoxville. When his military map for the defense of Knoxville was finished, he made several copies for commanders of different branches of the military service. Then he was assigned to make a plane table survey of Strawberry Plains, an area about 15 miles northeast of Knoxville and about halfway to Jefferson City, Tennessee. The field work and the map were completed and sent to the adjutant general at Knoxville by the end of May. Major General John

Captain Cleveland Rockwell in uniform. (OHS Collections)

...e of original maps made for defense of Knoxville, 1863-1864. NA RG
  Ofc. of Chief of Engineers, T-71-1. Mr. Edgar M. Howell, Curator
Military History, Smithsonian Institution, located the map and his
)ert assistance is acknowledged with thanks.

Schofield relieved Rockwell of military duty in the Department of the Ohio on June 2, 1864.[19]

From that day until early October, over four months, Rockwell's activities and whereabouts are unknown. The Annual Report for 1864 gives no information, nor does his personnel record, which indicates his assignments and leaves with or without pay. He was still an officer in the Engineers and still on special call for duty under General Foster. Rockwell may have been sent on a secret assignment for the army which was therefore not reported by the Coast Survey. Occasionally an uncompleted project will only be reported two years later, but that is not the case here. The Annual Report for 1865 throws no further light on the subject.

On October 8, 1864, Sub-Assistant Rockwell joined a party just beginning work under Assistant H. L. Whiting. The project was the topography of the Hudson River from Nyack and Sing Sing northward to Haverstraw and Croton village. Whiting describes the terrain:

> The circular crest of hills from the 'Verdiretige Hook' to 'High Tor' (seven hundred and thirty and eight hundred and twenty feet respectively) rises abruptly from the river shore at an angle impossible to ascend, with perpendicular cliffs at the summit crest. This narrow ridge of the entire line of summits, with the steep slope of descent westward, of from four hundred to six hundred feet, to the undulating fields at the base, forms one of the most striking natural features in the whole of the river topography. As a subject for contour, it is the most remarkable that has come within my experience in Coast Survey work.

Rockwell worked with the party until the season closed at the end of November. Superintendent Bache reported Assistant Whiting's warm commendation of Rockwell's "energy in meeting the difficulties peculiar to the work of the season . . ."[20]

In the autumn of 1864 Rockwell's chief, Superintendent Bache, sustained a stroke. He had been head of the Coast Survey since 1843. In those 21 years he had the respect, admiration and individual affection of all associated with him. As pointed out, Bache recognized Rockwell's ability and dedication to the Survey, and printed the favorable reports of heads of the parties under whom the young and surely adventurous man worked. Plaudits given Rockwell by leading generals of the army, too, found their way into Bache's annual reports. Bache worked side by side with Rockwell and their mutual respect had grown into friendship.

Bache did not succumb at once, but he could no longer function as head of the Coast Survey. His position was taken over in the interim by Assistant Julius E. Hilgard about the end of the 1864 season.

Captain Rockwell's final military adventure was in 1865. He joined Sub-Assistant F. W. Dorr for service with the army of Major General William T. Sherman. Making plane table surveys, Rockwell was to precede the army as it moved northward in Sherman's "March to the Sea" — the concluding campaign of the war between the states. The Annual Report for 1865 relates Rockwell's intimate participation in the final three and one-half months of the struggle:

> While military operations were in progress in the vicinity of Chattanooga, several of the topographers of the Coast Survey were engaged in making plane-table surveys under the direction of Colonel O. M. Poe [under whom Rockwell had worked in 1864 making the Knoxville, Tennessee military map], of the corps of engineers, and their aptitude had to some extent identified them with the movements in that quarter. Of these, Sub-Assistants Cleveland Rockwell, and F. W. Dorr rejoined the army of Major General Sherman of Savannah [Georgia], and again reported to Colonel Poe, the first-named on the 10th, and the latter on the 22d of January. Two aids, Messrs. W. W. Harding and Franklin Platt, were assigned to assist in any plane-table surveys that might be needed in the intended march of the army northward across the State of South Carolina. The parties left Savannah on the 26th, and two days after rejoined headquarters, then at Pocotaligo. During the stay at that point a plane-table survey was made of the rebel works and of the approaches

to them. Proceeding with the right wing of the army, Messrs. Rockwell and Dorr reached Columbia, South Carolina, on the 17th of February, and Winnsboro' on the 21st. There, joining the left wing, they crossed the Catawba [River] on the 24th, at Rocky Mount, and again met the right wing on the 4th of March at Cheraw. Fayetteville, North Carolina, was reached on the 11th, where the army halted until the 14th of March. In the arsenal at that place some topographical instruments, which had been used by the party working on the coast of North Carolina previous to the year 1861, were recovered and forwarded to the office.

The forward movement of the army being opposed only at Averysboro', where the enemy made a stand on the 16th, but gave way in the night, the columns moved on and occupied Goldsboro' on the 23d of March. Here a plane-table survey was at once commenced on two sheets, the intention of the commanding general being, if necessary, to hold the place with a small garrison. Sub-Assistant Dorr surveyed the ground west of the Wilmington and Weldon railroad, and Sub-Assistant Rockwell the section lying east of that line.

General Sherman's second campaign was opened on the 10th of April by a movement on Raleigh, North Carolina, which was occupied without resistance three days after, and on the day following the forward movement was terminated by overtures for surrender from the commander of the rebel forces in North Carolina. Messrs. Dorr and Rockwell accompanied the army in its march on Raleigh, but the capture of a detailed map of the defences of that city rendered it unnecessary to resume work with the plane table. The parties were relieved from further service with the army at Raleigh in the latter part of April and reported at the Coast Survey office.[21]

Captain Rockwell returned to civilian life after his five exciting and stimulating years of playing a unique role in the defense of his country. In the confusion that ensued he was uncertain as to the future and whether he should continue with the Coast Survey. At this point he was recommended as a member of a party of Coast Survey engineers to work in South America.

The project had its inception in August, 1865: Manuel Murillo, President of Colombia, applied through the U.S. Minister at Bogota, Allen A. Burton, to President Andrew Johnson for the services of "two competent engineers of the United States Survey" to examine and estimate the "proba-ble cost of certain contemplated improvements in the brazo [arm] connecting Lake Santa Marta with the Magdalena River."[22] General Eustorjis Salgar represented the Colombian government, and Col. Samuel A. Gilbert and Capt. Preston C. F. West (detached from the Coast Survey), the American government. The contract was forwarded by the U.S. Minister in Bogota to Secretary of State William H. Seward.

The contract described the work to be done and indicated that Gilbert and West were to select four other qualified engineers, experienced as to astronomy, topography and hydrography. For the six-month period involved, from December 1, 1865, the engineers were to be paid $800 a month and were to be furnished suitable subsistence, lodging and space for their baggage, instruments and stores.

Cleveland Rockwell volunteered to join the party after being recommended by the Washington office of the Coast Survey. His war experiences and his association with Assistants Gilbert and West, who were heading the project, made him a likely choice. He wrote to J. E. Hilgard, Assistant then in charge of the Coast Survey from Cleveland, Ohio, December 5, 1865, indicating that he would join the survey party.

Rockwell met the others in the party in New York City, and they sailed for Colombia on December 11 on the mail steamer *Tamar*. The voyage was uneventful until the vessel tried to enter the harbor of Santa Marta at night. The captain ran the vessel up and down the coast and "twice . . . thought he had hit the harbor, as also did local citizens of Santa Marta who were aboard." In each instance the ship had to be backed out, a risky maneuver because of the danger to the propeller in striking bottom or running against a rock. Rockwell and his companions were shocked at this primitive navigation and the danger which could have been obviated for all ships by the installation of a beacon light. Captain West related the experience and suggested a beacon of two different colored lights, one over the other, be placed on Morro Island in the harbor to indicate the entrance.[23] The suggestion was subsequently adopted.

On arrival in Santa Marta the group was stunned by unanticipated demands. They received written instructions from the Colombian Secretary of State to investigate the richness and probable extent of certain coal beds and to furnish to the executive power a report embracing all data for cost of a railroad necessary to work the mines and any other details required for forming an exact judgment on the matter. Gilbert and West lodged a protest for the party with the Colombian Secretary of State for Internal Affairs, stating that they had not come prepared to engage in mining engineering.[24] The impasse was settled by withdrawal of the coal mine survey orders.

Other difficulties followed when the party proceeded to the base for their survey operations. Housing and storage facilities provided proved to be grossly inadequate. Another protest and conferences followed which eventually resulted in satisfactory quarters. Then the Colombian government proposed to pay the engineers' monthly salary in Colombian gold dollars, worth considerably less than the U.S. gold dollars called for by contract. (The initial payment made in New York City before the party departed had been in U.S. gold.) Again an exchange of letters in stiff and formal language satisfied the necessary diplomatic protocol, and finally led to resumption of payment in American gold dollars.[25]

Little detailed information is available concerning the proposed connection between Lake Santa Marta and the Magdalena River. It took extra time "to put in proper shape"

the results of a 400-mile reconnaissance of the Magdalena River "from its mouths [sic] to the head of steamboat navigation . . . which was made *over & above* what was called for in our agreement or instructions, beside the thorough study required in examining surveys of a region of country some hundreds of square miles in extent, in order to properly project routes, make estimates, etc., etc."[26] In spite of problems and vexations, the work was completed on time and the party returned to the United States.[27] Rockwell wrote to J. E. Hilgard again from New York on June 11, 1866, after his return from South America, that he had

arrived in this city from South America, with our whole party, on Saturday [June 9]. I am happy to say we have all enjoyed excellent health. Since my arrival, I have been suffering from a bilious attack, but I hope to be better in a few days.

I wish to go to my home in Cleveland for a short time and will report myself from there, if there is no objection to such a course.

I should like to hear from you privately, about C. S. prospects and if any parties are on the coast of Maine, and, what my chances would be. Also what are the prospects of promotion for us young men. I am glad to hear appropriations do not fail. Hope to hear of better general C. S. prospects. I shall stay quietly here until I am better . . . .[28]

After Rockwell's recovery in Cleveland, he received the desired assignment on the coast of Maine for the balance of 1866. He was made head of a party to resume the topography of Muscongus Bay there, and, as reported,

turned in two plane-table sheets containing the outline and most all the topographical features between Crotch Island on the east and Round Pond on the west side of the sound. In the latter part of the season his work was furthered by the transfer to him of the schooner *Bowditch*. The mainland and islands represented on the two sheets sent in by Mr. Rockwell show an aggregate of sixty-two miles of shore-line, ten miles of road, and about eleven square miles of detailed topography. The work was prosecuted between the 6th of August and the 10th of November.[29]

Rockwell lost a friend and elder colleague when, on February 17, 1867, in Newport, Rhode Island, Alexander Dallas

Bache died. His stroke in 1864 had caused a long period of suffering and paralysis. Bache was succeeded by Prof. Benjamin Peirce, librarian at Harvard College and faculty member there until his death in 1880. Noted as astronomer and as America's leading mathematician, Peirce was Coast Survey superintendent from 1867-1874, carrying on his work at Harvard at the same time.[30]

Between November 10, 1866 and March 6, 1867, Rockwell's whereabouts are not known. The four and one-half months are not listed in his record of occupation or leaves.

In March, 1867, Sub-Assistant Rockwell began a topographical survey of St. Catherine's Sound, Georgia, using the schooner *Bailey*. He was relieved on April 6.

On May 1, 1867, at 30 years of age and after 11 years of service, Cleveland Rockwell became an Assistant in the U. S. Coast Survey. He also received a transfer to the West Coast. He was to work under his friend, Assistant George Davidson, who was in charge of the Coast Survey office in San Francisco.

CHAPTER II: NOTES

1. *Annual Report, 1861*, pp. 1, 9. The two Coast Survey vessels mentioned were seized in Charleston Harbor.
2. *Annual Report, 1861,* p. 10.
3. *Ibid.,* 47.
4. *Annual Report, 1862,* p. 50. Isaac Ingalls Stevens served as executive officer to Bache on the U.S. Coast Survey, 1849-1853. Then he was the first governor appointed to the Washington Territory created in 1853 by dividing Oregon Territory. General Stevens was killed in the Battle of Chantilly, Va., Sept. 1, 1862.
5. *Annual Report, 1861,* pp. 39, 40.
6. *Ibid.,* p. 40.
7. The brief background of Civil War history herein reported to coincide with Rockwell's activities is taken from *Encyclopedia of American History, op. cit.,* pp. 228-45.
8. *Annual Report, 1861,* pp. 267-68.
9. *Annual Report, 1862,* pp. 50, 51, 23.
10. *Annual Report, 1863,* p. 41.
11. *Ibid.,* p. 210.
12. *Annual Report, 1863,* p. 42.
13. Coast Survey Employment Record, National Archives, Record Group 23.
14. *Annual Report, 1863,* pp. 13, 22, 31.
15. *Ibid.,* 21, 22.
16. *Annual Report, 1863,* p. 42; *1864,* p. 23.
17. This information comes from his Grand Army of the Republic membership application to Garfield Post No. 3 (Portland), Department of Oregon, August 5, 1884.
18. *Annual Report, 1864,* p. 31.
19. *Ibid.*
20. *Annual Report, 1864,* p. 20.
21. *Annual Report, 1865,* pp. 21, 22.
22. Except where otherwise noted, the documents quoted and referred to concerning the South American work come from RG 59, National Archives, General Records Dept. of State, Dispatch No. 236 (with 13 enclosures). A seven-page contract between the governments of Colombia and the U.S. stipulates terms and conditions.
23. Preston C. F. West to the Resident Minister (A.L. Burton), Bogota, April 13, 1866, A.L.S.
24. S. A. Gilbert and Preston C. F. West to A. L. Burton, Santa Marta, Dec. 29, 1865.
25. P. C. F. West to Allen A. Burton, U.S. Minister at Bogota, March 9, 1866, A.L.S.
26. P.C.F. West to J.E. Hilgard, Assistant in Charge, Boston, Mass., Dec. 25, 1866, A.L.S.
27. Allen A. Burton to William H. Seward, Bogota, May 30, 1866, A.L.S. Stamped receipt date of August 7, 1866.
28. NA, RG 23. Rockwell's letter was written on stationery of Kent & Co., proprietor of which was George Kent, husband of Cleveland's sister Matilda. Rockwell used this address as his mail address, and referred to it as his office in New York City. George L. Kent and Kent and Co., listed variously as Merchants, Grocer and Broker, was located at 1 Front St., 1852-1857; 54 Broad St., 1858-1868; 35 Broadway, 1869-1871; 79 Front St., 1872-1879; 49 New St., 1880-1882; 49 Exchange St., 1883-1884. George Kent's residence was in Brooklyn. He married Matilda D. (du Plessis) Rockwell (born June 1832, died 1864) on June 1, 1852. Three children: George Rockwell Kent, Alice Kent and Frederick Cleveland Kent. George L. Kent died Dec. 22, 1884. There was no successor to his business firm. (Information from James J. Heslin, Director New-York Historical Society.)
29. Annual Report, 1866, p. 11.
30. The summation in the *Dictionary of American Biography* quotes a later Coast Survey superintendent, J. E. Hilgard, who commented in 1881 that Peirce began "the extension of the survey of the coast to a great geodetic system, stretching from ocean to ocean... laying the foundation for a general map of the country entirely independent of detached local surveys."

CHAPTER III

PACIFIC COAST: WORK IN
CALIFORNIA, OREGON & WASHINGTON TERRITORY

CLEVELAND ROCKWELL entered a region new to him on the Pacific Coast. Perhaps he never had occasion to think of the West during his busy days on the northern and southern Atlantic Coast, exciting Civil War experiences and South American engineering adventures. Yet the Pacific Coast was to become his home. His place in West Coast Survey work, too, becomes clearer with some background outlined for both the Survey there and his new superior, George Davidson, under whom Rockwell had worked before in the Civil War defense of Philadelphia.

Born in Nottingham, England, May 9, 1825, George Davidson came to the United States with his family in 1832. He received primary schooling in Philadelphia, then attended Central High School. Head of the high school was Alexander Dallas Bache, graduated 15 years before from West Point. Already an important figure in education, Bache was an administrator and scholar of physics, astronomy and geodesy (geological science). A lifetime of admiration and professional alliance ensued. Professor Bache recognized and directed his pupils' abilities. In 1840 the school was given a telescope and other astronomical equipment. George Davidson became a student assistant. After graduation he became magnetic observer at Girard College, Philadelphia, under Bache's direction. When Bache accepted the chair of chemistry and natural philosophy at the University of Pennsylvania in Philadelphia, Davidson followed as his assistant.

At 20 years of age he joined the U. S. Coast Survey. That was in 1845 — two years after his mentor had become superintendent of the Survey.

Davidson worked along the gulf from Florida to Texas, then in New England. For several years he spent winters in the southern states and summers in New England as an astronomical observer with Superintendent Bache's party. In various field parties he was engaged in reconnaissance, triangulation, latitude and longitude observation and field magnetics. He also served under Robert H. Fauntleroy, a brilliant engineer, whose daughter he was to marry.

The California Gold Rush was the great stimulus to West Coast activity of the Coast Survey. Hundreds of ships converged on San Francisco from all over the world: but there were no lighthouses, buoys or markers along the western U. S. coastline to guide them. In use were maps from schoolbooks, charts based on British George Vancouver's visit of 1792, and those from the 1841 American expedition commanded by Charles Wilkes.

The United States Coast Survey, spurred on by the frequent wrecks on the West Coast, dispatched the U. S. schooner *Ewing,* under command of Navy Lt. William P. McArthur, to California in October, 1848. Journeying around the Horn, she arrived in California almost a year later in September, 1849. Within a year, a three-sheet reconnaissance chart extending from San Diego to the Columbia River was published by the Survey. Then Lieutenant McArthur died in Panama on his return trip to Washington.

In May, 1850, with George Davidson as head of the party, a second expedition was sent via the Isthmus of Panama to San Francisco. They were to prepare accurate and detailed charts of the coastline from the Mexican border to Puget Sound. The hydrographic portion was in charge of Lt. James Alden, Jr., a naval officer then stationed on the coast and a veteran of the Wilkes Expedition nine years earlier.[1]

Davidson's party determined by astronomical methods the true positions of the more prominent headlands of the coast, specifically Points Conception, Pinos and Loma in California and Cape Disappointment at the mouth of the Columbia. Charts of these regions were published in 1852 and found immediate use in the heavy ship traffic of the West Coast.

The Survey continued working; in 1853 the *Active*, a larger and more seaworthy steamer, replaced the little *Ewing*. In 1854 a third reconnaissance sheet was published covering the Umpqua River northward to the Canadian border.

These 1854 charts were of special interest. Their great usefulness was augmented by pictorial representation of the most important headlands, entrances to rivers, bays and straits, a feature of inestimable value to ship captains who had never seen the region before. Another unique feature was that the views mentioned were genuine etchings on copper plate. They were done by the great American artist, James McNeill Whistler, the only such etchings he did during his brief employment with the Coast Survey. Whistler had failed chemistry at West Point Academy and briefly took a position with the Coast Survey before deciding to be a professional artist. He did not visit the West Coast but made the graphic representations from photographs and drawings, some by George Davidson.

Assistant George Davidson, head of C.S. West Coast office, was visiting Rockwell when this sketch was made, 1868. Graves Collection sketchbook.

Fixing the exact geographical locations was Davidson's responsibility. He also made recommendations as to location of lighthouses. In 1855 Davidson returned to Washington, D.C. after five years of strenuous West Coast fieldwork. The next summer, 1856, he returned to measure a base line at Port Townsend similar to one he laid out at San Pedro three years earlier. In 1857, despite severe rheumatism which incapacitated him much of the year, he spent what time he could in the field on the Sonoma County, California, coast. His comprehensive "Directory for the Pacific Coast" was published in the Coast Survey Report for 1858.

On October 5, 1858, George Davidson married Ellinor Fauntleroy at Whiteport, Virginia. The 21-year-old bride began her honeymoon with a voyage to California via the Isthmus of Panama. On her arrival, despite her frailty, she bore the hardships of survey life in tents and primitive camps. In 1859 their first child was born. He died from a fall in 1861, after they returned to Washington.

Seven years later, the Civil War was concluded and his old chief, A. D. Bache, was dead. Davidson acceded to new Superintendent Benjamin Peirce's plan for him to assume charge of the Coast Survey's sub-office in San Francisco. Meantime he made a survey of Alaska and reported in person to Secretary of State William H. Seward, Secretary of the Treasury Hugh McCulloch, the chairmen of the Senate Committee of Foreign Affairs, the Senate and House Finance committees. His 140-page report was published as Appendix 18 in the Coast Survey Report for 1867. It was given wide acclaim as influential in the consummation of the purchase of Alaska from Russia.

By the fall of 1868 Davidson was back in San Francisco in charge of the U. S. Coast Survey office, on Sansome Street between Washington and Jackson streets. As a veteran of the Coast Survey he was certainly the best informed on the West Coast from the Mexican border to and including Alaska. This was the man to whom the newly appointed Assistant Rockwell reported for work.[2]

Assistant Rockwell began his first West Coast assignment in charge of a party to survey a portion of the San Francisco peninsula. The entire project was to meet specifications of the Engineering Department for the military defenses of the city of San Francisco and to conform and connect accurately with previous surveys. Assistant A. F. Rodgers, like Davidson a Pacific Coast Survey veteran, was already at work in the interior of the peninsula. Another section of the peninsula was the objective for the season of Assistant Rockwell, his aid, L. A. Sengteller and party.

In his Annual Report, Superintendent Benjamin Peirce buried Rockwell's work in a portion of a single sentence making Rockwell subservient to Assistant Rodgers.[3] For the first time since joining the Survey there was no commendation for Rockwell in the Annual Report of the superintendent. Rockwell felt discouraged when he saw the publication.[4] He had reluctantly accepted an assignment on the West Coast far from family and friends. In the East he had received praise during his wartime experiences; now he was relegated to obscurity by distance from Coast Survey headquarters and a new superintendent with whom he had little in common. The work was difficult and frustrating, and even as a full assistant his pay was only $100 a month, with no allowance for room and board.

Rockwell mentioned a protest about the low rate of pay in a letter to George Davidson from Camp El Coxo, California, written March 23, 1869:

I have been sick in bed a week with your consolation rheumatiszmm [sic]. I think some regard might be paid to the comfort of Coast Surveyors

Cleveland Rockwell, Assistant

Date and Place of Birth.	Residence when Appointed, Date of Appointment.	COMPENSATION.		
		FROM	TO	AMOUNT
Nov. 24, 1836	New York City (July 1, 1856	Nov. 1, 1858	$15. per month & board)	
Youngstown, Ohio.	July 1, 1856 Nov. 1, 1858	Nov. 1, 1859	$25. per month & board.	
	Aid Nov. 1, 1859	July 1, 1860	35. " "	
	June 1, 1862 July 1, 1860 Sub Assistant	Jan'y 1, 1863	40. " "	
	May 1, 1867 Jan'y 1, 1863 Assistant	June 1, 1863	50. " "	
	June 1, 1863	July 1, 1864	800. annum	
	July 1, 1864	July 1, 1866	900. "	
	July 1, 1866	May 1, 1867	1.000 "	
	May 1, 1867	Jan'y 1, 1869	1.200 "	
	Jan'y 1, 1869	July 1, 1870	1.500 "	
	July 1, 1870	Jan'y 1, 1872	1.650 "	
	Jan'y 1, 1872	Apl. 1, 1873	1.850 "	
	Apl. 1, 1873		2.120 "	

DATE.	Cleveland Rockwell	FILE NO.
1882. August 5th	Compensation increased from "2120 to "2232" per annum	1521.
1883 July 1	" " "2232 to "2292 "	1570.
1885 Oct. 9	Oath of Office	1834
1886 March 9	On 'waiting orders', February & March 1886.	1952.
1887 July 11	Salary fixed at $2400. per an. from July 1, 1887.	2083
1886 Aug. 24	Bond, dated August 6, 1886, for $200000	2111
Oct. 8, 1888	Salary fixed @ $2400 Per Annum.	2262.
Aug. 29, 1890	" " 2.600 " from Aug. 30, 1890	2839.
Sep. 1, 1890	Prom. Amended so as to take effect from July 1, 1890	2841.
June 1, 1892	Resignation as Assistant to take effect from and after May 31st, 1892.	3085.

From NA, RG 23, Compensation Record.

in camp without any lumber for floors.

I sent through you a communication to the Superintendent requesting increase of pay — whatever you may think of my action in making such a request, I rely upon your good offices so far as not to feel it necessary to request that you do not oppose it. The communication explains itself and I mean the whole of it. I think quite hard of the Supdts. action; when Mr. H[ilgard] having known of my services in the army (when I was Chief topt. Engr. of Shermans raiders) in the Coast Survey, found the opportunity of increasing my pay, he immediately cut it down.[5]

Some time later Rockwell evidently read Peirce's 1867 Annual Report. He wrote again to Davidson on March 25, 1871, from San Simeon Bay, California, and included a letter to Superintendent Peirce — to be forwarded or retained as Davidson saw fit. Rockwell wrote Peirce:

It was with surprise and mortification that I read in the Coast Survey Report for 1868,[6] the very slight mention of my service in the survey of the peninsula of San Francisco.

According to my instructions I came out to the coast in charge of a party — my first duty being a survey of part of the peninsula of San Francisco under the general supervision of Assistant Rodgers. I did not come to "join the party of Asst. Rodgers with an additional plane table."

The name of my aid at that time, Mr. Sengteller, is not mentioned. I feel deeply mortified at the public slight of my services, when I recall the very complimentary and flattering letter addressed to me under date of July 6th, 1868, commendatory of these same services — a letter I have treasured with satisfaction and pride.

May I be permitted respectfully to enquire the reason for the public and official depreciation.[7]

Davidson was the only one to whom Rockwell could blow off steam and vent his anger and frustration. He understood Rockwell and made him feel that he was largely in agreement. At the same time he calmed him down and caused Rockwell to bide his time. His answer to Rockwell shows, in part, why all of the men in his West Coast jurisdiction loved and trusted him and found strength in Davidson's guiding hand:

Dear Sir:

I have yours of Mar 25 with letter to the Supt of same date. As you ask me to, I retain the letter to the Supt, if I see nothing to disprove of the tone or substance. I have retained it. The tone of the last paragraph appeared to me harsh, and I think you might modify the general tone of the whole, if you persist in making a protest. As your friend, and looking at it for your interests and not knowing who is to blame, I would advise you to let the matter sleep — if you will exhume it do so after more reflection, and when no sign of anger can be found in your letter.[8]

Meanwhile, from January into May, 1868, Assistant Rockwell had continued his topographical survey for the defense of San Francisco. The area between School-House Station and Millbrae was mapped by early May. Rockwell and his aid, L. A. Sengteller, next proceeded to Oregon on a five-day stagecoach trip.[9]

The mouth of the Columbia River had not been surveyed from 1852 until the 1868 season. The hydrography of the Columbia River was especially requested by Major General Andrew Humphries, Chief of Engineers. All aspects of the survey were made to conform to the requirements of the Corps of Engineers as stipulated by Gen. Barton S. Alexander. He worked closely with the survey and provided the use of the steam tug *Katy* to Assistant Edward Cordell in charge of the U.S. Coast Survey party.

Depth soundings indicated remarkable changes at the entrance to the Columbia River. A new channel above Astoria was discovered with two more feet of water than the old channel. There were also great changes about and on the bar. The north channel was the permanent main channel, while the south channel, the *apparent* main channel, was temporary. In the meantime, Sand Island had moved eastward and the north channel widened until it had become the only usable one. Assistant Cordell reported: "It is more crooked and contracted than formerly, and the depth of water on the bar has decreased from five to three and three quarter fathoms [30 to 22½ feet]. During strong northwest winds it [the sea] breaks completely across the bar."

The Columbia bar was considered one of the most treacherous in the world. One practical and immediate result of the survey was the removal of the sea buoy from the entrance of the north channel and its placement off the south channel entrance. In addition, a first class red buoy was installed near the entrance at the point of Clatsop Spit for the guidance of vessels clearing that point.

For special use of the Engineering Department, Assistant Cordell made a triangulation of the mouth of the Columbia, marking as stations Cape Disappointment, Chinook Point, Point Adams and Sand Island. The stations were secured by blocks of sandstone. Results of the triangulation including distances and geographical positions were furnished to the United States Engineers and to Cleveland Rockwell. Comment on the not uneventful work noted that

The prosecution of soundings on the Columbia River during the winter was attended with danger . . . Freezing weather in January followed by strong northeast winds, filled the lower part of the river with large fields of floating ice, and though Mr Cordell hastened to get the *Marcy* into a place of shelter, a considerable part of the copper sheathing was torn off and the planking was cut two inches deep by the ice drift in less than half an hour. The vessel was saved by being beached at Young's Point. No disaster occurred to the members of the party, although the night of the 8th of January was passed in great personal peril, not only to them, but to the crews of the other vessels in the river.[10]

Danger and peril constantly accompanied the work of the Survey. The "close shaves" were not reported. In the season just preceding Rockwell's arrival in Oregon, a catastrophe took place on the survey of Tillamook bar, about 45 miles south of the mouth of the Columbia:

Sub-Assistant Julius Kincheloe had essentially completed the hydrography of the bar on the 20th of May. The water being smooth at 2 p.m., that opportunity was taken to run a concluding line for the general verification of his previous soundings. In doing this, and while in seven fathoms water, the boat was suddenly swamped by a breaker, and in the next instant capsized. Five of the crew were washed from the bottom

of the capsized boat by succeeding breakers, and ultimately Mr. Kincheloe from the mast. The only survivor, James Steel, clung to the mast of the boat until rescued by a lad named George W. Clark, who bravely risked his own life in a very small canoe to save those whom he saw to be in more imminent peril.[11]

Assistant Rockwell and Aid Sengteller arrived in Astoria. By July 1, 1868, the party was organized and began their first season's work in Oregon. The plane table survey, taking over the triangulation markers set up by Assistant Cordell, began at Astoria and was carried eastward beyond the mouth of John Day's River in Clatsop County, and westward to include part of the Pacific seacoast beyond Point Adams. Probably it was Rockwell's description that the Annual Report quoted:

"The whole country is not only covered with a heavy growth of the largest evergreen timber, but densely clothed with thick and impenetrable bushes, chiefly of the berry-bearing class. This dense jungle is the principal impediment in prosecuting the topographical survey. The north (or Washington Territory) side of the river is very bold, almost mountainous. Cliffs and precipices occur at almost every point.

"Above the remarkable neck of land called Tongue Point, where the river widens into a large sheet of water known as Cathlamet Bay, there are again large areas of tide lands, or swamps, intersected by numerous channels. Some of these channels are navigable, and are used by the small steamers plying between Astoria and Portland.

"The smoke from fires in the forest became quite troublesome at the end of August, and soon after enveloped the whole country, obscuring the sun and seriously impeding navigation even at sea. For this reason no work could be done on a third plane-table sheet, which was projected to include part of the north side of the Columbia, above Cape Disappointment."[12]

During the winter of 1868 and spring of 1869 Rockwell traced and inked his maps of the Point Conception, California area. Point Conception angles out into the Pacific Ocean and forms the northern and western limit to Santa Barbara Channel. Then in carrying the topography northward, a landing was attempted at El Coxo. After many delays and with great difficulty the landing was accomplished. In addi-

tion to the usual shore topography, Rockwell was instructed to include the crest line of the coast mountains behind Point Conception light as viewed from seaward with contours of 100 feet. To accomplish the tertiary triangulation Assistant Rockwell was required to measure a base line of 1,500 meters. The work was completed in May, with the help of Sub-Assistant L. A. Sengteller and party. In San Francisco Rockwell supervised the repairs on the schooner *Humboldt*. The financial complications which ensued were to become an annoyance to him for several seasons and again strain his relations with Survey headquarters in Washington.[13]

Returning to the Columbia River on July 30, 1869, Assistant Rockwell, accompanied by Sub-Assistant Sengteller, used the Coast Survey schooner *Humboldt* to travel up the coast. The work began at Cape Disappointment and proceeded northward along the ocean shore to Point Grenville. The bold headlands at the river's mouth gave way to a low sand beach broken only by the entrances to Shoalwater (Willapa) Bay and Gray's Bay. On the inner shore of Cape Disappointment, forming Baker's Bay, the work was carried to beyond Chinook at the time of the season's report. A military post had been established at the extremity of Cape Disappointment since the survey of 1851. The many changes constituting the post made the resurvey advisable. Rockwell found "the interior of Cape Disappointment so densely wooded and covered with undergrowth as to be impenetrable for ordinary operations with an observing instrument. The first part of the season was smoky from the great fires raging in the forests of Oregon and Washington Territory. Early rains extinguished the fires, and were succeeded by fogs. The latter part of the season was favorable."[14]

In August Assistant George Davidson visited Astoria when returning from Alaska. He reoccupied the triangulation and secondary astronomical station at Astor Point and in one night observed the transits of 16 stars with a new meridian instrument. He connected the longitude of the station with San Francisco by transporting 16 chronometers. The purpose was to refine the readings of the exact location at Point Astor. The triangulation of the Columbia River survey would depend for its accuracy on this determination.[15]

That fall, 1869, Rockwell continued his topography of the Columbia's north shore. In May, 1870, his party resumed the survey of shores and islands of the river. He used the triangulations made in 1852. Included were both banks and numerous low, marshy islands in the river up as far as Cathlamet Point. Great care was taken to delineate the low water lines. Work closed in November, 1870.

Assistant Rockwell, his aid, George H. Wilson, and party moved in January, 1871, to San Simeon Bay, California. Here they measured a line of 816 meters and extended a triangulation therefrom to include San Simeon Bay and the shore to the westward. At the end of March the party returned to Oregon. Triangulation and topography of the Columbia River was resumed in May with difficulty. The shores were "covered with heavy timber, through which at high points, lines of sight were required to bring stations into view that otherwise would be hidden by the dense growth of timber on the islands in the river." The work was extended to Westport, about 12 miles above Cathlamet Point by river. The plane table survey sheet included both banks of the Columbia, with all the islands between Cathlamet Point and Puget Island. The river banks were shown as "being high, abrupt and broken, densely timbered and covered with thick underbrush." There was no river valley in that area, for "the shores have a steep pitch to the water line. The basin of the Columbia is from two to five miles wide and area between shores

filled with an intricacy of low marshy islands, which are covered with spruce, cottonwood and alder. The islands are overflowed by freshets and by high tides." Rockwell determined and included the positions of notable mountain peaks and ridges in view from the stations occupied for his work. As usual the dense smoke from summer forest fires retarded the work. Seventy-one miles of shoreline were surveyed and recorded. When the season closed, Rockwell returned to San Simeon Bay.[16]

Cleveland Rockwell spent the winter of 1871 in San Francisco. He completed and inked five sheets pertaining to the preceding season. He resumed work on San Simeon Bay, advancing beyond Piedras Blancas. On April 20th, the party left and returned to the Columbia River for the 1872 season. In spite of freshets, fogs and smoke, good progress was made. The survey advanced to include all of Puget Island and both river banks as far as Westport, 35 miles of shoreline.[17]

Rockwell wrote Davidson from Camp Cathlamet, Washington Territory on July 24, 1871: "My father, now an old man, expects to come out in the fall and perhaps stay all winter and if I have the opportunity of seeing him while here I shall not require a leave of absence this year."[18] In 1874 Rockwell stated that he had not taken leave since being on the West Coast and that it was then eight years. Therefore, he did not take a leave in 1871. There is no subsequent mention of his father. Presumably he did not come to San Francisco.

In 1873, work began in February at Point Piedras Blancas and continued the coast triangulation and topography northward near the Santa Lucia range of mountains. Rockwell made a reconnaissance of the seaward face of this range for 18 miles beyond the Arroyo San Carpofero. The position of Harlech Castle Rock was reconfirmed. The wreck of the

Sierra Nevada was located and shown on the plane table sheet. The Arroyo La Cruz and the San Carpofero were both sizable streams with deep channels running between hills of 500 and 600 feet elevation. The triangulation was carried to Valenzuela. George H. Wilson, his aid, was commended for zealous and efficient service. The party was transferred to the Columbia River in May.[19]

Cleveland Rockwell was married in 1873. His bride was 14-year-old Cornelia Flemming Russell. She was born in Nashville, Tennessee, the daughter of William A. Russell and Susan Fudy (or Fudge), also born in Nashville.[20] Her father and uncle were respectively a state senator and governor of Tennessee.[21] Her parents were strongly opposed to the marriage. They objected to Cleveland Rockwell as a son-in-law because of his Union army activities and in particular, his involvement with Sherman's raiders. Perhaps, too, they felt that Rockwell at 36 was too old for their 14-year-old daughter. At any rate, in an effort to keep the marriage from her family, they were married on a ferryboat between San Francisco and Angel Island in the Bay.[22]

Looking at the dates of Rockwell's field assignments, the wedding could have occurred in April, May or June. In April, 1873 he was granted a pay raise of $270 making his total pay $2,120 per annum. This was almost three times larger than the periodic increments he had been receiving and may have reflected his increased need as a married man.

Since Rockwell first arrived in California, he had retained a room in a boarding house, then in 1873 he moved into the Cosmopolitan Hotel for the next few years. When he was single, his room was simply a place to keep his possessions and civilian clothes since he was engaged in field work in California as soon as the season permitted. After office work, according to his established pattern, he would leave

for Oregon and his work on the Columbia River by May or June. With his marriage in 1873 he would doubtless have had a somewhat larger suite in the Cosmopolitan Hotel.

From a letter written several years later, Rockwell recounted that in 1873 he had traveled from San Francisco to the Columbia River by stagecoach and rested at "Sissions in Strawberry Valley" in June. This may well have been their honeymoon trip between Rockwell's spring and summer assignments. Sissons, a resort named for a pioneer family, lay at the base of Mount Shasta with a view of the mountain only a few miles away. In Oregon, Rockwell's new bride could have remained at a hotel in Astoria while his surveying activities were within a few miles so that he could see her on weekends. It is also possible that from 1873 on she shared his life in the camps from which he worked along the Columbia River. She had doubtless heard from Assistant George Davidson's wife, Ellinor, of her experience doing the same thing 20 years earlier.

In June the Rockwell party was at work on the Columbia River. It was important to adjust the survey of the Columbia by observing at a point for latitude. The topography was halted and triangulation was pushed forward on the Washington shore from Westport to Kalama, a distance of 32 miles. There the Northern Pacific Railway track left the Columbia River and turned northward toward Puget Sound. Again the sheer banks, marshes and dense forests made the work difficult. A boat was the only means of transportation, and the early summer run-off from melting snows made movement difficult. Lines of sight had to be cut through trees and underbrush and most of the lines ran through sloughs.

George Davidson had visited Point Astor in 1869, using complicated new equipment in combination with older and established methods to refine the longitude (east and west

Rockwell's painting of "Lassen Butte and Big Meadows, California."
Courtesy Edward Eberstadt & Sons, N.Y.

location) measurements. First, time was compared on an accurate bank of chronometers, then by telegraph between Cambridge Observatory in England and San Francisco. With permission of the Mayor of San Francisco, a temporary observatory was set up in Washington Square. The Western Union Telegraph Company cooperated by connecting one of their main lines to the observatory. Other stations were set up. Observations ensued from February 15th through April 4th by means of signals exchanged between Cambridge and San Francisco, Omaha and Salt Lake City. The telegraph time was correlated with sightings of the stars. In August, 1869 similar determinations were made at Astoria. This set of determinations was transferred to Kalama, Washington to eliminate magnetic disturbance in the signals at Astoria. Then in August, 1873, the Western Union Telegraph Company again granted free use of their lines. At Kalama transit readings on the stars were made on 18 nights and time signals transmitted on six nights.

This is a simplistic explanation of the procedure. The result was accurate longitude determinations which were extended to Puget Sound, British Columbia and Alaska. All figures in Rockwell's surveys were made exact and meaningful by the process.[23]

At the end of February, 1874, Rockwell and party were in the field north of Piedras Blancas in California. The coast was ragged and bluff, backed by gentle contours to the foot of the coast mountains. Along the northern limit, the mountain rises immediately at the coastline to 300 feet in height. At one point the party encountered and had to work across a mountain range of about 3,000 feet elevation above sea level. Five miles of the survey was completed when work closed on April 25th.[24]

While working in the field in California, Rockwell received word that his father had died February 25, 1874. Edward Rockwell had become increasingly weak and feeble and died at age 73.[25]

The Annual Report closes with June 30th for the year 1874. To determine what occurred in the last half of the calendar year from this point on, one must consult the next annual report.

Rockwell was in camp at Oak Point with his party on the Columbia River in May, 1874. Within a week a case of smallpox occurred in one of the members. The man was isolated, no other cases appeared and in early July the hand returned to work. Weather made it a poor season, but the survey was advanced to Smith Island, an estimated 20 miles (43 miles of shoreline surveyed). The season concluded the middle of October. Mr. George H. Wilson again was aid.[26]

Cleveland and Cornelia Flemming Rockwell's first child was born on July 20, 1874. Named Gertrude Ellinor Rockwell, she was christened at Trinity Episcopal Church in San Francisco by Rector Hiram W. Beers, D. D. Sponsors were Olivia Hoff, M. D., Mrs. Ellinor Davidson and Mrs. Elizabeth Stevenson.[27] Presumably Dr. Hoff was the obstetrician, Mrs. Ellinor Davidson was George Davidson's wife and Mrs. Elizabeth Stevenson remains unidentified. She may have been a sister or other relative of the mother; otherwise, no member of her seemingly unforgiving family was present. The baby did not live long.

A comic opera was played out on the rocky coast of California in 1875. Rockwell, the distraught hero, relates the experience. The survey was a continuation of work already done by the Coast Survey. However, the Lighthouse Board required the area of Point Sur to be meticulously surveyed in larger than usual scale and wanted Rockwell's recommendation for the location of a lighthouse and foghorn which would not only be visible while out at sea but also up and down the coast as far as possible.

Rockwell went to Monterey to obtain from the lighthouse service the use of the tender *Shubrick* to transport the party, their instruments, supplies and camp equipment to Point Sur. Unfortunately the *Shubrick* was laid up for repairs. So a second vessel, the *Gypsy,* smaller and more easily managed, was contracted from a local company. The *Gypsy* broke down on her trip to Monterey where she was to be loaded with the men and cargo. A third vessel, the *San Luis,* was engaged and left Monterey on the 1st of March with the party, supplies and equipment aboard. The *San Luis* was delayed in Monterey Bay by a southerly storm for two days and arrived at Point Sur on the morning of the 4th. A first small boat containing instruments, baggage and some blankets, as well as Rockwell and two of his men, landed safely, but the second load containing provisions and some instruments was capsized. These were partially recovered, but in water-soaked and damaged condition. A third load declined to land and returned to the *San Luis.* The *San Luis* lay off the point all day under steam. The wind did not abate and that evening she left on her way to San Diego. She took with her the cook, one of the hands, nearly all of the supplies and the remaining instruments and tools.

Fortunately there were two abandoned dairy shanties and in these the stranded party took shelter. The *San Luis* on her return from San Diego carried the men and supplies. When the vessel passed Point Sur, on the 17th of March, a northwest gale was blowing and the captain refused to anchor. She passed on her way and left everything at Monterey and continued to San Francisco. Rockwell rode up to Monterey and bargained for a small vessel of four tons — the fourth vessel. She did arrive with part of the things on

the 23rd of March and landed the load safely. The lost cook and one of the hands hiked into camp from Monterey. On the next trip down, the boat landed the balance of the supplies but then broke her mooring and was reduced to splinters on the beach. By this time it was the 25th of March, almost two months and four vessels since the party had assembled and attempted to start the season's work.

A base line was measured by 20 meter chain on favorable ground near the point and signals were erected in weather that would not permit the use of instruments. The wind blew morning, noon and night, and according to Rockwell's journal, there was no respite from the 10th to the 22nd of March. Much of the rock surface was so exposed and steep that both the men and the instruments were in danger of being blown off. At last the wind quieted for some days and allowed work to proceed, though such fog came in that they were unable to see a distance of 100 yards. However, levels were run and pegs driven at five-foot successive elevations up and down the main ridges. Where the slope was too steep for instruments or men, the lines were subsequently sketched in by tension lines from stations of known elevation. The result was a valuable survey and map on a scale sufficiently large to make vertical or horizontal sections of any part of the rock with great accuracy. Bearings were taken up and down the coast. The measurements were found to be absolutely indispensable for the determination of the site of the lighthouse and fog signal. Though the survey was incomplete, Rockwell decided it was useless to continue when he was prevented from working day after day by wind and fog.

During the survey party's stay, on April 21 at 8:00 p.m., the steamship *Ventura* ran on the rocks in the fog, a mile north of Point Sur. Ship and cargo were a total loss. Though it was only 100 yards from shore, Rockwell and party were helpless to assist.

On May 7 Rockwell rode to Monterey and telegraphed Goodale, Nelson & Perkins Steamship Company to send a vessel down at once to take off his party. The fifth vessel of the season, the steamer *Santa Cruz,* arrived on May 13. The party with their supplies and equipment were taken aboard and arrived in San Francisco on May 15.

On June 1 Rockwell sent the original plane table sheet of Point Sur and included his recommendations for a first and second choice of locations for a lighthouse and fog signal. The work was acknowledged as a "most beautiful specimen of topographical work with everything clearly and artistically delineated." The wreck of the *Ventura* clearly demonstrated the need for the lighthouse and fog signal at Point Sur.[28]

Rockwell's leave, after 20 years in the Coast Survey, began June 1, 1875. The first four months were with pay and he brought all charts up to date during that time. Then he was granted the eight months following without pay, which would end his leave period June 1, 1876. He had asked for leave with pay "for the reason that I have always inked all the sheets I have ever made since my first attachment to the Coast Survey and do not like to trust them in other hands than my own." He added: "I have not had a leave of absence since I arrived on this coast which will be 8 years next June. In order to protect myself, it may become necessary for me to give my personal attention to some matters of private interest and importance to me, which I can not do when engaged in the Coast Survey."[29]

There is no record to indicate where Cleveland Rockwell went during his leave nor information regarding his "private interests." It would seem likely that his father's death a year before created some estate problems. His father had extensive interests in land and the Cleveland and Pittsburgh Railway and investments in New York City. Rockwell's small salary would not have permitted him to accumulate the wealth which he later possessed.

In Portland, Oregon, there is the belief that he visited Europe and pursued his art career with further instruction. The period of September, 1875 through May, 1876, seems to be the only leave long enough for this purpose. He could have arranged his affairs in Cleveland and New York or Connecticut and then proceeded to Europe. Whether or not he did so is open to question.

The scarcity of personal letters has been reported. The letters from assistants to the superintendent consisted of a monthly report and sometimes a private letter to discuss matters other than Coast Survey business. The National Archives have microfilmed the letters through 1875, though many are missing. There is a gap from 1875 to 1887 when the letters have not been microfilmed.

He rejoined the Survey in June, 1876 after his leave, and with Assistant William Eimbeck joined Professor Davidson in the Sacramento Valley. Assistant Davidson was locating and surveying a base line of nearly 11 miles. It was named "Yolo Base" since it was located in Yolo County, and served to connect the prinicpal triangulations then proceeding in California.[30]

Assistant Rockwell did not return to work on the Columbia River for the next two years. In August, 1876 he started a reconnaissance of the area above the Russian River. The overall plan was to extend a chain of quadrangles further northward and westward along the coast of California. Rockwell and party traveled on horseback, using pack animals for their gear. Rockwell became ill at Cloverdale, recovered and rejoined the party in November. Main stations and subsidiary points were located. The coast series of primary triangles were to be related to triangulations in the mountainous interior. At the end of the season, on December 7th, the reconnaissance had progressed northward to the region of Cape Mendocino.

Early in April, 1877 Rockwell continued the work. He selected points to form desirable quadrilaterals. Forests of redwood timber covering even mountain summits made the task of opening lines of sight a formidable endeavor. Numerous stations were located and many summits were marked. The last location would carry the triangulation to the region of Cape Blanco on the Oregon coast. By the second week in October heavy rains caused the streams to swell. Crossings became dangerous. The party returned by way of Portland and Astoria to San Francisco.[31]

Rockwell returned to the Columbia River. He took over the *Kincheloe* at Astoria the last of April, 1878. The party aboard, they proceeded to Kalama where the survey had terminated two years before. Heavy rains for two months were followed by August forest fires. The air was dense with smoke and the white ashes of burned ferns. The survey established a string of stations to a point near Willow Bar, eight miles below the mouth of the Willamette River. The survey had advanced 17 miles by January 13, 1879 at the close of field work.

Rockwell added a comment quoted in the superintendent's report: "The bar at the lower end of Sauvie's Island near Saint Helen's, and extending down to Columbia City, is one of the few very shoal places in the Columbia, and is of much importance. A channel is maintained across the bar by dredging, which is done yearly under the direction of the United States Engineer Department."[32]

The year 1878 saw Assistant Rockwell's last duty in California for more than a decade. He had become entrenched in his Columbia River survey and must have been relieved in not having to transfer his party twice a year. For twelve years San Francisco had been home base. He had made friends there. In the five years since their marriage, he and Cornelia had established a congenial circle of friends, including the George Davidsons.

He was no longer directly under Davidson. The latter still had a fatherly interest and in several letters reminded Rockwell to "be sure to get the monthly reports in to the superintendent on time." Rockwell received his own separate annual appropriation.

The San Francisco directories listed him for the year 1878, but not for 1879. Then, as an afterthought, for 1880 his listing was: "After July 1st, Albino [sic] Oregon." Oregon was now the Cleveland Rockwells' new home.

1. James Alden, Jr. and James Madison Alden, his young nephew, are most frequently confused. James Alden, Jr., later an admiral, was not an artist. His nephew, James Madison Alden, served as artist on the hydrographic portion of the survey along with William B. McMurtrie. Later, in 1857-61, James M. Alden was the artist on the unfinished United States-Canadian boundary survey from the Pacific Coast to the summit of the Rocky Mountains.

2. This outline is derived from *George Davidson, Pioneer West Coast Scientist,* by Oscar Lewis (Berkeley, 1954).

3. *Annual Report, 1867,* p. 38.

4. Peirce's report, dated in December, 1867, was transmitted by the Secretary of the Treasury to Congress in May, 1868, and finally published in 1869. Probably Rockwell saw the 1867 report in 1869 or even later.

5. A. L. S., among 151 IN letters of Rockwell to Davidson, 1868-1888, located in the George Davidson Collection, Bancroft Library. There are 33 volumes of Davidson's OUT letters, largely U.S. Coast Survey correspondence. All were gleaned for information showing behind the scene details to cast some light on personal relations between Davidson and Rockwell, their wives and their private lives. My wife and I became quite proficient in reading George Davidson's scrawl. The paucity of non-survey related material comes from the fact that both men were highly dedicated to their work. If there was much warmth in either of them, it does not come through in their letters. (March 23, 1869 letter quoted by permission of The Director, The Bancroft Library, Univ. of California, Berkeley.)

6. Evidently Rockwell meant the 1867 report, for it is the one which omits mention of Sengteller, who is mentioned, as is Rockwell at some length, in the 1868 report.

7. Rockwell to Peirce, March 25, 1871, A.L.S. (Quoted by permission of The Director, The Bancroft Library, University of California, Berkeley.)

8. April 9, 1871, Davidson to Rockwell, letterbook v. 18. (Quoted by permission of The Director, The Bancroft Library, University of California, Berkeley.)

9. *Annual Report, 1869,* pp. 47-48.

10. *Annual Report, 1868,* pp. 34, 35.

11. *Annual Report, Report, 1867,* p. 39; see also p. 11.

12. *Annual Report, 1868,* p. 34.

13. *Annual Report, 1869,* pp. 47, 48. The financial complications appear in the Davidson Collection at Bancroft.

14. *Annual Report, 1869,* p. 54.

15. *Annual Report, 1869,* p. 54.

16. *Annual Report, 1871,* pp. 57, 62.

17. *Annual Report, 1872,* pp. 43, 44, 47.

18. A.L.S., George Davidson Collection. (Quoted by permission of The Director, The Bancroft Library, University of California, Berkeley.)

19. *Annual Report, 1873,* pp. 51-52, 57.

20. Montana State Bureau of Vital Statistics, Certificate of Death, Missoula County, #745. Register number 87 shows Mrs. Rockwell's maiden name, names of her parents, date and city of birth.

21. Several sources reported this allegation, a statement often repeated by the Rockwell daughters to their friends. The Tennessee State Library and Archives, Nashville, were consulted, but reported that the early census records are not indexed. The Russell and Fudy (Fudge) families were not identified.

22. Their marriage on the Angel Island ferry is reported by several persons who knew the two Rockwell daughters. In addition, Mr. and Mrs. Lloyd Graves of Seattle in 1945 talked to Col. Patrick Mullay, the second husband of the eldest daughter (Gertrude). The Graves kindly reported the interview. Official records for the marriage are not available (recording would depend on where the license was obtained). The entire year of 1873 was searched by the Marin County Clerk with no results.

The San Francisco County Clerk's office reports that all records were destroyed by fire, and the State of California Vital Records of Marriages were not kept until shortly after 1900.

23. *Annual Report, 1873,* pp. 52, 57; *1869,* p. 54.
24. *Annual Report, 1874,* p. 38.
25. *Obituary Records of Graduates of Yale College, op. cit.,* p. 124.
26. *Annual Report, 1875,* p. 63.
27. Vital Records, Trinity Episcopal Church, San Francisco. Typescript volume based on newspaper records, p. 96 (Sutro Library, San Francisco). After the 1906 earthquake and fire, the women of Trinity Episcopal Church recovered the destroyed records as far as possible. There is no other source for these records.
28. The involved tale of difficulties at Point Sur is reported in the Annual Report for 1875. The firsthand account is available in Rockwell's monthly reports and letters to Coast Survey Superintendent Carlile P. Patterson. The version here given is based on letters of April 24 and May 21, 1875, from National Archives RG 23. Journal of Occupation and Report at Point Sur.
29. Rockwell to C. P. Patterson, Superintendent of the Coast Survey, San Francisco, Jan. 12, 1875, A.L.S. NA RG 23.
30. *Annual Report, 1876,* p. 55.
31. *Annual Report, 1877,* p. 56; *1878,* pp. 48-49.
32. *Annual Report, 1879,* pp. 57-58.

CHAPTER IV

PORTLAND, OREGON; SURVEY OF COLUMBIA & WILLAMETTE RIVERS

CLEVELAND and Cornelia Rockwell were living in Albina, Oregon in 1879. Albina and East Portland had not united with west side Portland. A moorage and a base for supplies had been established at Albina. Here the Coast Survey sloop *Kincheloe* was moored during the winter. Rockwell and his wife may have lived aboard until they established a residence in Portland.

A child was born to them on March 19, 1879. The little girl died 15 days later of scarlet fever.[1] This was the second child which did not survive and, if family friends are correct, may have been the third or fourth child which the Rockwells lost owing to prematurity and childhood disease.

That year Rockwell seems to have remained at home until June. He was engaged in office work. The year's work extended the Columbia River survey from Kalama, Washington Territory to Columbia City on the Oregon side of the river. The survey covered eight miles of river, the islands and both banks. The *Kincheloe* served as transportation and quarters. Field work was concluded on December 8, 1879 and the survey vessel moored at the mouth of the Kalama River, secure from floating ice. With that season's work, the detailed survey of the Columbia had moved about 75 miles upriver.[2]

It is not established where Mrs. Rockwell lived during the working seasons in Oregon. In 1880, at least, she may have returned to San Francisco. The *Kincheloe* required repairs which prevented field work until August 5. Cleveland Rock-

well supervised the repairs and when completed, found the triangulation points had been swept away by unusually high water which was still much above normal in the Columbia River. He confined his operations to triangulation on the high ground near Columbia City and St. Helens. The work sheet included the channels of the Lewis River, Lake River, Willamette Slough, Scappoose Bay and high land on both sides of the basin of the Columbia. The character of the basin of the river had changed from the abruptly perpendicular sides of the lower river to a plateau of 60 to 100 feet on the south side and low, marshy lands on the north bank of the river. Details of the survey were furnished to Lieutenant Colonel G. L. Gillespie of the Corps of Engineers, in charge of river improvements.[3]

The San Francisco directories, as noted, listed Oregon as the Rockwells' residence after July 1, 1880. Their first listing in the Portland directory was in that for 1881. They were living at 151 Pacific, near the riverfront adjacent to Sullivan's Gulch in East Portland. His work, closer to his home each season, was now only a few miles away. In 1882 he was engaged at the mouth of the Willamette River, only ten miles away. They had moved their residence to 193 Sixth between Yamhill and Taylor, just two blocks from the Portland Hotel near the center of the city.

On July 10, 1881 a daughter, Gertrude Ellinor Rockwell, was born in San Francisco, the first of their children to live to maturity. Her birth occurred in the middle of her father's working season and for this reason she was born in San Francisco. Also, Mrs. Rockwell may have wanted Dr. Olivia Hoff, her previous obstetrician, to attend her again.[4] The Cleveland Rockwells' second daughter, Cornelia, was born 15 months later, October 4, 1882, also in San Francisco.[5] She, too, was a healthy sparkling girl. From childhood on she was called "Neely."

Cornelia's birth — in October — was not scheduled to coincide with her father's work. Rockwell was engaged in field work in Oregon until October 28. Then he was ordered to the sub-office in San Francisco for inking and duplicating records of field work. Presumably his wife and the two little girls remained there with him until June of 1883 before returning to Oregon.[6]

Assistant Rockwell's assignment changed. In accordance with instructions received in early July, 1883, he left Portland and traveled to Nestucca Bay. He organized a party for the survey of that bay and of the Big and Little Nestucca rivers, the junction of which forms the bay. The survey was to continue north to Tillamook Bay. This portion of the Oregon coast had never before been surveyed. A base was measured, signals erected at points selected for stations of the triangulation and a tide gauge established to obtain a point of reference for the soundings. Careful triangulation and topography were done as part of the general coast work, and the survey was completed September 27.

Rockwell reported that the country was mostly rolling and steep hills, long denuded of timber and then covered by fern and grass. Forest fires following settlement of the country by the whites had "swept over the whole area from the coast back to the Willamette Valley, and the coast range of mountains presents from the ocean a desolate array of tall and bare white stumps and trees." There was evidence "that in former times the Big Nestucca entered the ocean opposite Haystack Rock, but the drifting sand filled in the coast line, forming the long sand peninsula to the north of the entrance, and pushing the entrance to the two rivers down towards the rocky bluff to the south."

Because of the continual breakers on the bar and his lack of boat or crew, Rockwell found it impossible to examine the bar. "The heavy swell from the southwest which set in during the middle and latter part of August closed the bar nearly up, so that at low water, on viewing it from the bluff, the white water would roll across for a hundred yards or so. Shoal water extends a long distance outside, as shown by the heavy rollers."[7]

October found Assistant Rockwell back in Portland assuming the tertiary triangulation of the Willamette River from its mouth up to Portland. The *Kincheloe* was used and by December 15, 1883 the topography and hydrography of the Willamette was completed beyond the city of Portland. Being within a maximum of 10 miles from Portland during this phase, and having the *Kincheloe*, Rockwell was able to spend weekends at home for the first time since the couple's marriage. He was engaged in office work in the winter of 1883 and spring of 1884 in Portland.

From April 9 to mid-May, as shown by his dated sketches, Rockwell found time to visit and sketch the British Columbian and Alaskan coasts. In the latter part of May, 1884 he resumed the Columbia and Willamette low shore area survey. The water rose with spring runoff from melting snows and covered the low lying shores. Rockwell ran the *Kincheloe* up the Willamette to the city of St Johns and was engaged there when the fiscal year ended in June, 1884.[8]

The survey of the Willamette River through Portland was hailed by local citizens and businessmen. The excellence of

Rockwell's work was generally recognized. Particularly his 1884 survey was of interest to Portland. There were two sheets. One was from Willow Bar on the Columbia, a few miles below the confluence of that river and the Willamette. In this instance the shore details were included for a mile back on each shore. The sheet extended up to the head of Swan Island on a 1:20,000 scale.

The other sheet, in larger scale of 1:10,000, embraced the west side of the river from the head of Swan Island to the south limit of the city near the foot of Ross Island. It extended from the waterfront to include the first range of hills back of the city. This second sheet was of greatest local interest and it was made on a scale readily adaptable to the surveys of the City Surveyor's maps by a simple modification of scale.[9]

Captain Rockwell was becoming a well-known figure in Portland despite his conservatism and reticence. His patriotic services in the Civil War were known. The Coast Survey *Annual Reports* were available locally and those who read them passed the details on by word of mouth. Cleveland and Cornelia Rockwell and their little children resided in Portland. Cornelia had begun her role in Episcopal Church activities even as a young matron. Rockwell's paintings were admired and discussed. Those fortunate friends who had received them as wedding gifts or as tokens of friendly esteem were pleased and proud to hang them on their walls.

Rockwell continued his Willamette River survey. Tide gauges were set up at Vancouver, Washington Territory, at St. Johns and at Albina. Simultaneous readings were made at each station for 24 consecutive hours. Fluctuations were very small and the readings were deemed adequate. Permanent benchmarks were set up at the stations mentioned. The *Kincheloe* was employed for the hydrography from Ross Island down to Bachelor's Island. When the season closed at the end of September, 1885 the work, in addition to all else, included 17,782 depth soundings.[10]

In the autumn of 1885, Davidson conducted an inspection of the field parties in Oregon and Washington. He used the opportunity to obtain data and make sketches for the forthcoming new *Pacific Coast Pilot*. He visited Rockwell at Portland and Albina, satisfying himself as to the amount and good quality of hydrography executed by that officer. "Davidson studied the Columbia River up to Portland [the superintendent, F. M. Thorn seemed not to be aware of the geographical facts of life — *i.e.*, Portland was on the Willamette River] and remarked that the deep sea traffic is increasing in an extraordinary manner on account of the great wheat growth of eastern Oregon and eastern Washington Territory."[11]

George Davidson revisited Oregon in 1886, and occupied Balch station near Portland.[12] He was determining the latitude and the azimuth of a connecting line of the triangulation. Cleveland Rockwell served with Davidson. Readings were compared with similar sets of observations in 1870 and in 1881 at the same location. In order to align the readings to the triangulation of Puget Sound, Davidson then moved to Rainier on the south bank of the Columbia. Rainier station was a common point to the large triangulation of both Columbia River and Puget Sound and Rockwell was occupied for the entire year of 1886 in assisting Davidson and doing office work.[13]

Like some other services, the U.S. Coast Survey had problems of administration, personality, etc. After Bache died, there had been five superintendents in 23 years. The average term of service was about four and one-half years. Each seemed qualified in the eyes of the President, the Secretary of the Treasury and the Congress, from whom all appointments and appropriations flowed. Not all were scientists, and most had never seen the West Coast. All were unacquainted with the assistants and each was barely seasoned when, for varying reasons, he was replaced.

J. E. Hilgard was acting superintendent from the time Bache was incapacitated in 1864 until 1867. Then the position went to Benjamin Peirce for six years, during which time he held several other positions. Peirce resigned in 1873 and was succeeded by Carlile Patterson. He had five years' service in the United States Navy, a degree in Engineering, then 12 years with the U.S. Coast Survey. After a lapse of 11 years as captain of a Pacific mail steamer, he returned to the Coast Survey in 1861 and in 1874 became superintendent. He enlarged the scope of the service, which became the Coast and Geodetic Survey. He died in office in 1881. J. E. Hilgard, Bavarian-born scientist, after 40 years with the Coast Survey became superintendent in 1881. He was accused of maladministration, bruised by an investigation but absolved. He then resigned, after four years in office, in 1885. Frank Manly Thorn, a New York attorney who had engaged in law practice and journalism, succeeded him. He became chief clerk of the Bureau of Internal Revenue in 1885. A few weeks later he was appointed superintendent of the Coast and Geodetic Survey. He was charged with investigating and correcting certain irregularities, and his administration was credited with saving $50,000 per annum. He was not a scientist and left the Survey after four years, in 1888. Then followed Thomas Corwin Mendenhall, a scientist and educator of Quaker background. His family came to America with William Penn and pioneered the settling of the Mississippi Valley. He was Professor of Physics at Ohio University, then held the same post at the Imperial University of Tokyo, Japan. He made many contributions in applied science, published widely and became a member of leading scientific societies. He was superintendent of the U.S. Coast and Geodetic Survey from 1889 to 1894.

It was difficult for Cleveland Rockwell, after a life of hardship and physical strain as well as repeated significant accomplishments, to justify his professional existence to each new superintendent. Rockwell was just a name among the many assistants in the field. In most cases he did not personally meet the new superintendent during his term of office. New regulations and rules, often not justified, were instituted. The scope of the work was expanded and the appropriations reduced. Rockwell felt that his expertise based on his seasoned competence was frequently ignored. With the passing years the situation became worse.

The Oregon coast was the subject of Rockwell's endeavors again in 1887. The topographical reconnaissance of the Pacific shore from the Yaquina River to Tillamook Bay proved difficult and fraught with complications. Some of his reports to the Coast Survey office are available to relate the situation in Rockwell's own words. He reported to Superintendent Thorn from Nestucca Bay on July 6, 1887:

In November last, I submitted a full report of the execution of a hydrographic survey of the Columbia river above Columbia City. After that date, I was awaiting Instructions until May 1st when I received your orders of April 16th, to make a plane table reconnaissance of the coast of Oregon from Tillamook bay to Yaquina. I commenced immediate preparations for that work, and on the 16th of May, the party left Portland for Newport, Yaquina Bay.

The party was composed of 3 hands (one of whom was engaged in the capacity of foreman and packing) 1 cook and the chief of party. Transportation was effected by means of pack-horses, riding horses and saddles were not provided, even for the Chief of the party, all hands following the coast afoot. Camp outfit was restricted to the very bare necessities of the work in order to avoid delay in moving and to save expense of many animals in hire and forage. Up to June 30th no expense for forage has been incurred, animals subsisting upon the natural grass. Two light tents with a single pole cut on the ground, two champagne baskets to contain the simple cooking apparatus, a roll of blankets and clothes for each man, instruments and stationery composed the impedimenta of the party. Considerable difficulty was found in procuring horses from the Indians. The Siletz reservation extends along the coast from Yaquina pt. northward and no white settlers are allowed. The trails are consequently neglected, worn down, grown over with brush and obstructed by large fallen trees.

A great deal of time was necessarily expended in work with the axe on the trail to make it even possible for packed animals to pass through.

I observed the sun for time and azimuth, using a 3 inch Casella theodolite, at the light house at Yaquina Pt: the latitude having already been fixed by the C&G Survey, no further observations were required. I observed the sun for time and azimuth at Siletz bay and attempted to observe for latitude at noon. In these observations I used Alt. Az. theod. No. 138, which was sent to me by the Office as being admirably adapted to the work I had in hand, but I found it provided with a rectangular eye-piece so long that the telescope would not permit the measurement of a vertical angle greater than 63° direct or 65° in reversal. I was consequently unable to observe circummeridian altitudes of the sun for latitude. Moreover the horizontal wire was so slack in the damp climate of the Coast, it could not be used, and I had to put in another from the bushea [?], secured by a little dissolved mouth glue. The vertical wire could not be used in the early morning unless the instrument was warmed by the fire until the wire was stretched straight. Notwithstanding which difficulties, I think I obtained good results at Siletz bay for Azimuth. The plane table was used for the topographical reconnaissance, the work being done on a scale of 1:40,000. The Country is very wild and broken, heavily covered with timber and brush and in many places the work was not pushed through without great physical hardship and labor. No very large amount of provisions could be carried at a time, and it was not safe to cache supplies on account of the great number of black bears. Supplies had to be obtained from a distance of 25 to 50 miles. This party has not been able to procure a potato to eat since the 18th of May, and even beans could not be procured for the last two weeks.

On June 30th the first sheet of work was completed, extending from Yaquina point to the summit of the cape called Cascade Head.

On account of the lack of proper drawing materials and instruments, I am unable to present a sketch to accompany this Report, and trust its absence will be excused.

At the date of this writing, my party has cut its way through the forest of Cascade Head and made a junction with the work at Nestucca Bay

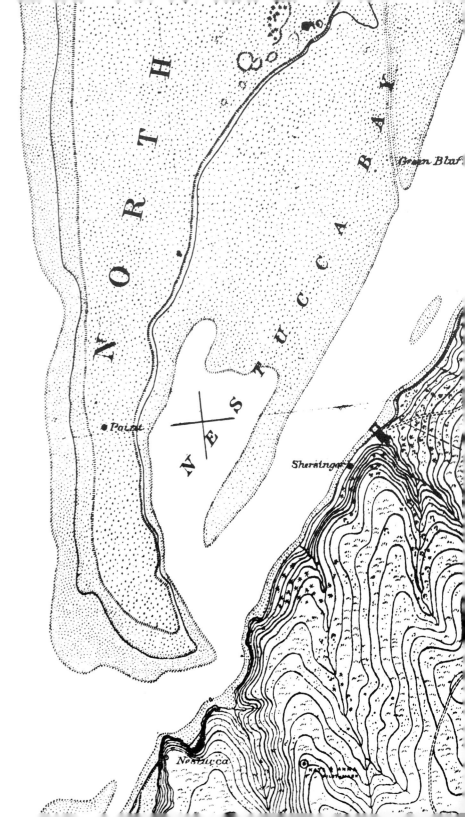

Part of Rockwell's 1883 chart of "Nestucca Bays and Rivers." (OHS)

done by me in 1883, and the work is in active progress toward the objective point, Tillamook Bay.[14]

In his July 6, 1887 report to Thorn, Rockwell is politely chiding the superintendent. He states that the preceding year's field operation was completed and results submitted in November, 1886. He waited to receive his orders. Finally written on April 16, the orders reached him on May 1, 1887. From November to May he had no assignment. Then it took 16 days to assemble the party and their supplies and instruments and leave Portland for work on the Oregon coast. Five and one-half months were lost by a superintendent stressing economy and dedicated to saving money, yet negligent in planning the basic work for Rockwell and his party.

There is a note of sarcasm throughout the letter though couched in formal tones of mock respect. He is implying: "you wasted five and one-half months in not issuing my orders. Yet my operation is restricted to the barest of necessities, no saddle horses for transportation for the party or even myself, no feed purchased for the pack horses until June 30, shortage of food, lack of drawing materials and instruments, etc. all to satisfy a burst of inconsistent and unjustified economy." Rockwell is angry.

On August 15, 1887, Rockwell reported again, from Portland:

I have completed — on the 8th of August — the planetable reconnaissance between Yaquina & Tillamook bays. I left the party at Garibaldi, on Tillamook Bay, to return on the first steamer leaving for Astoria, and am looking for their return to-day. I came to Portland by stage, arriving here on the 10th. I thought it best to discharge the men from pay while I was necessarily employed in bringing up my accounts and Reports with essential sketches, which I had neither materials nor facilities, situated as I was in the field, to properly prepare. I also required all blank forms and stationery for accounts, journals and reports as well as new forms and note books and proper instruments for the observation and recording of Magnetics, Latitude and Azimuth. I have not received from Assistant Davidson detailed instructions and upon their receipt will be enabled to make estimates for the proposed detailed topographical survey. The party and outfit will necessarily be composed quite differently from the meagre outfit of a reconnaissance in the dry months of summer. No instrument competent to use in Meriadian [sic] observations of the sun for latitude reached me while in the field — though one sent to me by Assistant Pratt is on its way to Tillamook. Mr. Pratt informed me that the theodolite was broken and could not be used until repaired, and as there was no one near him competent to repair it suggested that I have it repaired in Portland — which I will do when it returns from Tillamook.

My wife, who forwarded me the instrument from here, did not know it was broken and consequently useless without repairs or she could have had it repaired before sending. The instrument, however, could not have reached me before I had completed the plane table work. I would respectfully enquire now, if I will be required to make sketches both for my report to the end of the fiscal year or will the sketch made to accompany the Report on the completion of the whole reconnaissance be considered sufficient?

I had some time since been informed by Prof. George Davidson, Assistant, that it would be proper for me to make a special report upon the adaptability of Cape Lookout for a site for a light house and will therefore submit such a report with sketch as soon as I can find time to do it.

Rockwell is pointing out his economy in operating the party and the lack of forms, stationery for accounts, journals and report forms. He was also lacking in certain needed instruments. Supplies had never been so reduced before. The tone of his letter indicates his opinion of the superintendent as a penurious man who places frugality above all else.

Rockwell was requested to make a special examination of one coastal section for use of the lighthouse board. He found Cape Foulweather lighthouse not to be on that cape. The middle and most prominent part of Cape Foulweather was eight and one-half miles north of the light. His recommendations, in a special report, urged the site at Cape Lookout rather than Cape Meares for the lighthouse location. A good harbor with suitable anchorage where a lighthouse tender could readily discharge freight was a cogent reason.

Another main point was the excellent visibility up and down the coast. His report included a notebook of sketches of prominent capes, headlands and groups of rocks within the area of the survey, which was sent to the Washington office.[15] Assistant George Davidson backed Assistant Rockwell's findings in a letter to Superintendent Thorn.[16]

The season ended in mid-August with the party at Cascade Head. Assistant Rockwell was at home when, on September 16, 1887 the *Morning Oregonian* published the following article on "The Northern Pacific coast":

Washington, Sept. 16 — A notable reconnaissance of that nearly unknown and uninhabitable portion of Washington territory lying between Cape Flattery and Gray's Harbor, has just been completed, and is most satisfactory in all its details. *Assistant Gilbert has just finished a similar reconnaissance from Tillamook to Yaquina, Oregon.* The chart of the inland waters of Washington territory, which was issued about a year ago, has met with such favorable consideration that the issue of 600 copies has been disposed of, and a second edition is now being prepared.

Rockwell reacted with a sharp letter to Thorn dated September 20, 1887, enclosing a clipping, " An *associated press* dispatch from Washington and I would respectfully inquire if the reporters from the associated press obtain their information from anyone connected with the C. & G. Survey office in Washington."[17] There is no available record of the Superintendent's reply.

The 1888 work continued from Cascade Head and by August 8 the party was on Tillamook Beach completing the survey. Included on one of the sheets was a list of regional names and corresponding Tillamook Indian equivalents.[18]

During the fall of 1887 and until April, 1888, Captain Rockwell remained at home with his family. Neely was six and Gertrude was eight, both were in school and both were taking piano lessons. At the end of April he reported to the sub-office in San Francisco to work on the fourth edition

Cape Lookout projects into the ocean for a mile and a half, with 400-foot high promontory at seaward end. Rockwell chose this as a lighthouse site. His 1888 sketch above, Graves Collection.

"Finn Town, Astoria, Oregon," 1889. Watercolor painting, Lt. Col. Mrs. Alexander W. Chilton, Jr. Collection.

of the *Coast Pilot of California, Oregon and Washington Territory.*

George Davidson had been foresighted in taking views (sketches, probably by using a camera lucida). Other assistants had done the same. A few photographs were used. Of about 400 views available, 350 were reduced in size and put in approximately equal scale by Cleveland Rockwell. They were redrawn on bristol board and made ready for reproduction, and he "imparted his artistic touches to the sketches."[19] Rockwell was credited with the drawings of the headlands, points, islands and rocks in the preface of the fourth *Coast Pilot.*

Assistant Rockwell next began a resurvey inside the mouth of the Columbia River adjacent to Astoria. Political and commercial interests attempted to use him and impugn his work as superficial for their own interests. But Rockwell was his own man, and with right and justice on his side, he did triumph in the end!

The 1889 *Annual Report* (p. 72), notes that Assistant Cleveland Rockwell, towards the end of April, 1889, was instructed to resurvey

the river channel near Astoria, Oregon, covering the river from Tongue Point to Tansy Point, and also the areas of Young's Bay and parts of Young's River, and of Lewis and Clarke [*sic*] River, together with an examination of the shorelines of the vicinity, and a resurvey of the same wherever necessary. These resurveys and examinations had been called for by the Astoria Chamber of Commerce, and, at the request of Senator Dolph,[20] had been authorized by the Superintendent. Assistant Davidson, in his special instructions for the work, had included in it the delineation of the contours and outline of the prairies on Scarborough Hill, and the fixing of the position and the general contours of Coxcomb Hill on the Astoria Peninsula, both of these hills being noted landmarks for the Columbia River entrance.

Upon further consideration of the scope of his special instructions, Mr. Rockwell decided to make a complete resurvey of the localities covered by them.

On April 8, 1889 Rockwell wrote the Superintendent:

If it is intended to keep me on field work this season (which I desire), I write to suggest that the necessary instructions be issued in good time, so that I can submit the usual estimates for approval before the completion of the present work, and make any other preparation for the new work, such as projections, etc. . . If such instructions are sent to me for continuous field work, please inform me if I shall take the necessary time to complete the full plotting and drawing of the hydrography or to merely plot the sextant positions of boat and transmit the sheet with the record books, etc. . . I write this early in order to obviate the necessary and oftentimes vexatious delays consequent upon correspondence at such long distances.[21]

The letter has a slip of paper across its face as follows: "Assistant in Charge — Hold for the next Superintendent — B.A.C. — 4.22.89." B. A. Colonna was the Assistant in Charge. Frank M. Thorn had given up the post.

Ten days later Rockwell repeated his request by telegram. The following day he dispatched a letter to Thorn, not having been informed that he was gone:

I telegraphed to you yesterday to know when I could expect the projection and other data (for which I made requisition March 25th) and the advance of funds and special authority to cover transportation more than 50 miles, for which I asked in my letter of March 21st. My object in telegraphing is to gain time — for if I can be sure that my requisition has been received and not miscarried in the mails and if I can know (nearly) the date on which my data will be mailed, I do not need to wait here, but can gain much time by starting at once down the river to put in the new wharves, etc. and occupy the intervening time in the necessary work of erecting the tide gauges and hydrographical and topographical signals near Astoria. The weather is now very favorable for field work. As I have heretofore intimated and stated, I do not think any resurvey is required, or indeed that much should be done in this work, and I base my opinion on the statements made to me by the river pilots who inform me that though some changes have probably been made, they are not in anyway detrimental to the navigation of the river. The Astoria *"Chamber of Commerce"* may think it desirable to let the public know that they are alert to the interests of the port, etc., but I rely more, as I have stated, on the judgment of the pilots than the Chamber of Commerce. If I find after running a number of trial sounding lines, that no resurvey is required, I desire to know if I shall close the examination and discharge the party without special and further orders, or if I shall consider it my duty to wait upon the result of a correspondence with the office upon the subject.

I am resolved, if possible, that there shall be no misunderstanding of orders on my part, and my desire is to execute my instructions fully and to the letter. My instructions of November 2nd are rather vague and uncertain in tenor and call for further information instead of stating specifically what is required. Since their receipt I have endeavored to state in many letters to the Assistant in charge and to you, the requirements in this case, but have so far not elicited any corresponding freedom of expression from the office nor anything more explicit in my instructions.

If I am permitted to go on with the field work of the Columbia or Willamette river, it would be an advantage to not discharge the whole of my party for completing the office work.

The early reference to the foregoing matters will materially enlighten me as to my duties under the only instructions I have, those of date Nov. 2nd, 1888.[22]

Receiving orders at last, Rockwell organized his party and departed: "in order to obtain data for inserting on the charts of the river new wharves, canneries, and landings along the shores, not in existence at the time of the original survey, he ran down the river in his boat, and added the improvements on the way."

In the meantime, he sent other letters to Superintendent Thorn to clarify several specific vague points not spelled out in his original instructions. He had no confidence in Thorn and wished no loophole for misunderstanding which could result in his being accused of not carrying out orders. His agitation is revealed in his handwriting. His usually good script becomes almost unreadable when he is emotionally upset.

Rockwell and party were in Astoria by May 13, after including on the charts all new improvements along the water's edge. They had to locate points of the former triangulation, some of which had been carried away by high water and had to be replaced. The U. S. Engineers under Thomas B. Handbury, assisted by supplying records of tide readings, other records and a boat for transportation when needed.

When the hydrography was completed on June 25, 15,268 soundings for depth of water had been made. By July 10 the topography around the shores of Young's Bay and Point Adams, and the work around Scarborough and Coxcomb hills had been completed. Three sheets resulted.[23]

Rockwell wrote Thorn again from Portland, Oregon on July 12 for instructions regarding completing the three sheets. The reply came from T. C. Mendenhall. After three months, Rockwell was finally advised of Thorn's replacement. Rockwell seemed to hold the new superintendent in higher regard than Thorn — at least at the beginning of his term. Cleveland Rockwell's monthly and yearend report of July 30, 1889 includes material to fill in the new superintendent:

I have the honor to submit the following Report of the work done by the Party under my charge, in pursuance of your predecessor's instructions dated April 27th, 1889. These instructions looked to a re-survey or examination of the river channel near Astoria, Oregon covering the water from Tongue Pt. to Tansy Pt., including also the area of Youngs Bay and parts of Youngs and Lewis & Clarkes [sic] rivers, together with an examination of the shore lines of the vicinity and a resurvey of the same wherever necessary. This survey had been called for by the Astoria Chamber of Commerce and at the request of Senator Dolph had been authorized by our department. My instructions also contemplated by request of Assistant George Davidson, the delineation of the contours and outline of the prairies on Scarborough hill and the fixing of position and general contours of Coxcomb hill on the Astoria peninsula, both noted landmarks for the Columbia River Entrance.

In estimating for the time the party would be in the field work, I contemplated an hydrographic examination of the channels and shoals but after having received a letter dated 1889 from Assistant Davidson, in charge of the details of work, etc., I decided to make a complete re-survey of the locality covered by my instructions.

These instructions have been completely carried out — the hydrographic work is a finished re-survey — the shore lines of the topography have been examined thoroughly throughout and the present shore lines retraced or resurveyed wherever any changes were found to have taken place. In addition to the letter of my instructions, I thought best also to re-survey the shore line from Tansy Pt. (the limit of the work mentioned in my orders) to and around Pt. Adams, to include the site of the jetty now under construction, which together with the extension of the wharf at Fort Stevens has caused important changes in the outlines of that Point. I hope that my actions in respect thereto may not be disapproved, the additional work being limited to but two days.

The party was organized in Portland on the 22nd of April, leaving there on the 23rd and consisted of myself and 4 hands. In order to carry out previous instructions regarding the insertion on the printed charts of new wharves, canneries and landings along the shores of the river, not in existence when the original sheets were made, I decided to row down the river in person with my crew in the 28 foot boat belonging to the party and add the improvements on the way. This work took 3 days the distance being 100 miles. The sheets containing these additions will be forwarded as soon as I have time to draw and compile the necessary notes.

The 26th and 27th of April were employed in making some necessary repairs to my boat which having been stored a long time and also being quite old, developed some leaks and weaknesses on the way down the river. The first work of sounding was done on the 13th of May, the intervening time from April 30th having been occupied in hunting up triangulation points (mostly destroyed), erecting the hydrographic signals and fixing their positions with the plane table. The 2nd, 3rd, 4th & 6th of this month proved so rainy and stormy that not even signals could be erected during the time, and the first days work sounding was interrupted at 2 p.m. by so violent and unusual storm of rain, wind and lightning, that the party was forced to take refuge in a cave in the rocks and haul the boat out of the water. The weather during the remainder of May was moderately fair and during the month of June was generally fair except the 26th, 27th & 28th when a violent gale and rainstorm prevailed.

My sounding party was organized as follows, viz: I occupied the coxswain's seat, steered the boat, called time and observed the right hand angle. Mr. W. S. Haven, temporary Aid, observed the left hand angle and kept the record book or rough journal. Four hands at the oars and the leadsman completed the boat's crew. The employment of a tide observer was obviated by using the record of the self registering gauge kept by Mr. Louis Wilson, formerly observer for our service at Astoria. The sheets from the S. R. gauge were scaled off and transcribed into the tide book by Mr. Haven and the records of the machine were compared with the readings on the staff on frequent intervals.

The season proved very windy indeed, so much so that only on very few days could the sounding work be prosecuted the whole day and very often but a few hours in the morning could be used in the work. My boat proved totally unsuitable for the rough water of the Bay or river (although it is suitable for the upper river) her bow being so sharp and low that with the leadsman in his place and going against a head sea, she would plunge her nose under and take in quantities of water, compelling us to abandon the work for the day.

On June 25th the work of sounding was completed and on the 28th my Aid, Mr. Haven, having fixed up his tide record, I paid off and discharged him. His duties as sextant observer and recorder were performed to my satisfaction and had he been at all proficient in orthography and penmanship, I could have utilized his services in duplicating records for some time longer. The duplicates and fair journals, however as also the plotting of positions on both the rough and finished sheets are done by my hand.

By the 10th of July the plane table work around the shores of Youngs Bay and Point Adams, the work around Scarborough and Coxcombs hills had been completed. Some parts of this work were prosecuted at odd times when sounding could not be done or during the sickness of the Recorder. In addition to the determination of the prairie outline and contours of Scarborough and Coxcomb hills I have, on the 20,000 sheet endeavored to give the approximate contours of the peninsula of Astoria and the hills opposite. This work could have been much better done on a projection scale of 1-40,000, as requested in my letter of March 25th addressed to the Office, instead of the 20,000 scale sent, the reason being obvious that as the crest of the hills opposite Astoria could be fixed only by occupying points on the Oregon side of the river, the scale of 20,000 being so large, would not permit the points to be fixed and the points from which the observations to fix them should be made to be upon the plane table at the same time! I have done the best with the subject that the projection would allow.

The next day after the completion of field work, July 11th, I packed up Instruments and tools and got my boat on board the steamer and the same evening left for Portland with my party and on the 12th, after having temporarily stored the boat, tools and instruments, I paid off and discharged the hands.

The results of the survey are, one large hydrographic sheet, scale 1/10,000, extending from Tongue Pt. to Tansy Pt. including Youngs Bay. On this sheet will also be found the corrected shore lines drawn in ink showing the new shore lines surveyed to and around Pt. Adams as also the jetty tramways, railroads, wharves, etc., comprising the improvements in prosecution of the U.S. Engineer Dept. The contours around Coxcomb Hill and the peninsula of Astoria are also sketched on this sheet. The changes in the channels and shoals in the vicinity of Astoria, if any, will be developed only by a comparison with the Cordell survey of 1868 and as the office desires me to only plot the positions and lines of soundings, and moreover the tracing of the Cordell field work being on one-half the scale of my survey, I make no mention of them. The changes in the shorelines are however more considerable than I anticipated. The changes of the shores from Tongue Pt. down to Smiths Pt. and around to Youngs Bay are, from the nature of the shores which are shingle or rock, insignificant, but the tide land shores have generally worn away by the action of the waves. The point between Cooks Slough and the mouth of Youngs river has grown; the shore inside of the point being now as much as 90 meters outside of the former shoreline, covering what was formerly a few patches of tules. From Cooks Slough to Lewis and Clarkes river the shore has generally receded from 10 to 20 meters. The shore line from the small creek just west of Lewis and Clarkes river for half a mile or so has undergone but little apparent changes, but from Marsh Pt. triangulation to the mouth of Skipanon Creek, the changes are very marked, being generally from 20 to 35 meters. From Skipanon Creek to Tansy point no erosion whatever has taken place, the mud flats appearing higher than in 1868, and the tules also extending further out from the shores which are sloping instead of bluff, indicating that the land is making (rising). This portion of the shore is protected moreover from the prevailing wind and the closing of the mouths of Tansy and Alder creeks by diking the lands has checked the action of the tides toward and from those streams. The sandy beach from Tansy Pt. west for a mile has changed but little but from that point to Fort Stevens wharf, the changes are very great, the present shore near the wharf being 580 meters east and 720 meters north of the old shore while 200 meters have been washed away from the point a short distance from the Fort. The jetty is constructed to a point 2665 meters from the Fort flagstaff of 1873 and is progressing rapidly. A sand shoal, bare at low water seems to be forming South of the jetty and parralel [sic] to it for a long distance out.

The second hydrographical sheet, scale 1/10,000, contains Youngs and Lewis and Clarkes rivers. The soundings in these two streams were made generally on lines running from stakes set in place by the topographical features. The projection was evidently laid to facilitate carrying the work further up those rivers than was done in 1868. My instructions, however did not mention any new work and I did not consider it proper without authority to extend the shores of either of those streams. The soundings were therefore only carried to the limits of the topographical survey. None except trifling changes could be observed in the shores of these two streams.

The projection 1/20,000 contains only the work around Scarborough hill and the hills back of Pt. Ellice, etc. The prairie on Scarborough hill is a very bright and prominent mark from the ocean but it makes but

a pretty small patch on a 20,000 scale. While in Astoria I learned incidentally from sailors and others of the alleged discovery of a rock or ledge, and also a 14 fathom bank off the Coast of Oregon near Nestuggah river. The information I considered important and promptly communicated it to Assistant Davidson at San Francisco — I append the statistics of the work done and a sketch map, scale 1/100,000 showing the locality.

In conclusion I would state my acknowledgement of courtesies received from the U.S. Engineer department under Major T. H. Handbury who furnished the party transportation on their tow boat whenever desired. The records of the S. R. tide gauge at Astoria, kept by Mr. L. Wilson was also placed at my disposal through direction of that officer. Although I did not have occasion to avail myself of it, the tender of the boat and crew at the life-saving station at Fort Canby was made to me by Maj. J. T. Blakeney, in charge of the service, by whose standing order I could have called for it at any time. I have also, at all times, given to both those departments, whenever requested, such information from the results of my work as was desired by them. I would mention, incidentally, that Major Handbury intends, at once, to make a survey of the Bar and Entrance to connect with my survey at Tansy Pt. just completed.

I am at present employed upon the office work of the surveys just completed which, having no Aid, will all be done by my hand.[24]

Rockwell made his conclusions regarding the crossing of Young's Bay in a letter to Superintendent Mendenhall. This is the letter which was distorted by the omission of two words and then the attempt was made to discredit Cleveland Rockwell and his work. Rockwell's original letter of August 26, 1889 follows:

In conformity with the instructions of your predecessor, Mr. F. M. Thorn, dated April 27th, 1889, I have the honor to make the following Report upon the crossing of Youngs Bay by a proposed R. R. bridge and trestle. This bridge is to be constructed by the Astoria and South Coast Rail Road Co., a line commencing at Astoria running along the Columbia to Smiths Pt., crossing the bay by the most direct course and running along the tide lands to Clatsop plains. The projected route is thence by a pass near the head of Lewis and Clarkes river to the Nehalem, Tillamook Bays, etc. The road is of standard gauge. I append a clipping from a Portland paper to show that the Company have filed an acceptance of the terms of the act regulating the bridging of navigable waters, etc. I have obtained from the Chief Engineer the following details of construction.

Total length of trestle and bridge, 8400 ft. Bents, of 4 piles each, to be 15 ft. 6 inches between centres. Piles 16 to 20 inches, diameter at large end. The draw-span across the channel will be 254 feet over all. The opening or clear span will be 110 feet. The pivot pier will be 26 ft. wide and the abutment piers will be each 6 ft. wide.

In considering the effect this bridge will have upon navigation of the Columbia and of Youngs, and Lewis and Clarkes rivers, the future interests and importance of the port of Astoria demand recognition and protection, far more than the present. While for the present the great transcontinental railroads have made such combinations that Puget Sound, as an ocean outlet and terminus, is their objective point, it does not seem probable that the Columbia river will long remain unnoticed. The completion of the stone jetty will probably greatly improve the entrance to the river, so that in the near future vessels of the largest class may enter and find secure harbor within, 10 or 12 miles only from the sea.

A large city may, therefore be reasonably be expected to be located at or near Astoria. Youngs Bay, in that event, would afford the best facilities for wharfroom and mooring of vessels. Wharves and piers could readily be built out over the flats to the channel through the bay — This channel already very fair could be improved and maintained by dredging, affording abundant room for shipping, and for manufacturing establishments. Youngs river is mainly a tidal estuary, extending 6 or 7 miles to the head of tide water, and a short distance above that point the river falls from a height of 60 or 70 feet, affording a good water power. At present the commerce of Youngs river is small, a mill for the manufacture of wood pulp is the only manufacture established. The river is navigable to nearly the head of tide-water. The tide lands along the shores are partly reclaimed by diking and being very productive, are valuable. Lewis and Clarkes river is navigable to about the same distance as Youngs river. The falls just above the head of tide water is not quite so high as that in the former stream. Valuable deposits of fire and pottery clays are located on this stream, and the material is loaded on barges and towed to the works at Portland. The bottom in Youngs bay is generally very soft, and though the sounding lead indicates hard bottom in places it is probable that boring or driving piles would develop a soft silt bottom. There is no doubt that the obstruction presented by this long trestle would have the effect to shoalen the water in the bay to a very considerable extent and the pivot and abutment piers would also have a similar effect in the channel. The section opposed to the flow of the currents would be represented by 542 bents, or say 2000 piles 16 to 20 inches in diameter besides the section of the pier and abutments. In my opinion, in the advanced practice in building bridges with long spans, 110 feet is an inadequate width of span. The draw should be at least 150 feet in the ocean. I append a section of the C&G Survey Chart showing the location of the crossing. I am unable to give the present depth of water in the channel, as developed by the survey I have just completed, for lack of time to make the plot of soundings. The Astoria and South Coast railroad could easily be built around the head of Youngs bay, and would then be able to cover both the rivers by a very moderate draw span in each bridge. In connection with the obstruction of Youngs Bay by this bridge, I would call attention to the obstructions caused by the numerous weirs or traps (as they are called here) for the catching of salmon. These are built of small piles on stakes driven in the bottom in about two fathoms of water near the edge of a shoal; to the piles a net of small meshes is suspended, which acts as a fence to lead the fish into a pound or purse. They resemble very closely the shad nets in the Hudson river, New York harbor. Though not a permanent obstruction, while down they have a large tendency to retard the flow of the currents and leave deposits of sand which is always drifting along the bottom. In some localities they doubtless do much injury to the channels. One of these traps located on the Upper sands opposite Upper Astoria will undoubtedly increase the heightened area of that shoal.[25]

On the first page of the original letter is a notation: "Sent — 1 copy to Senator Dolph, 1 copy to Chamber Com., Astoria, 1 copy to Astoria & S.C. R.R. Co. (signed) B.A.C." B. A. Colonna, as mentioned, was the Assistant then in charge of the office. Apparently he was following the superintendent's orders.

On October 19, 1889, *The Astorian* attempted to discredit Cleveland Rockwell under the headline "Rockwell's Mistake." The newspaper article was based on Assistant Rockwell's report of August 26 to the Superintendent. Rockwell turned to his superior officer for explanation, writing to Mendenhall on November 6, 1889, from Portland:

I have been savagely attacked by the local press of Astoria for the opinions expressed in my report to you upon the crossing of Youngs Bay by the rail-road trestle and bridge. The "Astorian" which is the leading journal at that place, printed my Report in full with the headlines "Rockwell's Mistake" and in the leading editorial of the same issue, headed "An adverse report" criticises it severely, saying it had no weight for the reason that my observations were superficial as virtually admitted by me in the report, and then quotes "I am unable to give the present depth of water in the Channel for lack of time to make the soundings." On the 2nd inst. I wrote to the Astorian, substantially as follows — "My attention has just been called to the issue of your paper of the 19th Oct. containing a copy of my report to the Supt. Coast & Geodetic Survey on the crossing of Youngs Bay by the A. & S.C. R.R. Co. The report, while generally quite correctly printed, omits a word which is very essential to the sense of the matter, and on which you base the assertion that my observations were superficial and therefore carried no weight. You print "for lack of time to make the soundings" — whereas I wrote — "for lack of time to make the plot of soundings" — .

In fact, I was employed most of the six weeks I was at Astoria, in making the soundings in person, and the depth of the water in the channels was known by me at every cast of the lead. I was especially informed, however, that the plot on chart of soundings would be made in the office at Washington. Trusting you will make this correction, I am, very truly yours," (sd.) C.R.

The following is a copy of a reply to my above letter. "Astoria, Ogn. Nov. 4, 1889. Mr. Cleveland Rockwell, etc., Yours of the 2nd recd. The report in question was printed in exact accordance with its verbiage, as furnished me by Senator Dolph. *The Astorian* printed what you wrote. In proof of this and in denial of your assertion in your favor of the 2nd inst., I hold the copy. I, this morning, saw a second copy sent the Secretary of the Astoria and South Coast Railway Co. that reads precisely as did the copy I received and which appeared in the Astorian exactly as written. I, also, saw a third copy this afternoon, sent to the Astoria Chamber of Commerce. That, also, is of the exact verbiage of the one sent me and the one sent the railway Co. All three are exactly alike; all three say "I am unable to give the present depth of water in the Channel, as developed by the survey I have just completed, for lack of time to make the soundings. Your assertion is in direct opposition to the fact. Yours respectfully, (signed) J. F. Halloran," (Editor).

I have to ask you to see if in my report to you I wrote "lack of time to make the plot of soundings" or "lack of time to make the soundings." In my written Copy Book, the former is clearly written. I will also ask for the assurance that my views and opinions, expressed in my report are concurred in by the Office, or not. I feel called upon to state, in regard to the competency of my opinion, that I was employed in 1856-7-8 in the surveys for the preservation of New York Harbor by the State Commission, and later, in those of Boston harbor, both made by our service, and was cognizant of the views, opinions and practice of my superiors at that time in reference to those important harbors.

I will respectfully request that, if my report is written with the verbiage as I have stated, and if an incorrect copy has been supplied to Senator Dolph by the Coast Survey Office, and by him to the press and Chamber of Commerce of Astoria and to the Secretary of the A. & S. C. Railway Co., then in that event, due correction be made by the Office, in the matter, through Mr. Dolph, to all parties concerned.[26]

Mendenhall responded in a letter dated November 18, 1889:

In response to your letter of November 6, I enclose to you herewith a letter from Miss Kate Lawn, Typewriter, which is attested by the official seal of the Assistant in Charge of the Office as to its correctness in being a true copy from your report of August 26th last. I have furnished a copy of Miss Lawn's letter and of this to Senator Dolph, to the Editor of The Astorian, to the Secretary of the Astoria and South Coast Railway Co., and to the President of the Astoria Chamber of Commerce, and these gentlemen will readily see upon comparing the copies of the report which have been furnished them that they are triplicate copies made upon a Remington typewriter and that therefore any mistake which would be in one would necessarily be in the others — the papers will be found facsimiles in every respect so far as the machine is concerned.

I regret exceedingly that so awkward a mistake should have been made in the copies of your report which were furnished and hope that the matter will give you no further annoyance.

"U.S. Coast and Geodetic Survey Office
Washington, D.C., November 15, 1889

Prof. T. C. Mendenhall,
Superintendent U.S. Coast and Geodetic Survey,
Washington, D. C.
Dear Sir:

Referring to the letter from Assistant Rockwell dated November 6, in which he refers to his report on the work at Astoria, Oregon, dated August 26, 1889, I have to give the following correct quotation from the original MS.-

"I append a section of the C. & G. Survey Chart showing the location of the crossing — I am unable to give the present depth of water in the channel, as developed by the survey I have just completed, for lack of time to make the plot of soundings. The Astoria and South Coast rail road could easily be built around the head of Young's bay" — thus showing that in my previous "copy" made in triplicate, I made the mistake of leaving out the words "plot of" which entirely destroyed the sense of the sentence as written by Mr. Rockwell.

Yours respectfully,
(Sd.) Kate Lawn
Typewriter."

Superintendent Mendenhall's letter seemed to express a minimal quantity of "regret." His expressed "hope for no further annoyance" hardly constitutes an apology. It was, after all, his own secretary who made the strikingly curious error and he who directed that copies of Rockwell's altered report be sent to Senator Dolph, the Astoria Chamber of Commerce and the Astoria South Coast Railroad.

Mendenhall well knew who and what was behind the request for the resurvey near Astoria. He even mentioned Senator Dolph, the Chamber of Commerce and the proposed railway trestle across Young's Bay in the Annual Reports. Though only Rockwell's letters are available today, they tell the story. Rockwell was given every opportunity to join the interests promoting the construction of the railroad. He failed to alter or amend his opinion and forthrightly set down his opposition to the trestle across Young's Bay.

That Mendenhall's secretary should accidentally omit two words which completely altered the meaning of Rockwell's report seems a questionable coincidence. That Mendenhall should send out the result in triplicate without reading it, certainly suggests that he was either involved or inept.

Rockwell had sent along with his report of August 26, 1889 a clipping from an unnamed Portland newspaper. The Astoria and South Coast Railroad had filed their acceptance of the terms of the State of Oregon for building the trestle across Young's Bay. The railroad was constructed across the bay, although it was after several years of problems and several stages of refinancing.

In the meantime, relations between Cleveland Rockwell and his Superintendent had come to a low ebb.

Rockwell had received a letter from the Superintendent criticizing him for sending in a partially inked topographical sheet. Assistant Rockwell's reply is cold and formal:

It may perhaps be only necessary for me to state that I have never seen the late circular directing that such work should be completely inked and lettered before sending to the office; nor have I heard of it from others, otherwise I should have complied with its requirements. The last circular I have seen relating to the subject, especially enjoined the non-inking of sheets, for the reason that it was intended to produce direct reductions by the process of photolithography, etc.

I always preferred to ink my field sheets and when several years since the late Mr. Edwin Hergesheimer, Chief of the drawing division, was here, he informed me that it was especially understood at the office, that, owing to my recognized skill as a draftsman, I was to have been made an exception to the requirements of that circular. I will thank you to cause to be sent to me the late circular mentioned in your letter and hereafter will be pleased to comply with its provisions. Regarding the last paragraph in your letter respecting the plotting of hydrographic work, etc., it seems to me there may be some misunderstanding arise, as conflicting with "General Instructions in regard to Inshore Hydrographic work of the Coast Survey" 1878, — par. 157, where the hydrographer is required to plot the soundings in pencil, draw the curves in colors and otherwise complete the sheet fully in ink, save the inking of soundings.

I was informed however by the Assistant in Charge that the Office preferred to select and plot the soundings, and as I was under orders for the field for the work upon which I am now engaged, I decided to spend no more time upon the office work than necessary.[27]

Meanwhile, Cleveland Rockwell and his party were again continuing the triangulation of the Columbia River. From mid-August to the end of October, 1889 the work included the river, Hayden Island and Vancouver, Washington and up to the foot of Government Island, all shown on a sheet. It is presented here in reduced scale. By establishing a base line of known length and measuring the angles of sightings from the line, distances are easily computed.

Rockwell left Portland April 3, 1890 for California. He was to join Assistant George Davidson and his party for the connecting of the primary base line at Los Angeles with the main triangulation. There he was instructed to return to San Francisco and take charge of a party lacking a chief, the result of the sudden death of Assistant Charles M. Bache.[28]

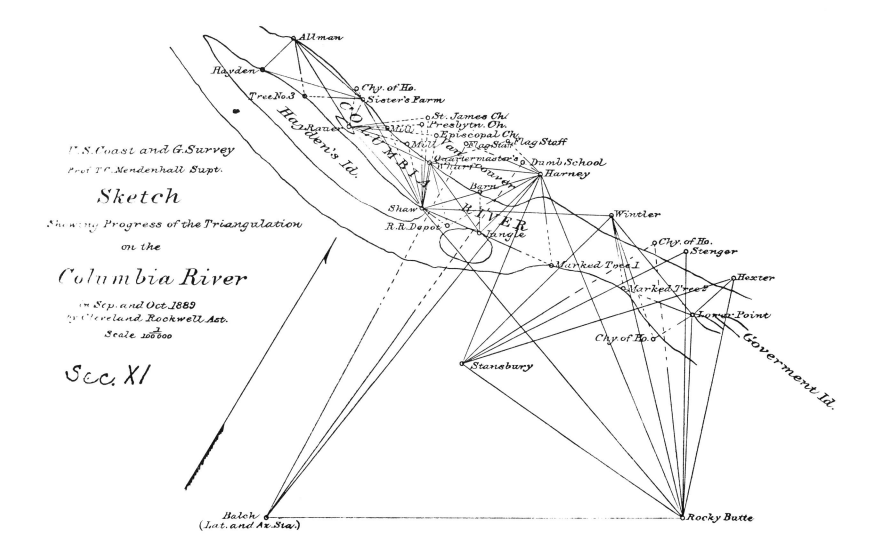

U.S. Coast and G. Survey
Prof. T.C. Mendenhall Supt.

Sketch

Showing Progress of the Triangulation

on the

Columbia River

in Sep. and Oct. 1889
by Cleveland Rockwell Ast.

Scale $\frac{1}{100000}$

Sec. XI

The above, taken from the printed *Annual Report,* contrasts with Rockwell's agonized handwritten report:

I arrived in San Francisco April 5th, and after completing preparations for the shipment of the camp outfit, instruments, horses and men of the party, I left with them on the 8th and arrived at Anaheim on the 9th.

I immediately got the party into camp at S. E. Base and assisted at the erection of the observing pier and tower at that station. By your instructions of April 11th I left Anaheim on the 18th of that month and returned to San Francisco to take charge of the topographical party left vacant by the sudden demise of the late Assistant C. M. Bache. While waiting at San Francisco for an advance of funds, I made every preparation to proceed to the coast below Point Sur in Monterey County, and left San Francisco on May 1st with 2 men, and arrived the same day at Jolon. A day or two delay at this place was necessary to wait the arrival of Sub. Asst. Nelson with the camp and animals belonging to the party.

I left Jolon on the 5th of May and arrived on the coast at Pacific Valley, my field of work on the 6th. Camp was immediately pitched and the work of the topographical survey was commenced.

The weather during May was so excessively foggy that scarcely any work could be done. On May 31, I made a special report to you upon the state of the weather for that month.[29]

Rockwell had never before given a superintendent such a tight accounting peppered with exact dates and with reference to weather and difficult working conditions. He seems to be leaving no possible basis for criticism. The verbal battle between Rockwell and Mendenhall continued with the former's August 12, 1890 letter from Portland:

I acknowledge the receipt of your letter of Instructions dated the 4th instant. Estimates, for the topographical work will be forwarded and submitted as soon as practicable. Separate Estimates for completion of the river survey to the Dalles will be sent later on. I have never contemplated carrying the work beyond the Cascades, and have not sufficient knowledge of that part of the river to enable me to make an estimate of the time or cost for its execution.

In regard to the asserted costliness of the survey of the Columbia river so far as it has been carried, I beg leave, at some future time to present a statement in refutation and explanation of the matter and to show that the assumption of extra costliness is partly due to the excessively difficult character of the subject; to the unfavorable times at which appropriations and allotments were available and largely to unfavorable prejudice and misrepresentation of the late Superintendent J. E. Hilgard and his advisors.

Owing to the contemplated tardiness of the disbursing office in adjusting party accounts, I will ask you to authorize an advance of funds for party expenses of $600. My party accounts for May and June are not yet settled, and my ¾ pay is not sufficient to meet my family expenses and of a party outfit.[30]

This letter lays bare the tension between Rockwell and Superintendent Hilgard, now deceased, and the unstated but implied prejudice and unfair criticism which Mendenhall is now heaping on Rockwell.

Rockwell's salary at the date of his letter was a net $2,400 per annum. The reference to ¾ pay is not clear. There was an economy effort at the Coast and Geodetic Office but no other reference to a pay cut is available.[31]

Cleveland Rockwell received orders in April 1891 for reorganizing his party and continuing the Columbia River survey. He operated from his camp on Fisher's Landing on the Oregon side of the river. It was located between Hayden and the lower end of Government Island. It rained for 20 days in June, slowing the work. By June 30, the triangulation and the first plane table sheet was completed.[32]

Rockwell wrote Mendenhall September 29, 1890 from Vancouver, Washington, asking for definite guidelines in determining how wide a margin of shoreline should be included for the section of the current survey. The Washington shoreline included the city of Vancouver and the adjacent military reservation. The width of margin would largely determine the cost. Rockwell had been scolded for the cost of the Columbia and Willamette river surveys where, in settled areas, a margin of one mile had been included. His survey of the Willamette had included up to two plus miles in the Portland city limits.

The point involved was that Rockwell was in the best position to make such decisions. He had years of experience and he was on hand to evaluate the facts in each instance. Mendenhall could not bring himself to grant Rockwell such authority. Rockwell was determined to have Mendenhall set down the terms in writing. It was a measure of Mendenhall as a poor administrator in being unable to delegate authority.

Rockwell indicated that Superintendent Peirce had left the extent of shoreline margin to Rockwell's judgment. Peirce's

successor, Mr. C.P. Patterson announced, on my request for a decision upon the matter, that the whole basin or valley of the river between the hills, including Sauvies and all other islands and the Willamette Slough must be represented. This decision would make the survey cover a vast area of land, intricate in details and difficult to cover with triangulation points, and entirely submerged during June & July freshets. I may remark right here, that a large part of the time consumed in bringing the work up from Kalama was the result of my carrying out instructions based on his decision, and I know of no other Assistant in the service who could have overcome the difficulties encountered in less time or at less expense. Prof. Hilgard instructed me to carry the survey to Portland as quickly as possible — and by dropping the plan of work laid out by Mr. Patterson and confining the margin of topography to a bare half mile or less, I was able to complete the survey from Willow Bar to Portland in one season, which was certainly fast enough.

Now the bottom lands, as you will see by an inspection of the original sheets I have sent in, are filled with an intricate mass of sloughs, ponds & lakes, swamp & forest outlines, details which it is impossible to ignore, upon the areas selected to survey; and the only possible way to avoid the time and expense of the survey is to limit the margin of topography. In respect of the sheet upon which I am now engaged, I am doing more than I would suggest being done on the sheets above this one, for the reason that it is so close to the city of Portland and includes the city of Vancouver and the most important military garrison on the Western coast. For the country above Vancouver I would suggest that the bottom lands be shown or surveyed to not more than one-half of a mile from the shore. The high lands of the river touch the river shore at Vancouver and from thence upwards no large areas of bottom lands occur on the north side; on the south side the bottom lands are wide as far as the Sandy River, 15 miles above Vancouver. On the present sheet, in the absence of any defined instructions, I am carrying the survey on the south side, which is on bottom land, to a full mile in width; and the north shore will require a mile in width to embrace the city of Vancouver and

Military Post. I am endeavoring to carry out your instructions to represent the topography without elaboration. There are, however, so many details which it is impossible to "blink" if the area is covered at all by a topo. survey that I again return to the original subject of this letter and ask you for a definite course to be laid out.[33]

Rockwell's report for the end of the calendar year of 1890 is found in his letter to Professor Mendenhall dated December 1, 1890. There are some salient features.

Rockwell furnished Major Thomas H. Handbury of the U. S. Engineers a shoreline tracing with triangulation points. This was for the purpose of making a hydrographic survey of the river with a view to improvement of the channel. Included was a sketch by Rockwell to show the site of the railroad and wagon road bridge being constructed. Also shown is the line of the Portland & Puget Sound Railroad, a part of the Union Pacific system. The sketch is on a scale of 1:100,000.

The total cost of the survey, not including the triangulation, which extended a considerable distance beyond the upper limits of the sketch, was $682, making the cost of the survey $28 per mile square. Rockwell noted that this was by no means average, since the city of Vancouver and suburbs and the Garrison of Vancouver increased the amount of detail work. Rockwell's statistics for the season's work, August 23 to November 1, 1890 are as follows:[34]

Number of miles of shore line	17½
Number of miles of shore (Hayden Island)	9⅞
Number of ponds, lakes, sloughs and creeks	59½
Number of miles Marsh outlines	8½
Number of miles of Roads (including Railroads)	70
Number of Square Miles, area	24

Rockwell completed the last half of 1891 working in the area of Government Island in the Columbia River. On September 2 he moved his camp to the village of Washougal. Rockwell remarks on the geology of the area, the source of

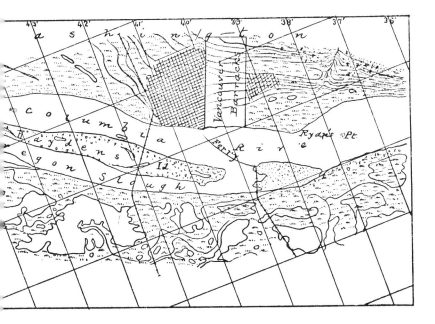

Sketch with Rockwell's Dec. 1, 1890 report to Superintendent Mendenhall, NA, RG 23.

great quantities of quarried basaltic augite used for the jetty and dikes at the mouth of the river. The season closed on October 19.[35]

Cleveland Rockwell was ordered to attend a Topographical Conference in Washington, D.C., in January 1892. He was instructed to serve as a member by direction of Superintendent Mendenhall. The conference adjourned in March and Rockwell returned to his home in Portland, Oregon. The face to face meeting seemingly did nothing to clear the air between Assistant Cleveland Rockwell and Superintendent Thomas Corwin Mendenhall. The rift must have been intolerable. Shortly after returning to Portland, Assistant Rock-

well submitted his resignation to take effect June 1, 1892. The Annual Report of 1892 contained the Superintendent's statement that in forwarding to Rockwell "a letter from the Secretary of the Treasury accepting his resignation, the Superintendent took occasion to express to Mr. Rockwell his appreciation of the great value of his services during the long period, nearly thirty-six years, of his connection with the Survey, the high esteem in which he was held by his brother officers being justified by the unvarying excellence of his work, ranking always among the best of its kind." Considering Rockwell's long and faithful service, the Superintendent could hardly do otherwise than make some recognition. That statement was Rockwell's "gold watch" after his 36 years of work.

A little over a year later Mendenhall, himself, resigned.

Three years later George Davidson was summarily notified of his dismissal by another new superintendent, General W. W. Duffield. The dismissal, by orders of a new Secretary of the Treasury, stated no reason. Dated June 30, 1895, the text read: "Services as an assistant in the offices of the United States Coast & Geodetic Survey will not be required after the 30th instant."[36]

CHAPTER IV: NOTES

1. Portland *Oregonian,* March 27, 1879, p. 2, col. 2.
2. *Annual Report, 1880,* p. 44.
3. *Annual Report, 1881,* pp. 42-43.
4. California State Dept. of Vital Records, City and County of San Francisco, State number 6178. Certified copy of death of Gertrude Ellinor Rockwell Mullay.
5. California State Dept. of Public Health, Certificate of Death of Cornelia (Rockwell) Kearney. State number 49-056478. Registrar's number 5526.
6. *Annual Report, 1883,* p. 58.
7. *Annual Report, 1884,* p. 67.
8. *Annual Report, 1884,* p. 68.
9. *Annual Report, 1885,* pp. 60-61.
10. *Annual Report, 1886,* pp. 75-76.
11. *Annual Report, 1886,* p. 77.
12. Danford Balch settled near what is now Willamette Heights, Portland, in 1850. Balch Creek was named for him and Balch station was near its confluence with the Willamette. Reputedly Balch was the first Portland citizen hanged. He killed his son-in-law and the hanging occurred Oct. 17, 1859.
13. *Annual Report, 1886,* pp. 76-77.
14. National Archives, RG 23 is the source of these reports.
15. *Annual Report, 1888,* p. 67. Unfortunately, the sketchbook was not located in the records at the National Archives.
16. Davidson to Thorn, Aug. 18, 1887, NA RG 23.
17. NA RG 23.
18. *Annual Report, 1888,* p. 67. See inside back cover.
19. *Annual Report, 1888,* p. 94. The 721-page volume with views and charts was published in 1889.
20. Joseph N. Dolph (1835-1897) was born and educated in New York, came to Portland and practiced law 1862-1883, served as U.S. district attorney 1865-1866, and as state senator 1866-1868 and 1872-1876. He was elected U.S. Senator (Republican) and served 1893-1895. Among his clients were the Oregon Steam Navigation Co., Oregon Railway & Navigation Co., Oregon and California Railroad, Ben Holladay and Henry Villard. See *Dictionary of Oregon History,* edited by Howard McKinley Corning (Portland, 1956).
21. NA RG 23.
22. Rockwell to Thorn, April 19, 1889, NA RG 23.
23. *Annual Report, 1889,* pp. 72-73.
24. Rockwell to Mendenhall, NA RG 23.
25. Rockwell to Mendenhall, NA RG 23.
26. NA RG 23.
27. Sept. 19, 1889, NA, RG 23.
28. *Annual Report, 1890,* pp. 65, 71.
29. June 30, 1890, NA, RG 23.
30. Aug. 12, 1890, NA RG 23.
31. NA RG 23, Compensation Records.
32. *Annual Report, 1891,* pp. 73-74.
33. Sept. 29, 1890, NA RG 23.
34. NA RG 23.
35. *Annual Report, 1892,* p. 74.
36. Duffield to Davidson, A.L.S., George Davidson Collection, Volume 33, p. 334. (Quoted by permission of The Director, The Bancroft Library, University of California, Berkeley.) The trouble in the Coast and Geodetic Survey came toward the end of Rockwell's service. Further detail is beyond the scope of this discussion. See also *George Davidson, Pioneer West Coast Scientist, op. cit.,* pp. 98-99; and *Centennial Celebration of the United States Coast & Geodetic Survey* (Washington, Dept. of Commerce, 1916).

RETIREMENT ACTIVITIES

Aғᴛᴇʀ JUNE, 1892 Captain Rockwell began doing the things he enjoyed most. By all accounts he was as busy as before, taking up new activities and placing new meaning on some of his old ones. He established new priorities as he settled down with his family. At this point Cleveland was 55 years of age and his wife Cornelia was 33, Gertrude was 12 years old and Neely was 10.

The Captain enjoyed the privilege of being with his family much more than ever before. His daily routine included going to his office and dressing in city clothes instead of his uniform of field clothes and boots. During the week his business and lunch encounters made him feel more allied with the life of the growing city. Sundays he proudly attended church with his wife and daughters and listened to the Rev. Thomas L. Cole's sermon.

His new life meant avoiding the extreme physical hardship which he had sustained for 36 years. The exposure to cold and sleeping on the ground or a few boughs had given Rockwell arthritis, as it had George Davidson and doubtless other assistants. No more dust, fog or hordes of mosquitoes — except when he chose to go fishing or hunting! When he pursued his profession privately on engineering assignments, the exposure was different than the six to ten months he had spent in the field each year.

Portland had fused with Albina and East Portland on July 5, 1891. The combined population of the three towns was 58,000 by the official 1890 census. A recount came up with a figure of 72,357 which the Census Bureau in Washington deemed to be inflated.

Captain Rockwell was widely acquainted in Portland and noted for his surveys of the Columbia and Willamette rivers and the Oregon coast which added immeasurably to the safety of navigation and the development of marine commerce. The tonnage of wheat and other grains, canned and preserved salmon, lumber and fruit was growing each year. Not everyone knew of his contribution to the economic progress of the region but many did and these were generally the leaders of the community.

The old office of the U. S. Coast and Geodetic Survey in the Portland Savings Bank Building was closed in 1892. The same space became Captain Rockwell's office and by 1894, he was listed in the city directory as Cleveland Rockwell, capitalist. His residence, which he bought in 1886, was at 395 Sixth Street. Today this is the southwest corner facing S. W. Sixth between Montgomery and Harrison streets. The old house is gone and the property is part of the Portland State University campus. However, this was the Rockwell home from 1886 to 1904. It was a good neighborhood and only about 10 or 12 blocks from the center of the city.

Captain and Mrs. Cleveland Rockwell were listed in the *Portland Blue Book,* a social register, from 1890 on. As dictated by the custom of that time, each family listed one day in the week when they were "at home" to receive their friends. Calling cards were invariably left on a silver tray at the termination of the formal and brief call. It was one of the ways in which the members of Victorian society decorously displayed their modish raiment and accessories and insured periodic contact with their friends.

Rockwell's listing as "capitalist" in the city directory of 1894 may come as a surprise. His maximum annual salary had been $2,600 per annum from 1890 until retirement in June, 1892. (See p. 24.) It is doubtful that he could have accumulated any appreciable amount of capital even with his Yankee frugality. Yet after leaving Coast Survey service he lists himself as capitalist. This implies lending money, buying mortages and commercial paper and making investments. He became a member of the board of directors of three Portland banks. In every instance he presumably had a substantial interest in the bank in order to be appointed to serve as a board member. In one case he owned 200 shares with a face value of $20,000. In this prosperous bank, the undisbursed capital was equal to the capitalized value. The current worth was nearer $40,000. His holdings in Portland bank stocks may have exceeded $100,000. He owned his home. He associated with substantial persons in the business and social community and the implication of significant wealth is sustained.

It is supposed that Captain Rockwell's inheritance from his father's proprietary interest in the Cleveland Pittsburgh Railroad, iron manufacturing and mercantile interests and land in the Western Reserve must have been substantial. Since his sister Matilda (Mrs. George Kent of New York City) died in 1864, Cleveland Rockwell was his father's sole heir. His father died in 1874 and in 1875 Rockwell had asked for a leave of absence. As noted, at that time he had written that it might become necessary for him to give "personal attention to some matters of private interest and impor-

Rockwell as he appeared during his Portland residence. (OHS)

tance..." He did take an eight month leave in 1875 and 1876 and his whereabouts were not accounted for; he was most likely settling his father's affairs then.

Captain Rockwell had a degree in Mining Engineering according to the *Circular of Information of the Portland School of Mines.* It may be that he obtained a degree from the College of the City of New York, though their incomplete records do not so indicate. The catalogue of the school of mines displayed a photograph of Rockwell and recorded his education at Troy Polytechnic School and the University of New York, his Coast and Geodetic Survey service and his rank of Chief Topographical Engineer on Gen. William T. Sherman's staff.[1] The 24-page catalogue describes the courses offered, and indicates that the term begins on October 1, 1897. Dated testimonials of graduated students included specifically mention their work of "the past winter," so the school must have been in existence in 1896.

Principal was J. H. Fisk, M.E., and Cleveland Rockwell, M.E., was instructor of mining engineering. Along with two other instructors, this was the faculty. The school taught all of the usual mining courses and assayed ores and coal. It also examined and made reports on mines and prospects.[2]

Continuing the private practice of his profession, Rockwell was called upon to travel throughout the Northwest. In this connection he seems to have made a trip to Alaska in 1892 just after he retired. Alaskan paintings, so dated, establish his presence there in 1892. Others bear later dates indicating several Alaskan trips.

Rockwell's survey of coal fields at Coos Bay, Oregon was deemed of such professional excellence and interest that it was published in *The Engineering and Mining Journal.* Illustrations consist of two photographs, Rockwell's map of the region and his drawing of the "Bunkers at Tunnel, Newport Mine, Oregon." The conclusions were not encouraging for coal mining on a large scale. The thoroughness with which the situation is analyzed is impressive. In his civilian engineering Rockwell evidenced the same capabilities apparent in his Civil War defense maps and his Coast Survey charts.[3]

Captain Rockwell's post-Coast Survey life was characterized by increased activity as a nimrod. It has been noted that he provided fresh meat and fish, when it was available, for his surveying parties in the field. His continued interest and his prowess is attested in an article titled "A Day with the Ducks." The history of duck hunting along the Columbia River is detailed. The heavy growth of wapato (wild potatoes) along the lakes and bottomlands insured the great flights of mallards, teal, canvasbacks and widgeons. The birds dropped down to feed as they flew north, and later south, each year.

For many years the hunters, with their retrieving dogs, crowded the riverboats. Then regular duck hunting runs were instituted. In the fall and winter months the hunting boat swung away from the dock at midnight and headed down the Willamette and in turn, the Columbia River. Frequently there were as many as 100 hunters aboard. Each was bent on a good day's sport over his own privileged ground. In the ladies' cabin the piano was kept going. Some of the hunters were sure to add the sounds of the mandolin, guitar and violin they brought for this purpose. The singing was invariably in perfect key!

Early hunting boats were the *Maria Wilkins, Commodore Perry* and *Salem.* The procedure was the same. After a pre-dawn breakfast aboard, the boat moved out, cautiously picked her way for fear of stranding on some hidden obstacle, and finally shoved her nose into the bank and brush. The sportsmen, in singles or groups, with their decoys, gun, hunting boat, rubber coat, ammunition bag and lunch descended the long gangplank, each jerking behind him the "best dog on earth." So the great load was let loose along the various lakes and sloughs. For a distance of twenty miles or more on either side of the river, each hunter had to be in his blind, a brush pile in circular form, as the first light of dawn made the flying birds visible.

Captain Rockwell, after his life in the out-of-doors, was perfectly at home when he first joined the traditional hunters' sojourn. Soon he was acquainted with all of the participants and had a reputation as an excellent shot: "Jack Knott, Sim Reed, Millard Lownsdale and Captain Rockwell have made the largest killings ever made on these birds. These gentlemen shoot over Bachelor's island, twenty-five miles down the Columbia from Portland."[4] One hopes that Mrs. Rockwell and the two daughters enjoyed eating wild duck.

Previous reference has been made to Captain Rockwell's membership in the Grand Army of the Republic. From 1891 on, he played an increasingly active role in the activities of Garfield Post No. 3 in Portland. There was a two-day encampment in April, 1891 at Astoria. The election and installation of officers included Captain Cleveland Rockwell on the Council of Administration. Subsequently he served as Commander of Lincoln Garfield Post.[5]

Captain Rockwell was active in Republican politics. As a member of the Fifth Ward Club of Portland, he took his place among his neighbors and friends. Other members of the club were: Joseph N. Dolph (U. S. Senator), David Dalgleish (unidentified), Melvin C. George (educator, lawyer and U. S. Congressman), W. H. Harris (proprietor, Portland Artificial Ice Company), B. P. Cardwell (real estate and Customs House broker), Wallace McCamant (attorney and Oregon Supreme Court justice), Russell E. Sewell (unidentified), George A. Steel (Portland postmaster and president of the

Metropolitan Railway Co.), Joseph A. Strowbridge (pioneer merchant, organizer of the Portland Library Association, and state legislator), Tyler Woodward (banker, co-builder of Portland Steel Railways, county commissioner and city councilman), A. L. Maxwell (ticket agent for railroads), Allen B. Croasman (real estate, timber lands and mining supplies, later police commissioner and postmaster), A. W. Witherell (unidentified), Clark Hay (insurance), William M. Ladd (son of pioneer banker, William S. Ladd), John Ring (building contractor), George E. Watkins (real estate, investments, loans and insurance, Portland councilman), William C. Noon (bags, bagging, tents, twine, awnings), Buell Lamberson (seed store), Edward H. Habighorst (hardware and logging supplies).[6]

That Rockwell maintained his lifelong interest in fishing is apparent, as indicated by his 1884 self-portrait fishing the Trask River in Tillamook County, Oregon. He refers to fishing along the Oregon coast and the Columbia River in his U. S. Coast and Geodetic Survey Annual Reports. Further documentation of his interest in salmon fishing is evidenced by his story, "The First Columbia River Salmon Ever Caught with a Fly."

In 1867 I was engaged in making a survey of the mouth of the Columbia and was anchored in the shelter of Baker's Bay, [not far from Forts Canby and Columbia] just inside of Cape Disappointment .... Well do I remember my first salmon taken in these waters. Equipped with a good two-handed English salmon-rod of ash, with lancewood tip, one hundred yards of braided line, and the best of flies, all furnished me by a valued friend, I left the vessel's side, alone in my dingy, to try for silver-side salmon.

No salmon had ever been known before to take a fly on the Columbia River, and I had very little hope of success. I had but a few hundred yards to pull from the vessel .... I took my rod and commenced casting. Though an old hand with an eight-ounce trout rod, I found a two-handed rod an awkward thing. However I soon succeeded in making a cast far enough away from the boat to hook a salmon. What a thrill of excitement accompanied striking the hook into the solid tongue of that first salmon — and how my heart rushed up into my throat as the alarmed fish made his first frantic rush for liberty![7]

Rockwell lost his rod overboard in six feet of water, then returned to the boat with a long pike pole to which a gaff hook was lashed and "almost immediately succeeded in fishing up the rod . . . ."

Of course I had lost my first salmon, and probably half my line, and silently and in sorrow I reeled it in, when, whizz! out flew the handle from my fingers, and away went my salmon, fresh for a second heat . . . . When finally I thrust the gaff into his shining belly and lifted him into the boat, a cheer went up from the shore, which, with the salmon thrashing around in the boat, made me feel quite proud of the adventure. He weighed twenty five pounds . . . . In a week every rooster on the military post presented a most forlorn appearance; necks and tails had both been plucked to make salmon flies!

Rockwell's humorous misadventure documents his being an old hand with an eight-ounce fly rod and in general with fishing poles and tackle. It is not likely that he ever lost his zest for fishing.

Cleveland Rockwell continued his fishing, hunting and mountain climbing activities. His sketches from the summit of Saddle Mountain and from the headlands along the Oregon coast and his large oil painting of the Canadian Rocky Mountains are confirmatory.

When Rockwell's U.S. Coast and Geodetic Survey work terminated on June 1, 1892, he and his family set off on a vacation trip. Visiting Puget Sound and specifically Tacoma and Seattle, they moved on to British Columbia. July found them seeing Harrison Lake, Banff and Mount Sir Donald. They visited the Canadian Glacier Park region and Alaska. Sketches and a significant number of finished paintings resulted from the trip.

From the time of his arrival in Oregon, he began writing about the Pacific Northwest. Naturally his attention focused on the Columbia River but he turned to other areas, as well. The writing varied from the whimsical to scientific and from fantasy to documentary. After he retired, he accelerated his writing, which he continued as long as he lived. Most of his writing appeared in the *Pacific Monthly* and *The West Shore* magazines, through the latter was careless about giving credits. Sometimes authorship is established by an accompanying illustration which can be recognized as Rockwell's.

While his art career will be dealt with in a separate section, from 1892 on, he certainly increased his sketching and painting and continued until his final illness. Until he came west, his painting seemed to have been an avocation and any sales were casual. Rockwell frequently gave away his work to friends and admirers. He did occasionally accept a commission to paint a particular scene for a fee. With retirement he had more time and his increased output continued to occupy his attention. He also began teaching painting. Evidence of this comes from Mrs. Earl Marshall of Portland. Her husband, now deceased after a career of civil engineering, was one of his pupils. Mr. Marshall's work shows a marked influence of his teacher's instruction.

Rockwell had developed a new way of life and according to all evidence at hand, enjoyed a position of trust and respect in his community. Suddenly a cloud loomed over the horizon.

In July 1893, Portland, Oregon was shaken by the closing of a number of banks. The Oregon National Bank closed, then the Northwest Loan and Trust Company, which was practically under the same management. At the same time, the Union Banking Company suspended operations and in a few days the Portland Savings Bank and the Commercial National Bank, with common ownership and management, followed suit. Since the latter two banks' largest stockholder also was associated with national banks in other Oregon cities, the pressure on these other banks was great. They were located in McMinnville, Arlington, The Dalles, Heppner and other cities in Oregon, and were included in a wave of suspension all over the state. Some of these institutions subsequently reopened.[8]

Earlier, in 1873, failure of the investment banking firm of Jay Cooke and Company, New York City, was followed by the failure of the Northern Pacific Railroad and banks throughout the eastern and middlewestern part of the country. The building of the Northern Pacific Railroad toward the West Coast was at first stopped, and then slowed, in its rate of progress. It was not until 1883 that the track was built all of the way to Portland. For the next ten years business expanded and banks kept pace. They so proliferated that in 1892 there were 41 national banks in Oregon. There were three national banks in Portland and several other states' chartered banks. All had shown substantial growth in the previous decade.

It may well be that the rate of business expansion of the preceding decade simply could not be maintained. Reappraisal of the situation, as late as 1967, reveals no culpable individuals. It certainly is true that as a result of these and other failures, banking laws were changed to maintain a greater liquidity in the ratio of cash to loans. There were few protective laws relating to state chartered banks, and, of course, there was no type of depositor insurance.

Once a single bank closed its doors emotions ran high, precipitating withdrawals of sufficient magnitude to put great pressure on the remaining banks. Most, although not all, ceased operations at least temporarily.

It was truly a period of panic. All who were connected with banks were subject to recrimination. Some of the allegations were completely ridiculous but those whose money was tied up in one of the closed banks were not expected to be calm or reasonable. Some idea of the extent of the hard times may be gained by the fact that the *Oregonian*, September 18, 1893, published a list of tax delinquent property to be sold at sheriff's sale. The list required five full newspaper pages of very small type.

The various stockholder meetings, receiverships, partial payments to depositors, ramifications and complications continued and it was 1905 before the last suit was settled and final payment was made.

At the time of the banking crisis, Cleveland Rockwell was on the board of directors of three banking institutions. The first was the Portland Trust Company, incorporated April 22, 1877. Its officers were Henry L. Pittock, President, Dr. A. S. Nichols, Vice President and Benjamin I. Cohen, Secretary. The board of directors consisted of A. M. Smith, Charles E. Sitton, W. W. Spaulding, Louis G. Clarke, Charles H. Woodward, A. F. Hildreth and Cleveland Rockwell.[9] The Portland Trust Company withstood the pressure and did not close its doors. It subsequently became the Oregon Bank.

The second institution with which Cleveland Rockwell was associated was the Commercial National Bank. It opened January 4, 1886, with a capital of $100,000, later increased to $250,000. President was D. P. Thompson, Vice President was Frank Dekum, and R. L. Durham was cashier. The board of directors were: Thompson, Dekum and Durham plus R. M. Wade, E. S. Kearney, George H. Williams, R. Jacobs, L. White, Henry Weinhard, Cleveland Rockwell, J. W. Hill, H. C. Wortman, J. B. David, W. F. Burrell and George H. Durham. The Commercial National Bank closed its doors the first week in August, 1893.

The third bank, the Portland Savings Bank, was organized

in 1880, and its first two years were largely

a matter of experiment. From a small beginning it has grown, however, to be one of the leading banks of the city....[Its] elegant bank building is at the corner of Washington and Second, where the bank occupies most attractive quarters. The president of the bank is Frank Dekum, who was also one of the incorporators of the institution. The other officers are W. K. Smith, vice-president, and H. C. Stratton, cashier. The board of directors is composed of D. P. Thompson, W. F. Burrell, Frank Dekum, W. K. Smith, R. M. Wade, George H. Durham, S. A. Durham, C. A. Dolph, Ward S. Stevens, E. J. Jeffrey and Cleveland Rockwell. The bank has paid up capital of $125,000, with a surplus and undivided profits of $120,000.

It can be seen that there is a considerable overlapping insofar as officers and board are concerned between the Portland Savings Bank and the Commercial National Bank. The extent of Rockwell's investment in the stock of the Commercial National Bank, where he served on the board of directors, as well as the Portland Trust Company, where he was also a director, cannot be stated from information at hand. In the Portland Savings Bank, however, Rockwell was also a director and owner of 200 shares of capital stock with a face value of $20,000 in January, 1894, according to the allegation of a suit Cleveland Rockwell instituted against the Portland Savings Bank and the other directors.

The heat of the controversy was recorded by the newspapers. The *Oregonian* carried daily reports for the first month. Few citizens were not touched and there seemed little else to talk about. Rockwell had brought suit for a nominal amount "apparently with the approval of the bank . . . and in connection with the suit asked for the appointment of a reviewer."[10]

With this action, Rockwell precipitated himself into the center of the upheaval. The Portland Savings Bank had suspended operations on July 29, 1893, reopened on May 1, 1894, and suspended again permanently on November 19, 1894. At the initial closing there were assets enough to pay creditors and depositors in full had there not been a run. The reopening was ill advised and claims were presented faster than notes, mortgages and other obligations became due. This forced the final closing. During the reopening, the bank paid creditors in full. Those who were trusting and loyal to the bank and did not draw out their funds were punished by a loss and it then required eight years to get the reduced balance of their funds.

The suit filed in Cleveland Rockwell's name had several purposes. He sued for the return of his own capital. He was not a banker except by investing part of his capital in the stock of the Portland Savings Bank. His position on the board of the bank was based on his reputation of honesty and integrity and the fact that he owned 200 of 2,600 shares outstanding — one-thirteenth of the capital stock.

He asked for receivership and pointed out that the total indebtedness of the bank was $2,514,573.29. Against this were assets "of valuable lands, buildings, notes, mortgages and other evidences of debt...but owing to the great and unusual scarcity of money at the present time . . . and the great depreciation in the market value of the properties and securities . . . [the bank] will not be able to pay the rest of its said indebtedness as it becomes due and is in imminent danger of becoming insolvent."[11]

It was further alleged that the greater part of the indebtedness to the bank would not come due for some months and that the corporation should be dissolved and a receiver appointed. It was held "That the property and assets of said defendant corporation are sufficient in value if properly secured and managed by a competent person acting under the appointment and directions of this Honorable Court, to pay and satisfy all of said indebtedness, and leave a large surplus in money and property to be divided among said owners and holders of its capital stock." David P. Thompson, one of the founders of the Portland Savings Bank who had sold his interest about a year before, was named as receiver and duly bonded for $500,000.

The petition served the purposes of the bank and the public by instituting an orderly process of collecting money from the numerous sources. Otherwise, only a fraction of the potential worth would be realized in a forced sale of assets during such hard times.

Rockwell's petition also asked for the return of his own funds and those of others in circumstances differing from regular deposition of the bank.

One claimant was the Chemical National Bank of New York City which on June 14, 1893, barely two weeks before the Portland Savings Bank closed its doors, had loaned the latter $25,000 — a loan supported by five notes signed by reliable Portland citizens. There was a similar note owned by the Western National Bank of New York City. A Mrs. Minnie Luchesi, too, had deposited three notes for a total of $13,000 for safekeeping and collection of interest. Mrs. Luchesi, a resident of California, had a local agent and the bank had caused interest on her notes to be deposited in the agent's personal account. Mrs. Luchesi wished her notes and the interest collected to be returned to her.

Approval was asked of a schedule for payments over the course of a year from the Commercial National Bank to the Portland Savings Bank for liquidating an obligation of $65,478.93.

Payments owing by Portland Savings Bank to contractors for adding additional stories and refurbishing their bank building were due. The cost was $80,000 of which a balance of $14,000 was owing. Other balances on the lighting, new elevator, etc., were overdue. There were several small amounts due for labor or services to the bank. A borrower had put up as security for a loan some stock of a Blaine, Washington bank. The stock was sold for an excess of about $2,000 above the amount owing on the loan. The owner wanted the excess returned.

There were numerous other instances involving special circumstances, labor and materials, money and notes placed in safekeeping, assets pledged for other obligations, none of which were the simple situation of depositors. Cleveland Rockwell divorced himself from the officers and board and yet part of his purpose was to clarify and define special instances in the interests of the bank. His name appeared as plaintiff in every instance. Similar to the modern concept of a class suit, his action gained special consideration for deserving persons. It also saved untold costs to the bank and the litigants over the expenses of individual suits and the defense thereto.

Under the caption, "Paying off Creditors," the *Oregonian* of August 23, 1893, p. 8, col. 2, announced that Judge Loyal B. Stearns had rendered a judgment for Cleveland Rockwell and the spate of creditors whom he represented. Though it was a moral victory, the entire episode was a shattering blow to Rockwell's rigid ethical standards from which he never completely recovered. Nor did he ever completely recoup his financial losses.[12] The receiver first paid 10% to the depositors. Then in May, 1894, another 30% was paid. Finally in January, 1902, a final 18% for a total of 58% was made as the receivership ended.

The Commercial National Bank closed and reopened. A controlling interest was purchased by Wells, Fargo and Company in 1894. Cleveland Rockwell was not listed on the new board of directors.[13]

When the Portland Savings Bank made its final payment and the receivership ended after almost nine years, the *Oregonian* bestowed its benediction: "It is such an old, old story that everyone will be glad to hear the end of it. But the matter has left scars on many which are not healed nor shall be as long as the sufferers live!"

Gradually Portland recovered from the bank closures and panic of the 1890s. So, too, did Rockwell continue his activities. He pursued his career as civil engineer. In 1896 he moved his office to the Commercial Block.

About this time, the battleship *Oregon* returned to the state and was visiting in Portland. The ship had served the United

Three Rockwell scenes were engraved as vignettes on the $25,000 sterling punch set for the Battleship *Oregon*. Only one shows here on the smaller bowl. (Silver set at OHS)

States Navy since 1893. Later she took a significant role in the Spanish-American War. At the battle of Santiago she fired the first shot; she sank the Spanish *Maria Theresa* and beached the *Colon*. The vessel became the flagship of the squadron in 1898.[14]

The Portland committee for the ship's visit in 1897 decided to present the *Oregon* with a silver punch bowl. Captain Rockwell was designated to furnish three of his pen and ink drawings of local scenes to be engraved on the two sterling silver punch bowls. The large bowl was to hold 80 pints. There was a smaller bowl, about one foot across, a ladle for each and a huge tray. In addition, the set included 24 silver holders for 24 crystal glasses. Around the base of each bowl were silver beavers in full relief, the state animal. On the rim of each bowl were two vignettes. On the large bowl, the enclosed space was engraved: "From the citizens of the State of Oregon to the U.S. Battleship 'Oregon' 1896." The opposite space is engraved with Cleveland Rockwell's drawing of Mt. Hood from the Columbia River and showing a part of Government Island. The drawing for this vignette has been preserved and is displayed in the exhibit. On the smaller bowl are engraved two other Rockwell drawings: "A Sailing Ship being guided across the Columbia River Bar," and on the opposite lip of the bowl, Rockwell's "The Falls of Oregon City."

The cost of the punch set was $25,000. The bowl was ordered through A. Feldenheimer, Jewelers of Portland. The bowl was manufactured by Gorham and Company. Funds were collected throughout the state. Each school child was asked to contribute ten cents and each adult twenty-five cents to pay for the set. The punch bowl and glasses were presented to the "Bull Dog of the Navy" when Governor William P. Lord visited Capt. Albert S. Barker, in command of the USS *Oregon*, on July 6, 1897.[15]

About 1895, while on a trip, Rockwell was importuned to paint a curtain for the recently constructed Opera House at Union, Oregon. This he did, choosing a version of his best known "Ship outward bound across the Columbia Bar." Sometime after 1900 the structure burned, and with it, the painting.[16]

Rockwell remained active in both his professional and art activity. The financial return from both endeavors became more important after his financial losses. A number of his large oils were painted in the last half of the 1890s. He also began keeping on hand a supply of smaller watercolors. These were marines, beach scenes with waves breaking on shore or ocean scenes, each with a ship or two in the distance. They sold for from $10 to $20. They were priced and on display. They were for visitors, whose interest in art was minimal, to purchase after being given a hospitable showing in his home studio. Most artists did this, in one way or another.

A social comment seems in order. It is a truism that interest in art never occurs in a community until a certain level of stability and affluence is reached. In Portland it was in the mid-1880s that a patron group began to develop. Characteristically, those early collectors sought marble statuary and painting from far away. European was best; next best, art from New York. The work of local artists was passed by with the notable exception of Rockwell. His established position in Portland, his social acceptance and the competence and charm of his work broke the rule for almost three decades. When those who were acquainted with him passed on, most of his pictures came down off the walls. Recent interest in his work is a revival after a hiatus of half a century.

The Rockwells' youngest daughter, Cornelia, was married

at her parents' home on March 1, 1899. Her husband was John Rittenhouse Stevens of Philadelphia, more recently from Shoshone County, Idaho, where, as an engineer, he was building a bridge.[17] John Stevens died at an unknown date. A son, Rockwell Rittenhouse Stevens, Captain and Mrs. Cleveland Rockwell's only grandchild, resulted from the union. He reputedly married the daughter of a Chicago professor about 1929 and lived in Boston until about 1940. This and other leads have been traced, but he could not be located.

Mrs. John R. Stevens remarried about 1930. Her second husband was Capt. Thomas A. Kearney, USN. He was living at Vallejo, California, and was in command of Mare Island Naval Base. He retired in 1932 and they moved to San Francisco and occupied the former Norwegian Legation House at 1901 Jackson Street. A friend describes her as a woman of great charm, wit and courage. She was slender, had lovely brown eyes and dark hair. Captain Kearney died in San Francisco in 1941 and Mrs. Kearney (Neely Rockwell) died July 29, 1947. They are buried in Arlington National Cemetery.[18]

Cornelia's sister, Gertrude, older by almost 15 months, first married John Rounsfell. No local marriage record has been located. Presumably she was not married in Portland. Her husband is said to have been a jeweler, and is believed to have died about 1910. There were no children. Gertrude Rockwell Rounsfell was remarried in 1913 to Col. Patrick Mullay, USA. He was subsequently in command at Fort Missoula. After his retirement they moved to San Francisco and lived in a house on Van Ness Avenue near her sister and Captain Kearney. Every wall was hung with her father's paintings. Both families entertained friends frequently. Gertrude Mullay was a talented pianist and once accompanied

Sketch of N(eely) and G(ertrude), from their Father's sketchbook. Graves Col.

Enrico Caruso when his own accompanist became ill before a concert in San Francisco. Mrs. Kearney sustained a stroke, recovered and lived for several years with an impairment of speech. She died September 4, 1936. Col. Patrick Mullay, USA (Ret.) lived until March 22, 1963. There were no children. Both are buried at the San Francisco National Cemetery at the Presidio.[19]

Mrs. Cleveland Rockwell was deeply committed to helping others and was particularly involved with assisting children and young people. She was instrumental in the founding of the Florence Crittenton Refuge Home, a branch of the International Florence Crittenton Refuge Mission based in Washington, D.C. When that institution was turned over to the State of Oregon, Governor George Chamberlain appointed Mrs. Rockwell to handle the funds for the home. She was President of the Home in 1911. Mrs. Rockwell also served with the founding group of the Children's Home, the city board of charities and the Oregon Humane Society.

Later she resided with her daughter, Mrs. John Stevens, then living in Philadelphia. Subsequently she joined Colonel and Mrs. Mullay in the Philippines, returning to Montana with them when the Colonel was made commanding officer at Fort Missoula.

Mrs. Rockwell was stricken with pneumonia, seemed to recover but relapsed and died March 19, 1922. Her body was accompanied to Portland, Oregon, by her daughter and there joined by her other daughter, Mrs. John R. Stevens of Chicago. Funeral services were conducted by Dr. A. A. Morrison at the Portland Crematorium on March 22, 1922.[20]

Cleveland and Cornelia Rockwell had purchased a new house in 1905 at 1100 Vaughn Street on Willamette Heights. He moved his office to smaller quarters in the Worcester Building. He did not go to his office every day, and his commissions as a civil engineer became fewer. But his painting continued; he still had a steady hand and keen eyesight. There are dated 1904 sketches, and he apparently continued his sketching trips each subsequent year. Some of the paintings in the current exhibit at the Oregon Historical Society are dated 1906 and 1907, and they show no deterioration in the quality of his work.

In early 1907 Captain Rockwell became ill with a severe respiratory infection. He was forced to remain in bed for several weeks and his condition worsened with the development of pneumonia. At 69 years, 3 months and 25 days, his vital forces failed and he died. The following day the *Morning Oregonian* stated: "Captain Cleveland Rockwell, one of Oregon's oldest and most distinguished citizens, died at 10:00 o'clock last night at his residence . . . ."

CHAPTER V: NOTES

1. Copies in the writer's collection and at OHS.
2. James H. Fisk is listed as assayer and chemist in the Portland city directories, and the school was at the same address as his office, 204 1/2 Washington Street.
3. See "The Coos Bay Coal Fields," by Cleveland Rockwell, in the *Engineering and Mining Journal*, Feb. 15, 1902, pp. 238-40, and Feb. 22, 1902, pp. 270-71.
4. "A Day with Ducks," by George L. Curry, in *The West Shore*, Vol. XVII (March 7, 1891), pp. 158-60. The article is suggested reading for local historians, duck hunters past 70 years of age, in fact all native senior citizens of Portland. It names an additional 100 duck hunters of 1891. Surely this list includes old friends and acquaintances and possibly some antecedents. Names which bring up unpleasant memories may be scanned hastily.
5. *The West Shore*, Vol. XVII (April 18, 1891), p. 260; *History of Oregon*, by H. K. Hines, *op. cit.*, p. 598.
6. *A Record of the Republican Party in the State of Oregon*, compiled and published with the approval of the Republican State Central Committee of 1894-1896, and the Executive Committee of the Republican League of Oregon for 1894-1896 (Portland, Oregon, 1896), p. 86.
7. The *Pacific Monthly*, Vol. X (October 1903), pp. 202-203.
8. The background story concerning the general economic situation, failure of Portland banks, etc., is a long and detailed matter. What is given in the text to explain Cleveland Rockwell's involvement comes from two sources: *Gold in the Woodpile, An Informal History of Banking in Oregon*, by O. K. Burrell (Eugene, Oregon, 1967), pp. 129-67; and the *Oregonian* clipping file index, which contains at least 50 references to Oregon's bank failures from 1893-1902.
9. The detailing of the officers and boards of the three banks named comes from Harvey Scott's *History of Portland, Oregon* (Syracuse, New York, 1890).
10. *Gold in the Woodpile, op. cit.*, p. 146.
11. References to the various legal proceedings are from the approximately 123 pages of Circuit Court documents of Multnomah County, State of Oregon, papers for the year of 1894 under the number 5558, Film File CC-337. Locating and printing of the old records was facilitated by Deputy Director of the Circuit Court, Harold Jensen.
12. As related by his two daughters, according to several close friends.
13. *Gold in the Woodpile, op. cit.*, p. 155.
14. *Dictionary of Oregon History, op. cit.*
15. See the Portland *Evening Telegram* of that date and pamphlet published for the occasion, Mary Walker Tichenor, author and compiler (OHS).
16. The story was related some years ago by Dr. Garwood H. Ostrander, Portland physician now deceased. He furnished the writer with a photograph of the curtain.
17. Multnomah County Marriage Records, Vol. 12, October 1897-September, 1899, p. 364.
18. Basic material of the life of Cornelia Rockwell Kearney comes from her official California death record, from friends and from Roland E. Lex, Superintendent of the San Francisco National Cemetery at The Presidio, San Francisco.
19. Information regarding the life of Gertrude Rockwell Mullay comes from her official California death record, from friends, from Francis B. Heitman's *Historical Register and Dictionary of the U. S. Army* (2 vols., Washington, 1903), p. 735, and from Roland Lex, Superintendent of the San Francisco National Cemetery at The Presidio.
20. Portland *Oregon Journal*, March 22, 1922, p. 15.

2.—GEOMETRICAL DRAWING.

A.—ELEMENTARY DRAWING.—*Calligraphy ;* Drawing of Lettering,—Plain and Ornamental.—*Model Drawing ;* Linear Drawing from Models, Simple and Complex Geometrical Forms in Plan, Elevation, and Section.—*Tinting and Shading ;* Use of India Ink and Colors ; Conventional Treatment of Wood, Stone, and the Metals ; Graining, Tinting in Colors.—*Copying* of Geometrical Drawings ; Construction to Reduced or Enlarged Scales ; Use of Tracing Muslin,—Transfer Paper.

B.—ARCHITECTURAL DRAWING.—Drawing of Roofs and Bridges, from Architectural and Engineering Structures in the City and its Environs ; Visiting, Measuring, and Sketching these Works ; Reproduction in the Graphical Rooms of Working Drawings in Plans, Elevations, Sections, and Details.

C.—MACHINE DRAWING.—The Elements of Machine Drawing ; Problems of Drawing in Plan and Elevation,—in Right and Oblique Projection,—of Wheels, Drums, and Axles, Cylindrical and Conical Gearing, Screws, etc.—Drawing of Special Machines ; Visiting, Sketching, and Measuring Machines ; Reproduction of Complete Working Drawings, elaborated in Tints, Grainings, and Projections of Shades and Shadows.

3.—TOPOGRAPHICAL DRAWING.

A.—GENERAL TOPOGRAPHY.—*Topographical Elements :*—Graphical Construction of Polygons from Line Surveys ; Conventional Treatment of Surface Representations ;—Natural and Cultivated Surfaces,—Structural Works,—Water,—etc. ; Hill Drawing ;—Different Modes of Delineation,—LEHMAN's Mode with Vertical Light ; Field Sketching.

B.—MAPS OF FARM SURVEYS.—Construction to Scale of Perimeters, from Notes of Line Surveys ; Topographical Delineation of the Surface from Notes and Field Sketches ; Execution of a Finished Map.

C.—TRIGONOMETRICAL SURVEYS.—Projection of the Geodetical Points and Lines of the Survey of an extended Area ; Principles of Procedure in the Drawing of Topographic, Hydrographic, and various Subordinate details.

D.—MAPS AND SECTIONS OF RAILWAY SURVEYS.—Topographical Field Sketching of the Line of Survey,—Graphical Construction of *Railway Topographical Plans ;* Construction of *Railway Sections,*—Profiles of Surface Line,—Geological Sections of Succession of Rocky and Earthy Strata.

E.—PLANS AND SECTIONS OF MINE SURVEYS.—Graphical Construction of Topographical Plans of Mining Districts.—Subterranean Plans of the Distribution of Mineral Veins and Mine Workings.—Construction of Profiles of Surface Contours, Sections of Mineral Veins and Mine Workings, and Geological Sections of the Succession of Rocky and Earthy Strata.—Finished Plans and Sections in Conventional Treatment of Mine Surveys, by the Method of Isometical Projections,—by the Mode of Rectangular Co-ordinates of MM. D'AUBUISSON and COMBES.

SCHOOL OF CIVIL ENGINEERING AND ARCHITECTURE.

Civil Engineering in charge of Prof. BULL. *Architecture in charge of* Prof. CUMMINGS.

THE Course in this Department comprehends Geometrical Drawing, the use of Instruments and Problems in Graphical Calculations ; Land Surveying and Levelling, with the use of Instruments, and field operations ; Descriptive Geometry ; Astronomical Observations and Calculations for determining Latitude, Longitude, &c. ; Geodesy, Marine Surveys, and Field Topography ; Linear Drawing, with Coloring and Shading, as applied to Engineering and Architecture ; Science of Masonry and Carpentry, of Machinery, and the Founder's Art ; Construction of Machines, Mill-work, Steam-engine Locomotives, etc. ; Principles of Architecture, with the elements of Design, Construction, and Estimates ; Construction of Bridges, etc. ; Construction of Railroads, location, curves, cutting, filling, laying track, etc. ; Railroad Management ; Construction of Canals and Aqueducts, Water-Works, Sewers, Drains, etc.

SCHOOL OF DESIGN.

In charge of Professor CUMMINGS, N.A.

THE Course in this Department embraces Elementary Drawing in Lead Pencils and Crayon, from examples from the Round (School of the Antique), from Nature, and from the living Models ; Painting in Oil and Water Colors, from examples from Nature, and from the living Models ; General Principles of Composition ; School of Ornament ; the Arts of Design—their application and advantages to the Mechanic Arts.

Pages from Rensselaer Polytechnic Institute 1854 catalog and Universit of City of New York 1856 catalog showing courses Rockwell probabl took.

THE ARTIST : CHAPTER VI

CLEVELAND ROCKWELL AS AN ARTIST

CAPTAIN Cleveland Rockwell's earliest instruction in art seems to have occurred when he attended Troy Academy in Troy, New York. By his own assertion he was in attendance during the years 1853 and 1854. The school cannot identify him as attending and their only positive information is a catalogue of 1854. A portion of the catalogue showing available courses is reproduced. Correspondence with K. J. Bauer, Rensselaer Polytechnic Institute Archivist, discloses that the instructor in drawing during 1853 and 1854 was S. Edward Warren. The course included calligraphy, model drawing, tinting and shading including use of India ink and colors, copying to reduce and enlarge scale and other allied courses. There was enough there to stimulate and guide a gifted student in fundamentals. It is not known whether Rockwell received private instruction. S. Edward Warren is not listed in American dictionaries of art, nor is his work known to *The Archives of American Art.*[1] Warren's early influence on Rockwell is a certainty.

Cleveland Rockwell next attended the University of the City of New York, now incorporated in New York University. He is listed as C. S. Rockwell, Cleveland, Ohio, a sophomore, in the *Circular and Catalogue of the University of the City of New York,* March 1856. This was presumably his second year in attendance but no 1855 catalogue or other record is extant. He is not listed in 1857 or 1858 records, although he was granted a degree of Mechanical Engineer which he later used.

In 1855 and 1856 (see catalogue here reproduced for courses and teachers) Professor Richardson Harrison Bull was Rockwell's teacher in drawing as applied to civil engineering. He is not found listed elsewhere in art sources consulted.

The University's teacher in their course of Design was Thomas Seir Cummings, 1804-1894, a founding member of the National Academy of Design in 1826. He continued in the activities of the Academy and was the oldest founding member at the time of his death in 1894. Thomas S. Cummings was a yearly exhibitor in the Academy shows from 1826 until 1860. He was a teacher at the School of the National Academy and a member of the Committee of Arrangements and a member of the Council. He specialized in portraits and miniature painting.[2]

In an obituary article, the Portland *Evening Telegram* for March 22, 1907 stated: "Captain Rockwell took up art as a boy and studied under the best masters in New York." The information may have come from a previous interview with Rockwell or from talking with his wife or his daughters. The reference may have been to Thomas S. Cummings. Rockwell was able to afford private lessons and Professor Cummings may have given him instruction. The exhibitions at the National Academy, the American Art Union and other art galleries then flourishing in New York City must have held great interest for a young artist in his formative period. He was exposed to the work of many of the best American painters from his arrival at the University in 1855 until his assignment to the West Coast, since his home was New York City. His sketchbooks were so inscribed.

The yearly exhibition of the National Academy of Design alone averaged 350 paintings.[3] Therefore, during Rockwell's years of living in New York City, from 1855 to 1867, the total available for his inspection was over 4,500. Figures for the American Art Union and other galleries, public and private, are not available.

The National Academy exhibition records cover the span from 1825 to 1860. During the years Rockwell was in New York, some of the exhibitors were John Woodhouse Audubon, Albert Bierstadt, George Caleb Bingham, George Catlin, Samuel Coleman, Vincent Colyer, Jasper Cropsey, Felix Octavius Carr Darley, Charles Deas, Seth Eastman, Sanford Robinson Gifford, Martin Johnson Heade, Winslow Homer, Eastman Johnson, John F. Kensett, Alfred Jacob Miller, Edward Moran, William Sidney Mount, William Tylee Ranney and Thomas Worthington Whittredge.

Cleveland Rockwell had every opportunity to see and know what was going on in American art. His Survey work on the coastal reaches from Maine to Georgia, as reported in the U. S. Coast Survey Annual Reports, reveals that there were several months each year before and after assignments when he had time and opportunity to contemplate the painting of contemporaneous artists and to endeavor to bring his own work to a higher state of perfection. His field trips afforded ample source material, which he set down in his sketchbooks.

Most painters turned their hand to marine painting occasionally and there were some who made this field their specialty. Robert Salmon, c. 1775-c. 1842, worked in Boston. Antoine Roux (French-born in 1765) and his three sons painted marine scenes in French and Mediterranean ports. Included in the paintings were American vessels and the paintings found their way to the United States. Fitz Hugh Lane, 1804-1865, Gloucester, Massachusetts-born, was a landscape and marine painter. The work of these men established basic ground rules and influenced most American marine painters who followed them.

Cleveland Rockwell's paintings bear some resemblance to single examples of the work of a score of his contemporary American painters. Not all were predominantly marine painters. Some were trained entirely in the United States and others were trained in Germany, France or Italy. In the writer's opinion these are Albert Bierstadt, John Frederick Kensett, Thomas Birch, William Sidney Mount, Martin Johnson Heade, George Harvey, Worthington Whittredge and three artists connected with New Bedford — William Bradford, Albert Van Beest and his pupil, Robert Swain Gifford.

Thomas Birch's "Delaware River Front, Philadelphia," 10 1/8 x 13 7/8 pencil and watercolor on paper dated in the 1800s, is owned by the Museum of Fine Arts, Boston (M. and M. Karolik Collection) and is strikingly similar to Cleveland Rockwell's sketch and completed watercolor of "Montreal Dockside. 1862-1904."

The conclusion to be drawn is that Cleveland Rockwell was well versed in the work of marine and landscape artists of his time. Of course he was more isolated after he left New York, although San Francisco was a hub of art activity. This was not true of Portland, Oregon. He probably sought technical answers in the works of other painters and could easily have sought instruction in overcoming specific problems he encountered in his oil and watercolor painting. Here and there are renderings of clouds, water effects and other details which present striking similarity to Rockwell's work. There are dissimilarities as well. Rockwell painted no huge raging waves and no dark angry seas. He did not seek to present nature as a clash of the elements. He was not a mood painter and was not influenced by such work. Nothing of the mystical or allegorical crept into his work. In this regard, Cleveland Rockwell had little in common with Thomas Cole, James Butterworth and Albert Ryder. In fact, Rockwell seems not to have been stongly under the influence of any-one.

Other painters may have grappled with the problem of how to present nature, but for Cleveland Rockwell there was only one way. He painted what he knew. He had spent years in the field, working along the coast — either from the sea looking toward the shore or looking out to sea. He knew every detail of the Columbia River. He had measured the height of every mountain and had climbed most. Since he lived in the scenes he painted, he had experienced the change in appearance from early dawn to the lighting from the sun's last few rays. When he needed to refresh his memory he turned to his sketchbook.

No examples of his completed work along the eastern seaboard have been located. There are only a few sketches along the coast of Maine. Eastern coast paintings most regularly show stretches of long level beaches. In the West, the coastal mountains are higher and the mountains and cliffs frequently come down to the sea. The difference is caused by the rising of the coast line along the Pacific Ocean. Rockwell, unlike Bierstadt who exaggerated his mountains in terms of the precepts of his Dusseldorf training, painted what he had seen and measured.

If Rockwell's beaches, river shores, waterways and bays seem empty and less populated than a comparable eastern coastal painting, it is that they were so. He was not striving to present an impression of loneliness. He was recording the solitude of the new and sparsely settled West and Alaska.

Rockwell seldom employed the standard academic devices of his time. He was exposed to the work of highly-trained contemporaries, as has been noted. The well-worn cover of a manual from the Acadamie Julien in Paris was in one of his sketchbooks and has his name faintly inscribed on it. The manual once contained figures by eminent French Academicians. Their names are legible and the illustrations were examples of poised figures and formal groupings. The manual is further evidence of Rockwell's exposure to elements of formal drawing and painting.

If Rockwell rearranged trees, rocks or hills to enhance a painting, it does not come to the viewer's attention. Each element in a painting is presented exactly as it occurred. Those of his paintings which contain human figures show fishermen on shore or in boats doing exactly what their work called on them to do. There is no grouping them in a classic arrangement. He does use one or more figures at times, as in walking on a beach, to give the scale of magnitude to his compositions.

No portraits have come to light except in his sketchbooks. One of George Davidson in casual dress and pose is shown. Another, which may be Edward Rockwell, his father, bears no title. Then there are two studies, each of a young girl. They could be his daughters and another sketch could be his wife — or they could be models at a sketch club session. Two labelled N (Neely) and G (Gertrude) are his daughters and are illustrated.

Some of his paintings portray a scene just after dawn, as "Salmon Fishing Grounds — Mouth of the Columbia." "Seine Fishing, Tongue Point" is painted in sunset colors.

No nocturnal scenes have been discovered. There are no story telling genre nor history scenes.

Much of his painting has a hard edge. This is true where distant mountains are silhouetted against the sky, where water meets land, except where the surf is portrayed. Only occasionally is there a leafy bower, as in "Whipping the Trask — Self Portrait" (color section). This, the closest effort to a self portrait, is painted on the Trask River in Tillamook County on the northern Oregon Coast. Rockwell's boats are hard edged and never partially obscured by fog except in "Smoky Sunset on the Columbia River."

As to color, he improves with age. His early oils tend to be gloomy, as "Mt. St. Helens from the Columbia River" painted in 1879, which suffers from lack of color in contrast to most of his later oils. His 1875 watercolor, "Ship at Sea," is very dark. If Rockwell meant to show an overcast day, he certainly succeeded!

His later watercolors are quite colorful but he never gets carried away with pigments. He introduces pink or purple reflections coming as from a prism in the clouds whch envelop the entire painting. Sometimes the atmosphere is colored, too, but always in believable hues. His colors are not so bold as those of Joseph M. William Turner or Frederick Church, whose bright hues sometimes clash. Rockwell's colors are controlled and in ordered harmony.

The oil paintings, also become more highly colored in the last 15 years of his life. Some of his oils are thinly painted with little impasto and in these, Rockwell lays on his pigments more like a watercolor wash. When he does this, his work seems not too far removed from cartography — albeit in color.

Cleveland Rockwell, like Frederick Church and a spate of other artists on the eastern seaboard, was influenced in

THE ART OF DRAWING

A COLLECTION OF ELEMENTARY MANUALS

FIGURES — JULIEN

PARIS

FRANÇOIS DELARUE, PUBLISHER

18, RUE J. J. ROUSSEAU

his painting by the dictates of a pervasive scientist. Baron Friedrich Wilhelm Heinrich Alexander von Humboldt, 1769-1859, was the great German naturalist, statesman and explorer of South America and Asia. He is credited with founding geophysics. His relationship to science was one of classification based on recording of all known physical attributes. Landscape painting, he felt, was the melding of science through the sensitivity of the painter's creative power in recording the peculiar and characteristic beauty of each place on earth.

Rockwell's scientific work in the West was measuring and recording the physical facts of the interrelationship of the Pacific Ocean and its river tributaries to the land masses which they abutted. In his art, again following the precepts of von Humboldt, he was depicting the natural beauty of each setting to which he turned his attention.

No paintings of the eastern coast are available for exhibition, comparison or comment. A few sketches are preserved from an 1862 trip to Maine and upper New York State. One of Lake George, New York and one of Mt. Desert, Maine, are reproduced. Rockwell was making a pilgrimage, since most painters of the eastern seaboard visited and painted these two locations. They are among the earliest of his sketches which have survived.

To review his painting activities, one has to skip from 1862 to 1867. When Rockwell came to San Francisco he began a two-season survey of the San Francisco peninsula. During the survey, sketches were made which resulted in a number of paintings. At least two are represented in the exhibit: "Fishing with Dynamite" (near Golden Gate with Pt. Bolinas in background), an 1868 watercolor; and "Golden Gate from China Beach" (showing Fort Point), also an 1868 watercolor. Both are from the collection of David S. Edwards, Capt. USN (Ret.)[4]

When young Captain Cleveland Rockwell, as he called himself socially, arrived in California, he seems to have stepped up the pace of his painting. It is difficult to estimate the volume of his previous production but it seems safe to assume that he did not have time nor opportunity to do much in the Civil War period. To be sure, there were artist-correspondents representing magazines and newspapers present. Yet sketching and painting might have seemed frivolous in a military topographer, At any rate, no finished paintings of the 1861-65 period have come to light.

Another important reason for his revived interest in sketching and painting was his advanced rank in the Coast Survey. As an Assistant in charge of a party, his sketching during the lunch break or after the day's work could hardly be questioned. Until 1863, when the Civil War was under way, he was only an Aid in the Survey. He would not have wished to incur the displeasure of his superiors, but as an Assistant he used his newly-acquired authority to make a pictorial record of every area where he worked.

He found San Francisco an art-conscious community and was stimulated by the presence of fellow painters with whom he could talk and compare work. Rockwell's interest and response was re-echoed by formation of the San Francisco Art Association. The formal organization was accomplished on March 21, 1871. The first exhibition of the new association was opened in the Mercantile Library Hall on May 14, 1871. There were 155 artist members.[5]

Another assessment of California art activity was given by the Honorable William Alvord, President of the San Francisco Art Association, at the third annual meeting on March 28, 1873:

It would hardly be an exaggeration to assert that in the last ten years California has become better known by the achievements of her artists than through any other medium, the press alone excepted. San Francisco is beginning to be recognized to some extent as an emporium, where artist and purchaser are brought together for their mutual advantage. It is the abiding place of forty resident artists, including historical, landscape, marine, genre, portrait and still-life painters; besides several sculptors, forty-four architects, forty-six engravers and eleven lithographers, all receiving an increasing patronage, and most of them constantly employed.[6]

The records of The San Francisco Association are fragmentary. After the first exhibit in May, 1871 there was a fall and a spring exhibit each year through 1895. Only a few of the catalogues could be located.

In 1873, the 4th, Spring Exhibition, Catalogue, indicated two Cleveland Rockwell paintings: "Columbia River" and "Tropical Scene."

The catalogue for the 5th, Fall Exhibition, 1874 is unavailable.

The 6th, Spring Exhibition, Catalogue, 1874 lists two Cleveland Rockwell paintings: "Mount St. Helens" (Washington Territory) and "The Big Meadows."

The next six exhibition catalogues are unavailable.

The 12th, Spring Exhibition, Catalogue in 1877 lists four Rockwell paintings: "Big Meadows, Plumas County," oil; "Mt. Desert" (Maine), oil; "Foggy Morning — Sunrise," watercolor; and "It looks like Clearing up," watercolor.

Then in 1883, after a gap of ten missing exhibition catalogues, whether Spring or Fall not stated, Cleveland Rockwell's "The Columbia Bar" is exhibited.

The exhibition catalogues of the San Francisco Art Association for the next 25 exhibits, except for Fall and Spring exhibit records of 1895, could not be located.[7]

Rockwell's paintings were shown in all but one of the exhibitions for which catalogues could be checked. Presumably he exhibited each year from 1873 through 1880 when he moved to Oregon and even after that time.

In the 6th Exhibit of the San Francisco Art Association, 1874, there were two paintings by A. E. Rockwell. This is not an error! She was a lady artist, did not paint in Oregon and was not related to Cleveland. She and J. G. Denny did (individually) some panels on tin for the salon of the steamship *Solano.* For years she was listed just beneath his name in the San Francisco directories!

The "Free Art Galleries" was a term coined to refer to the store windows facing onto the sidewalks of San Francisco. The windows belonged to art dealers and included such firms as Snow and Roos, as well as that of Currier and Winters picture stores, both located on Kearney Street. Marple and Gump's galleries and others exhibited artists' work without charge in their windows. Usually the work so displayed was criticized or commented on in local newspapers or one of the several art publications.[8]

A Rockwell was on display in one of the "free galleries" in 1873. "Rockwell has at Snow & Roos' a Columbia River scene, the best picture he has yet exhibited and which shows considerable progress over his past efforts. The drawing is good and considerable artistic perception is displayed, although there is an evident timidity in the use of color and shadow."[9]

Exhibition records of the older California State Fairs were sought for further evidence of Rockwell's activity from 1868 to 1880. Only a single exhibition catalogue for the California State Fair was located, no date given and Rockwell was not represented.[10]

The records of the Industrial Exhibitions of the Mechanics Institute of San Francisco are complete from the first, in 1857, through the 28th, in 1895, excepting the 3rd and 27th catalogues. Numerous entries by a host of California and visiting artists covering 38 years include paintings of the Northwest in almost every exhibition. No Cleveland Rockwell paintings were exhibited.

Let it be emphasized that we are referring to the activities of full-time professional artists. It is noteworthy that Rockwell, who was carrying out his assignments in the U.S. Coast Survey and was working in both California and Oregon each year, found time to sketch and paint. Despite missing exhibition records which would document his having shown other paintings, enough evidence has been produced to show significant participation in California art circles.

Before leaving Rockwell's California painting, there is a "Private & unofficial" letter referring to one which he wrote to his Chief on May 18, 1875:

Since my return from Point Sur, Asst. Rodgers has related to me his experiences of a trip to the summit of Mount Shasta, with a view of making it a Coast Survey Station.

From his account of the interest which you take in the Matter, I send you a painting of the mountain, which I beg you to accept as a token of respect & esteem. The painting is a very faithful view from "Strawberry Valley" from sketches which I made in June 1873, while resting at "Sissons" on my journey to the Columbia River.[11]

"California – Mount Shasta, from Strawberry Valley," was also painted in two other similar but not exact versions. One was used to illustrate Rockwell's story on Mount Shasta and appears as a two-page center spread in *The West Shore.*[12] The other is an oil painting exhibited by an anonymous Seattle collector (No. 28). It is a variation of the same picture.

Rockwell repeated paintings by varying the angle of sight, the medium and changing the details. The scene most repeated is his "ship leaving or entering the Columbia River Bar" in oil or watercolor, in sizes from 12"x20" to 20"x40", guided by the bar pilot and/or a tug and with one of several other boats in the painting. None were duplicates although half a dozen variations are known.

Rockwell was one of the organizers of the Portland Art Club in 1885. The membership changed as artists not locally based appeared on the scene and departed after a longer or shorter period of time. The membership list in 1886 included:

J. E. Stuart	H. Epting
C. Rockwell	J. Norman Biles
C. L. Smith	Clyde Cooke
John Gill	E. W. Moore
A. Burr	Lou Goldsmith
C. C. Maring	Edward Espey
G. T. Brown	James Pickett

In addition to Cleveland Rockwell, the members were: widely roving and prolific James Everett Stuart; Grafton Tyler Brown, an eastern-born black man who made lithographs in California and painted throughout the West; Edward Espey and Henry Epting, both of whom committed suicide within two years; James Tilden Pickett, the half Haida Indian son of Gen. George E. Pickett who died three years after the Portland Art Club was formed. Clyde Benton Cooke lived until 1933. A. Burr and the others seem to have disappeared from the files of Oregon art activity.

It is implied that there were four previous sketching sessions since the Club's founding in 1885. The "Fifth sketch night" included Rockwell's painting, "subject in oil, representing a brook with fir trees, and immense rocks in background, the quiet water and surroundings indicating the artist's idea of silence."[13]

The Portland Mechanics Fair of 1883, according to its catalogue, included among the works of local artists two paintings by Rockwell. One was of "Clatsop Beach" and the other was titled "Multnomah Falls." Two years later the Portland Mechanics Fair catalogue listed three Rockwell paintings on exhibit. Titles and owners as given were "Clatsop Beach," Miss Henrietta Failing; "Mount Saint Helens," Mr. W.T. Shanahan, a Portland dealer in art and in musical instruments; and "Columbia River," owned by the artist and writer John Muir. The catalogue of the Tenth Annual Portland Mechanics Fair of 1888 is in the writer's collection. Of the implied nine previous fairs, those of 1883 and 1885 have been reviewed as showing Rockwell paintings, leaving seven unlocated catalogues in which Captain Rockwell presumably exhibited. It should be noted that six Rockwell works were displayed in the tenth fair, three of which are mistakenly credited to Mrs. C. Rockwell, who did not paint. The items listed are:

"The Swans," watercolor	Cleveland Rockwell
"Mt. Shasta"	Cleveland Rockwell
"Ruins in South America"	Cleveland Rockwell
"Fishing Fleet off the Coast of Maine"	Mrs. [sic] C. Rockwell
"Marine"	Mrs. [sic] C. Rockwell

"Old Barn on the Slough of
Sauvie's Island"   Mrs. [*sic*] C. Rockwell

In September-October, 1889, the First North Pacific Industrial Exposition catalogue (at OHS) lists an oil painting by Rockwell titled "Off the Straits of Fuca." The Third Annual Portland Industrial Exposition of 1891 lists "Miss Durham's contribution of Capt. Rockwell's 'Snow Scene'," which "is frozen delicacy."[14]

If there were either previous or subsequent Mechanics Fairs or other exposition exhibitions, the catalogues have not been located. Such early trade fairs with their art departments occurred in Seattle, Tacoma and Spokane, as well. Their catalogues sometimes reveal art not elsewhere recorded, though the catalogues in the 1870 through the 1890 decades are difficult to find.

The Portland Art Club instituted in 1886 emerged 13 years later as the Sketch Club of Portland. The *Pacific Monthly* reported that the club would "hold an exhibition in the club rooms in the Worcester Block in November. There will be some new and excellent work exhibited by the members who have been painting in silence and solitude for a whole year and over."[15] The December issue (p. 87) reported that the Sketch Club had found its Worcester block quarters too small for the November exhibition, and accepted the Library Association's offer of "the large west room of the library building." The exhibition of "the club's work in oil, watercolor and charcoal for the year ... is by far the most creditable ever held in Portland." Of the 30 members of the club, 25 exhibited, including John Gill, who "shows a watercolor, a grey shore line with a grey sea rolling in under a grey sky. Miss Stephens has a number of pictures hung, both in water and oil ... Harry Wentz shows some striking woodland effects. The January issue of the *Pacific Monthly,*" it was

reported, would "contain a history of the Sketch Club." But perusal of the January and subsequent issues of the *Pacific Monthly* discloses no such history. It seems to be the old Portland Art Club with two new names added — Miss (Clara Jane) Stephens and Mr. Harry Wentz.

The Sketch Club was reorganized in 1891. Members were Harry Wentz, Albert E. Doyle, Joseph Jacobberger, John Reed, Morris Whitehouse, Seth Catlin and Fred Weber. Ladies admitted later were Anna Belle Crocker, Clara Jane Stephens, Caroline Dilly and Lillian P. Bain. Members of this "working club," interested in drawing and painting, had considerable effect on the later Museum Art School.

The Portland Art Association was founded in 1892, and its first officers were: "H. W. Corbett, President (1892-1903); Dr. Holt C. Wilson, Secretary (1892-1918); Henry Failing, Vice-President (1892-1898); Wm. M. Ladd, Treasurer (1892-1926); W. B. Ayer, Trustee (1892-1928); Reverend T. L. Eliot, Trustee, (1892-1927); C. E. S. Wood, Trustee (1892-1910)." Funds totaled $1,000, and "Collections" as yet were "None." In 1894 100 plaster casts of Greek and Roman sculpture arrived, a gift of Henry W. Corbett, "selected by W. B. Ayer on advice of Edward Robinson, Boston Art Museum; Charles Eliot Norton, Harvard; Robert W. de-Forest, President of the Metropolitan Museum." The next year the casts were installed in the upper hall of the then new Library building (Seventh and Stark). Henrietta H. Failing was curator until 1909. Admission cost 15 cents, and Thursday was free.[16]

The transition of names of the several organizations is somewhat confusing but there seems to be a progression because of the identical names of some of the officers and board members and professional artist members. The Portland Art Association became the Oregon Art Association in

1895. The following year, 1896, they held their First Annual Exhibition, Oregon Art Association in Portland. Officers of the Association were: Cleveland Rockwell, President, Miss E. M. Woolfolk, Mr. Lionel D. Deane, vice presidents, Mrs. L. Scott Bower, Secretary, Miss A. J. Smith, Treasurer. The officers were also members of the Board of Directors which included, in addition, Mrs. J. T. Haynes, Mr. W. E. Rollins, Mr. Jas. Anderson, Mr. C. E. S. Wood and Mr. A. Burr.

Captain Rockwell sold his paintings directly to buyers, though he also had dealers represent him. The earlier reference to his displaying paintings in Snow and Roos' "free gallery" windows in San Francisco meant that the firm also offered his works for sale. Later Vickery, Atkins & Torrey, San Francisco, also operated a Portland, Oregon branch. Their labels on the back of the frames of a number of his paintings suggest that they sold them as Rockwell's agent. Too, there was a friend and associate of Rockwell in Portland, William T. Shanahan, a dealer in musical instruments who also operated an art store. Rockwell's paintings hung on the walls of both establishments with prices displayed.

Seven of Cleveland Rockwell sketchbooks are available. From this source 370 sketches lay bare much about the artist, his sketching habits, where he traveled and when, the transition from sketches to his finished paintings. Here for the first time one learns of his 1884 Alaskan trip. One interesting facet of that sketchbook is the large number of completed scenes, pencil drawn and gone over with black and white wash. Each is a complete picture and together they form a most revealing and attractive kaleidoscopic report of his visit. Being on shipboard, Rockwell had the time to complete each pencil sketch. Other books are less complete and a high percentage of his sketches are simply line drawings of the contour of mountains and seashore. That seemed to be enough so that his memory filled in the details as he developed the sketch into a painting. This procedure is evidenced by finished paintings in the exhibition and the presence of a very simple sketch for them in the sketchbooks. Sometimes much more detail is given and color notes are set down in the sketch. His pen and ink renditions, some half-completed in his sketchbooks, strikingly illustrate his ability to transform a very scant pencil sketch into a detailed finished work. One suspects that often the degree of completeness was related to the available time — at least if he were surveying.

Obviously, because of the years and the regions not covered, these are only a fraction of his sketchbooks. Until more information comes to light, the knowledge of his sketching and painting in Maine, Massachusetts, New York, North and South Carolina and Georgia is almost a blank. His located South American work is limited to two paintings, a photograph of another and no sketches. Rockwell's western years are only partially covered in the sketchbooks. Little of his California sketching is shown — none from his survey north of San Francisco. His upper Columbia River and the Willamette River at Albina, East Portland and West Portland are missing. Several paintings of Indian activities and camps are known to have been executed but could not be located for this exhibit.

Nearly 130 paintings are listed from all sources. Those given away, sold or destroyed and record of the owners, lost by death or moving, account for another twenty. The ones here assembled for the Oregon Historical Society exhibit come from a wide area, indicating considerable scattering of his works. To answer a frequently asked question, it is likely that his total output was at least 500 finished oil, watercolor and pen and ink drawings.

"Street in Fort Wrangel, Alaska," from Rockwell Sketchbook (1884).
Graves Collection.

Cleveland Rockwell's hand was steady and his vision remained keen. He produced paintings of top quality until his death. A small watercolor of the Oregon coast is exhibited which was done in 1907. Rockwell's death, due to pneumonia from which he failed to respond, occurred on March 22, 1907. His age was 69 years, 3 months and 25 days.

The Portland *Oregonian,* in an obituary, called him "one of the most distinguished men in the West." Although his work covered both coasts of the United States and Alaska, he lived his last 26 years in Portland and many now viewing his work would like to add "Captain Rockwell was Oregon's best 19th century painter."

CHAPTER VI: NOTES

1. Since 1969, a division of the Smithsonian Institution. Information from Mr. Garnett McCoy, deputy Director-Archivist.

2. See *New-York Historical Society's Dictionary of Artists in America, 1564-1860,* compiled by George C. Groce and David H. Wallace (New Haven, 1957), p. 158; also *National Academy of Design Exhibition Record, 1826-1860,* compiled by Miss Bartlett Cowdry (2 vols., New York, 1943), Vol. I, pp. 104-108; also *History of the National Academy of Design, 1825-1953,* by Elliot Clark, N.A. (New York, 1954), several references.

3. *History of National Academy of Design, op. cit.,* p. ix.

4. Captain Edwards' grandmother married Assistant William S. Edwards of the Coast Survey. After his death she married Assistant Louis A. Sengteller, who worked with Rockwell during the years 1867 through 1870 on the survey of the San Francisco peninsula and the first two years of the survey at the mouth of the Columbia River. Five paintings obtained directly from the artist came into the family. They are exhibited and catalogued.

5. A contemporaneous disbound booklet, The San Francisco Art Association, consisting of pp. 7-13 (no printer or date indicated), in the writer's collection.

6. *The California Art Gallery,* Vol. I, No. 4, April 1873. This monthly publication consists of five issues in the California Historical Society Library. The run is January through May, and no other issues have been located. The abstracted material from this publication came from Dr. Joseph Baird, Professor of Art at the Davis Branch, University of California, consultant to California Historical Society and a leading authority on California art.

7. The review of the San Francisco Art Association Spring and Fall exhibition records is based on a 1965 search of Association holdings at The Society of California Pioneers, The Mechanics Institute and the Oakland Art Museum. The earthquake and fire of 1906 seem to have wiped out a most interesting record of art activity in San Francisco from 1871 to 1897 when, apparently, the exhibitions as such were terminated.

8. *California Art Gallery,* Vol. I, No. I, January, 1873. Citation kindness of Dr. Joseph Baird, previously cited.

9. *California Art Gallery,* Vol. I, No. IV, April, 1873.

10. Located at Society of California Pioneers.

11. Rockwell to C. P. Patterson, NA RG 23.

12. No. 242, Jan. 24, 1891, pp. 59-60.

13. *Morning Oregonian,* Feb. 13, 1886, p. 3, col. 3. No newspaper account of previous or subsequent sketch sessions have been located.

14. The catalogues of The Oregon Industrial Exposition of Oct. 28, 1899, of September-October 1893, and of October 1895 (at OHS) have no art section.

15. "The Month in Art," in *Pacific Monthly,* Vol. III (November, 1899), p. 30.

16. Portland Art Association, 50th Anniversary pamphlet, 1942.

LENDERS

Elinor Cushman Allen,
Los Gatos, California

Arlington Club,
Portland, Oregon

Dr. and Mrs. D. W. E. Baird,
Portland, Oregon

Mr. and Mrs. Thomas P. Binford,
Portland, Oregon

Mr. and Mrs. Eben H. Carruthers,
Warrenton, Oregon

Mrs. R. T. Carruthers,
Warrenton, Oregon

Lt. Col. and Mrs. Alexander W. Chilton, Jr.,
Portland, Oregon

Columbia River Maritime Museum,
Astoria, Oregon

Cheney Cowles Memorial Museum,
Eastern Washington State Historical Society,
Spokane, Washington

Mr. and Mrs. John A. DeFrance,
Portland, Oregon

David S. Edwards, Capt., U.S.N. (Ret.),
Bolinas, California

Glenbow-Alberta Institute,
Seattle, Washington

Mr. and Mrs. Lloyd O. Graves
Seattle, Washington

Mr. and Mrs. Edmund Hayes,
Portland, Oregon

Mr. and Mrs. George F. Jacroux,
Honolulu, Hawaii

Mrs. Robert E. Jacroux,
Seattle, Washington

Mr. Rudolf G. Wunderlich,
Kennedy Galleries, Inc.,
New York, N.Y.

Dr. and Mrs. Howard P. Lewis,
Portland, Oregon

Dr. and Mrs. Gene T. McCallum,
Salem, Oregon

Mrs. Earl A. Marshall,
Portland, Oregon

Oakland Museum, Art Division,
Oakland, California

Oregon Historical Society,
Portland, Oregon

Mr. and Mrs. Gregg M. Paterson,
Portland, Oregon

Mr. and Mrs. Ross T. Pierce,
Portland, Oregon

Mr. and Mrs. Robert Platt,
Portland, Oregon

Mr. Robert Rockwell,
Corning, N.Y.

Mrs. Elizabeth Howe Rogers,
El Paso, Texas

Seattle Collector, Anonymous
Seattle, Washington

Mr. and Mrs. Harold K. Steen,
Santa Cruz, California

Dr. and Mrs. Franz Stenzel,
Portland, Oregon

Mrs. Christine S. Tinney,
Santa Cruz, California

University of Oregon Medical School,
Portland, Oregon

The port of "Santa Marta, Colombia, South America," where Clevelan[
Rockwell and other Coast Survey engineers made a survey for the U.S
Department of State, 1866. Collection of Capt. David S. Edwards, USN
(Ret.).

"The Straits of the Farallones," 1868 watercolor just outside the entran to the Golden Gate of San Francisco Bay. Collection of Capt. Dav S. Edwards, USN (Ret.)

"Mount Hood from near the mouth of the Willamette," 1881 watercol
Collection of Dr. and Mrs. Franz Stenzel.

"Early Morning View of Tongue Point from Astoria (Oregon) Wate[r] front." 1883 watercolor. Columbia River Maritime Museum Collection.

Cleveland Rockwell.

"Salmon Fishing Grounds — Mouth of the Columbia River." Fishi
fleet waking up in early dawn. The "mother boat" which canned the fi
is shown in this 1883 oil painting. Collection of Dr. and Mrs. Fra
Stenzel.

"Whipping the Trask — Self Portrait." 1884 watercolor of the artist fly fishing. Collection of Dr. and Mrs. Franz Stenzel.

Whipping The Trout

Cleveland Rockwell 1887

"Crossing the Bar." The *Joseph Pulitzer*, bar pilot, leading a three ma
American sailing ship outward as a tug stands by. The middle of
bar lies between the red buoy and the lighthouse high on Cape Di
pointment. This (1884) painting formerly hung in the ill-fated Comme
National Bank of Portland. Collection of Dr. and Mrs. Franz Stenzel.

"Gill Netters near Rooster Rock," 1891 watercolor. Oregon Historical Society Collection.

"Mt. Rainier from the mouth of the Nisqually River," Puget Sou
Washington. 1891 watercolor. Collection of Mrs. Robert Jacroux.

Cleveland Rockwell. 1891.

"A British Bark picking up her Pilot on the Columbia River Bar," 1895. Watercolor from the Collection of Mr. and Mrs. Edmund Hayes.

"Mount St. Helens and Spirit Lake," watercolor painted in 1904. Published in *Pacific Monthly* in 1906. Collection of Mr. and Mrs. Harold K. Steen.

Lake George from Fort William Henry Hotel

Lake George, New York, as Rockwell saw and sketched it from his hotel window in 1862. He visited upper New York State and Mt. Desert in Maine, favorite haunts for artists of the eastern seaboard, and here produced some of his earliest known sketches. Graves Collection sketchbook.

Near Mt. Desert, Maine. This 1862 sketch reveals how a survey party operated. The transit is set on its base and a second triangulation station with an elevated pole can be seen on the point of land jutting out from the right. Graves Collection sketchbook.

"Fishing with Dynamite" near Golden Gate with Pt. Bolinas in background. (1868). Collection of Dr. and Mrs. Franz Stenzel.

"Golden Gate from China Beach," showing Fort Point. Watercolor. Collection of Capt. David S. Edwards, USN (Ret.).

The officers' homes at Fort Canby, Washington Territory, built in 1865 to protect the mouth of the Columbia River. Here it is in 1868, as seen in Cleveland Rockwell's sketch. Graves Collection sketchbook.

"Looking toward Saddle Mountain from Baker Bay," watercolor (1868).
Collection of Mr. and Mrs. E. H. Carruthers.

At top, undated view of Santa Barbara Mission, Calif. Rockwell worked in the area in 1871-1873. Lower sketch of Chinook canoe and Indians.

The Chinooks inhabited the shores of the lower Columbia River. 1868 sketch. Graves Collection sketchbook.

Cape Lookout from the south, Oregon coast landmark. From Rockwell
sketch in 1877. Graves Collection sketchbook.

"Haystack Rock and Cascade Head, and Sand Cape" was on Rockwell's survey route of the Oregon coast from Yaquina to Tillamook Beach in 1888. There were several "Haystack Rocks." This one is not so named at present. Graves Collection sketchbook.

Undated sketch of a survey camp, by Rockwell. Graves Collection sketch-book.

Hotel Banff and Twin Peaks, Alberta, Canada. From Rockwell's 1888 sketchbook, Graves Collection.

Glacier House, Glacier Park, B.C., 1888 watercolor. Collection of Dr. and Mrs. Franz Stenzel.

The Davidson glacier, Chilcat Inlet, Alaska.

"The Davidson glacier, Chilcat Inlet, Alaska." 1884 Alaska trip sketch from Graves Collection sketchbook.

View of "Adams, Mt. Edgecombe, Sitka Harbor & Village, Alaska," from
Rockwell's 1884 sketchbook, Graves Collection.

CHRONOLOGY

CLEVELAND S. ROCKWELL'S WORK WITH THE UNITED STATES COAST SURVEY

SINCE ROCKWELL made sketches in the areas where he worked and traveled and later executed his watercolor and oil paintings, a chronological table is helpful in dating those paintings which he signed but did not date. As noted, Coast Survey field work was planned for favorable weather; the winters were utilized for drawing, inking and labeling to complete the charts in the Survey office. References in the U.S. Coast Survey annual reports are given with year and page indicated.

1857 *New York.* April through October. Rockwell joined the U.S. Coast Survey as an aid. He served in the party of Assistant H. L. Whiting on the topography of a section of New York Harbor. (*Annual Report 1857* — pp. 50, 122)

1858 *North Carolina.* May through June. Survey of Charleston Harbor and parts of the coast of South Carolina under Assistant John Seib. (*Annual Report 1858* — pp. 74-75)

New York. July through October. Supplementary topography of New York Harbor along the shoreline of East River from Little Neck Bay westward to Hunter's Point under Assistant Whiting. (*Annual Report 1858* — pp. 55-56)

1859 *South Carolina and Georgia.* January-May. Worked in the party of Assistant John Seib making a shoreline survey from St. Helena Sound, South Carolina to the mouth of Savannah River, Georgia. (*Annual Report 1859* — pp. 66-67)

New York. June. Survey of a small region to complete the area near Jamaica, Long Island.

New Jersey. Topography of Hudson City and environs.

New York. Two mile stretch along west side of the Hudson River completed by Rockwell in October. The section was required for the finished map of New York Harbor. (*Annual Report 1859* — pp. 47-48)

1860 *South Carolina and Georgia.* January-June. Following the sudden death of Assistant John Seib in Washington, D.C. on December 23, 1859, Aid Rockwell was assigned the duty of continuing the coast topography from Port Royal entrance, South Carolina to Savannah River, Georgia, using the schooner *Bailey.* (*Annual Report 1860* — p. 59)

Massachusetts. July. Resurvey of a portion of Boston Harbor for the municipal authorities under Assistant H. L. Whiting using the schooner *Torrey* for transportation. (*Annual Report 1860* — pp. 36, 106)

1861 Rockwell had been instructed to complete the plane table survey of Port Royal Sound, South Carolina and Savannah River after the death of Assistant John Seib. The Treasury announced no funds were available. Hence field work stopped and Rockwell spent the spring working on inking of the charts, though incomplete. (*Annual Report 1861* — p. 47)

The Civil War began with the firing on Fort Sumter April 12th. Most of Rockwell's surveys of 1861 through part of 1865 were for military purposes.

Virginia, Maryland and District of Columbia. June-December. Rockwell mapped parts of Fairfax County in Virginia, Montgomery County in Maryland and the banks of the Potomac River, north of the District of Columbia were mapped for the defense of Washington, D.C. (*Annual Report 1861* – pp. 39-41)

1862 *South Carolina.* December (1861) to August. The area was now occupied by Union forces. The shore lines of rivers and bays were surveyed for military maps. (*Annual Report 1862* – pp. 50-51)

Maine. September-November. Rockwell continued surveying coastline near Winter Harbor. (*Annual Report 1862* – p. 23)

1863 *North Carolina.* (Military Department). February-June. Rockwell promoted to Sub-Assistant in the United States Coast Survey on June 1st. He surveyed the approaches to the city of New Bern, North Carolina. He then accompanied General Henry Prince to the Tar River, North Carolina to reconnoiter. (*Annual Report 1863* – pp. 41-42)

Pennsylvania. July and August. Rockwell began a survey for the defense of Philadelphia, Pennsylvania. He became ill. After recovery, he joined Assistant Whiting in topographical reconnaissance near Schuykill, Pennsylvania until mid-August. (*Annual Report 1863* – pp. 31, 42)

Maine. September and October. Rockwell arrived in Winter Harbor, Maine, September 9th and working from the deck of the schooner *Caswell,* completed his survey east of Frenchman's Bay for the United States Coast Survey. (*Annual Report 1863* – pp. 21-22)

Virginia. November. Completed survey of Sewall's Point adjacent to Fortress Monroe. The fort was to be a depot for prisoners. Rockwell completed the assignment within a month. (*Annual Report 1863* – p. 42; *Annual Report 1864* – p. 23)

Tennessee. December. Rockwell and his party traveled from Cincinnati through Cumberland Gap to Knoxville with their equipment arriving December 11, 1863. (*Annual Report 1864* – p. 31)

Rockwell was commissioned December 12th, a Captain of Engineers, Topographical Corps, Army of the Ohio, for the duration of the war.

1864. *Tennessee.* January-June. Rockwell's party made a plane table survey of the north side of the Holston River including city of Knoxville. After completion by the end of March, April and May were spent in a topographical survey of Strawberry Plains, Tennessee. (*Annual Report 1864* – p. 31)

Rockwell was relieved from further duty in Department of Ohio on June 2, 1864. (*Annual Report 1864* – p. 31)

No report covering his assignment, possible leave of absence from June 2 to October 8.

New York. October-November. Joined Assistant Whiting in the topography of the Hudson River, New York, until the end of November. (*Annual Report 1864* – p. 20)

1865 *Georgia and North Carolina.* January-April. Sub-Assistant Rockwell, already identified with the area because of his aptitude in making plane table surveys, rejoined the army of Major General William Tecumseh Sherman. Rockwell moved just ahead of the Union forces making plane table surveys of rebel works and approaches to them. Rockwell and Sub-Assistant Dorr reached Columbia, South Carolina on February 17th. Fayetteville, North Carolina was occupied on March 11th. Goldsborough was taken on March 23rd. Rockwell surveyed the ground lying east of the Wilmington and Weldon railroad tracks.

Sherman's second campaign began April 10 by a movement on Raleigh, North Carolina. Raleigh was occupied on April 13. The next day the commanders of the rebel forces made overtures for surrender. A captured confederate map obviated the need for Rockwell's services. On April 23 in Raleigh, he was released from further service with the army. (*Annual Report 1865* – pp. 21-22)

Maine. June-October. The plane table survey to the eastward of Mount Desert Island was resumed by Sub-Assistant Rockwell in June. The work was extended to the mouth of Gouldsboro, Steuben and West bays and a group of islands lying across from the main entrance from the ocean. (*Annual Report 1865* – pp. 11-12)

South America. December. Rockwell joined a party headed by Colonel S. A. Gilbert and Captain P. F. C. West and departed from New York on December 11, 1865 for South America.

1866 *Colombia, South America.* January-June. At the request of the Government of Colombia, represented by General Salgar, a survey of the Magdalena River was made. The survey extended from the mouth of the river to the head of navigation, some 400 miles. Rockwell and the party arrived back in New York City on June 9, 1866. (For references see discussion of Magdalena River Survey in text)

Maine. August to November. On Steamer *Bowditch* doing topography of Muscongas Bay.

Between November 10, 1866 and March 6, 1867, four and one-half months are unaccounted for.

1867 Alexander Dallas Bache, Rockwell's friend and Chief of the United States Coast Survey, died the 17th of February in Newport, Rhode Island. He had been superintendent of the United States Coast Survey since 1843. He was succeeded by Professor Benjamin Peirce. (*Annual Report 1867* – p. 330)

Georgia. March-April. Survey of topography of St. Catherine's Sound, Georgia by Sub-Assistant Rockwell on the schooner *Bailey.* On April 6 he was relieved and assigned to the Pacific Coast. The assignment carried a promotion for Rockwell from Sub-Assistant to Assistant.

California. June-December. Rockwell's west coast duty began in June. He joined a party conducting a minute topographical survey of the peninsula near San Francisco. The survey was for Department of Engineers in planning the military defenses of San Francisco.

1868 *California.* January-May. By the middle of January, Rockwell had mapped the area between School House Station and Milbrae on San Francisco peninsula. Topography of Point Conception and crest line of coast mountains immediately behind completed. (*Annual Report 1869* – pp. 47-48)

Oregon. June-July. Rockwell's first Oregon assignment. He was ordered to make a plane table chart of the southern shore of the Columbia River.

Oregon. August-November. Work started at Cape Disappointment. Survey completed between Chinook Point and Gray's Bay, northward to Point Grenville and including Shoalwater Bay and Gray's Bay entrances. Rockwell used the United States Coast Survey schooner *Humbolt.* (*Annual Report 1869* – p. 54)

1869 *Oregon.* May-November. Columbia River survey includes both banks of the river up as far as Cathlamet Point and Three Trees Point. (*Annual Report 1869* – p. 54)

1870 Completed in winter 1870 the office work on his three sheets of Columbia River topography.

California. January-March. Rockwell transferred his party to survey San Simeon Bay and shore to westward. (*Annual Report 1871* – p. 57)

Oregon. May. Rockwell party resumed triangulation of Columbia River. The preliminary work was carried to Westport, about 12 miles above Cathlamet Point.

1871 *California.* January-April. Continued triangulation and topography of San Simeon Bay. The work was advanced northward of Piedras Blancas. (*Annual Report 1872* — pp. 43-44)

Oregon. May-October. Detailed survey of shores of the Columbia River. Work included east and west of Cathlamet, including whole of Puget Island and both banks as far as Westport. (*Annual Report 1872* — p. 47)

1872 *California.* February-April. Resumed work at point Piedras Blancas, continued northward to southern end of Santa Lucia mountains. The wreck of the vessel *Sierra Nevada* was included on the plane table sheet. (*Annual Report 1873* — pp. 51-52)

Oregon. May. Triangulation continued from Westport to Kalama, a distance of 32 miles. (*Annual Report 1873* — pp. 57-58)

1873 *California.* February and April. Survey advanced about five miles northward from Piedras Blancas. (*Annual Report 1874* — p. 38)

Oregon. May-June. Rockwell party working on both shores of the Columbia River above Puget Island. (*Annual Report 1874* — ends with June 30th — p. 41)

1874 *California.* January-May. Assigned to work for Light-House Board to survey and determine the best site for a light house and fog horn at or near Point Sur. In mid-May the party departed. (*Annual Report 1875* — pp. 54-55)

Oregon. June-October. Work on the Columbia River resumed. Work advanced as far as Smith Island by mid-October. (*Annual Report 1875* — p. 63)

1875 *California.* January-May. Topography of Point Sur, California for Light-House Board. (*Annual Report 1875* — p. 54)

June. Leave of absence for 12 months from June 1st.

1876 *California.* June-August. Assistant Rockwell and Assistant William Eimbeck joined Assistant George Davidson in the Sacramento Valley, California, to establish a base line. It was named "Yolo Base" for the county in which it lies. (*Annual Report* — ending *1876* — p. 55)

California. August-December. Rockwell detailed in August, 1876 to make a reconnaissance above Russian River. Then he worked at Round Valley, Spruce Grove and Mount Pierce (near Cape Mendocino) locating points for primary triangulation in northern California. Operations closed in early December. (*Annual Report 1877* — p. 56)

1877 *California.* February-June. Continuation of selecting points northward to include Cape Blanco. Much of the region traversed was extremely rough and destitute of trails. (*Annual Report 1878* — p. 48-49)

1878 *Oregon.* April, 1878-January, 1879. Triangulation of Columbia River resumed near Kalama in April, 1878. Rockwell took over the sloop *Kincheloe* for transportation and quarters. In August the air was smoke filled. Lines of sight opened up to Willow Bar, eight miles below the mouth of the Willamette River. The party disbanded January 13, 1879. (*Annual Report 1879* — pp. 57-58)

1879 *Oregon.* January-December. Continuation of topographical work on Columbia River. By December the work had progressed to near Kalama River where the sloop *Kincheloe* was moored for the winter. The detailed survey now completed for 75 miles above the mouth of the river. (*Annual Report 1880* — p. 44)

1880 Work halted while the *Kincheloe* was being repaired.
Oregon. August-November. Following completion of repairs to *Kincheloe*, work on Columbia River resumed in August. Work on triangulation from Columbia City and St. Helens was accomplished and by November had been completed several miles above St. Helens. (*Annual Report 1881* — pp. 42-43)

1881 *Oregon.* April-June. Poor weather allowed time to re-erect markers washed away by high water in previous season. In June triangulation resumed and continued to one mile past Kalama. (*Annual Report 1881* — pp. 42-43)

Oregon. July-October. Work between St. Helens and the mouth of the Willamette River completed by end of October.

California. October-December. Rockwell went to San Francisco to ink and duplicate records. (*Annual Report 1883* — p. 58)

1882 *California.* January-June. In sub-office in San Francisco he continued work on charts.

Oregon. June-January 1883. Reassigned to Portland for work on Columbia River. (*Annual Report 1883* — p. 58)

1883 *Oregon.* July-September. The party arrived for the survey of Nestucca Bay and the Big and Little Nestucca Rivers. Triangulation and topography completed by end of September. (*Annual Report 1884* — p. 67)

Oregon. October-December. In October resumed tertiary triangulation of the Willamette River from mouth to Portland. This phase completed by the end of December using sloop *Kincheloe* for transportation. (*Annual Report 1884* — p. 67)

1884 *Oregon.* January-April. Office work. In part of April and until mid-May, Rockwell visited Alaskan and B. C. coasts. May-June. Topographical survey along Columbia and Willamette rivers. Spring run-off raised the water level as the party moved up the Willamette. (*Annual Report 1884* — pp. 67-68)

Oregon. June-October. Rockwell worked on topographical survey of the river through Albina, East Portland and Portland carrying it back about one mile from the water's edge. Later he worked on the lower river survey from just above the mouth to the head of Swan Island. (*Annual Report 1885* — pp. 60-61)

1885 *Oregon.* June-October. Continuation of hydrographic survey of the Columbia and Willamette river.

1886 *Oregon.* May-July. Columbia River. Reported for field duty to Assistant George Davidson at Station Balch near Portland, Oregon. They determined the latitude and the azimuth of a line to connect Puget Sound and Columbia River triangulations. (*Annual Report 1886* — pp. 76-77)

Oregon. September-November. Under detailed instruction from Assistant George Davidson, Assistant Rockwell took up the most needed hydrography of the Columbia from Columbia City to the head of Batchelor's Island. The field work was completed in November. (*Annual Report 1887* — pp. 70-71)

1887 *Oregon.* April-July. The assignment was a topographical reconnaissance of the Oregon coast between Yaquina River and Tillamook Bay. Mr. Rockwell submitted a progress sketch on a 1:100,000 scale, giving the name of the capes, creeks, bays and other topographical features. Field work was completed end of July. (*Annual Report 1887* — pp. 69-70)

Oregon. September-November. Columbia River. Hydrography resumed in September and completed in early November. (*Annual Report 1887* — p. 71)

1888 In conjunction with his topographical reconnaissance of the Oregon coast between the Yaquina River and Tillamook Bay, Mr. Rockwell submitted a note book of sketches of prominent capes, headlands and groups of rocks within the limits of his survey. These records, with original topographical sheets, have been deposited in the Archives. During his Oregon Coast reconnaissance, he made examinations at Cape Lookout and Cape Meares as possible sites for a lighthouse. His report recommended Cape Lookout as more useful than Cape Meares. (*Annual Report 1888* — p. 67)

California. January-April. San Francisco office. Office duties and working under Assistant George Davidson in preparation for the fourth edition of the *Pacific Coast Pilot.* (*Annual Report 1888* – p. 67)

Assistant Rockwell reduced between 300 and 350 views, drawing them on bristol board and "imparted his artistic touches to the sketches". This work was concluded in May. (*Annual Report 1888* – p. 94)

1889 *Oregon.* April-July. Astoria. A re-survey of the Columbia River from Tongue Point to Tansy Point, also the areas of Youngs Bay and parts of Youngs River and of Lewis and Clark River. A complete survey of the localities covered was begun and by early July was completed. Included were the jettys, tramways, railroads and wharves. (*Annual Report 1889* – pp. 72-73)
T.C. Mendenhall appointed Superintendent of the United States Coast Survey on July 9, 1889.

Oregon. Portland. Rockwell worked to complete the Columbia River survey near Astoria, sending results and charts to the office. (*Annual Report 1890* – p. 64)

1890 *Oregon.* Spring. Portland. Made a reduction of topography for a new edition of a chart of the approaches to New York Harbor. Left Portland in early April.

California. April-June. Reported to Assistant George Davidson for purposes of connecting the primary base line of Los Angeles with the main triangulation. He began work but was instructed to return to San Francisco to take over the party of Assistant Charles M. Bache, who suffered a stroke and died on April 10, 1890. Rockwell left May 1st for the coast of Monterey County. The foggy weather and the rough and mountainous character of the country made necessary the moving of the instruments by mule back. Only three and one-half miles of shore were surveyed. Field operations closed in mid-June. (*Annual Report 1890* – p. 65)

Oregon. August-November. Began at Vancouver, Washington in early August to continue the Columbia River survey toward The Dalles. (*Annual Report 1891* – pp. 73-74)

1891 *Oregon.* April-October. Columbia River. By mid-April the Rockwell party was organized and in camp at Fisher's Landing on the Oregon side of the river. Rain fell for 20 consecutive days in June slowing the work. (*Annual Report 1891* – p. 74)

In September, Rockwell and party moved camp to Washougal, Washington. The first triangulation sheet was completed to the head of Government Island. Field work terminated in mid-October. (*Annual Report 1892* – pp. 73-74)

1892 *Washington, D.C.* Assistant Rockwell reported to the national office in Washington, District of Columbia, as a member of the Topographical Conference convened by direction of the Superintendent.
"After returning home in March, Rockwell tendered his resignation as an assistant in the Survey to take effect June 1, 1892." (*Annual Report 1892* – p. 74)

CATALOG OF ROCKWELL'S KNOWN PAINTINGS AND SKETCHES

THIS CHRONOLOGICAL CATALOGUE includes all known Rockwell paintings exhibited, published and in private or museum collections. Desired information includes: title or description title; medium; size as sight measurement, height before width, in inches to nearest ¼ inch; whether signed; whether dated; present owner; provenance; where exhibited and when; and where published and when.

All of the above information, if known, is included. Descriptive titles, notes and dates (in parentheses) supplied by the writer are based on sketch records, chronology of the artist's work and travels, and notes from various sources collected over a 20-year period.

Paintings and sketches marked with asterisk after title appear as illustrations in color or black and white within this volume.

1. "Montreal Dockside"
   Watercolor 7-1/2x11-1/2 Signed: Cleveland
       Rockwell 1862-1904
   Owner:Mr. and Mrs. Lloyd O. Graves
       Seattle, Washington
   Exhibited: 1972 — Oregon Historical Society, Portland.
       (hereafter OHS)

2. "Fishing Fleet off the Coast of Maine" (1862)
   Exhibited: 1880 — 10th Annual Portland Mechanics Fair, Oregon.

3. "Mt. Desert"
   Oil (1862)
   Exhibited: 1877 — San Francisco Art Association, California.

4. "Santa Marta, Colombia, South America"*
   Watercolor 14x20-1/2 Signed: Cleveland Rockwell 1866
   Owner:David S. Edwards, Capt. USN (Ret.)
       Bolinas, California
       Provenance: U.S. Coast Survey Assistant William S. Edwards and
           Assistant Louis Sengteller
   Exhibited: 1972 — OHS, Portland.

5. "Tropical Scene" (Doubtless in Colombia, South America) (1866)
   Exhibited: 1873 — 4th Exhibition San Francisco Art Association.

6. "Ruins in South America" (1866)
   Exhibited: 1880 — 10th Annual Portland Mechanics Fair, Oregon.

7. "Magdalena River, Colombia"
   Oil 20x14 Signed: Cleveland Rockwell (1866)
   Owner:Edward Eberstadt & Sons
       New York, N.Y.

8. "Golden Gate from China Beach" (Showing Fort Point)*
   Watercolor 11x16 Signed: Cleveland Rockwell 1868
   Owner:David S. Edwards, Capt. USN (Ret.)
       Bolinas, California
       Provenance: U.S. Coast Survey Assistant William S. Edwards and
           Assistant Louis Sengteller
   Exhibited: 1965 — California Historical Society, San Francisco.
       1972 — OHS, Portland.

9. "Straits of the Farallones"*
   Watercolor 12x18 Signed: Cleveland Rockwell 1868
   Owner:David S. Edwards, Capt. USN (Ret.)
       Bolinas, California

Provenance: U.S. Coast Survey Assistant William S. Edwards and
Assistant Louis Sengteller
Exhibited: 1965 — California Historical Society, San Francisco.
1972 — OHS, Portland.

10. "Fishing with Dynamite" (near Golden Gate with Pt. Bolinas in
background)*
Watercolor   7x10   Signed: Cleveland Rockwell   (1868)
Owner:David S. Edwards, Capt. USN (Ret.)
Bolinas, California
Provenance: U.S. Coast Survey Assistant William S. Edwards and
Assistant Louis Sengteller
Exhibited: 1972 — OHS, Portland.

11. "Mount St. Helens" (1868)
Exhibited: 1874 — 6th Exhibition San Francisco Art Association.

12. "Scow Schooners on Young's River. Saddle Mountain in
Background"
Watercolor   14x20   Signed: Cleveland Rockwell   (1868)
Owner:Columbia River Maritime Museum
Astoria, Oregon
Provenance: Collection George E. Kaboth,
Santa Barbara, California
Exhibited: 1972 — OHS, Portland.

13. "Columbia River" (1868)
Exhibited:
1873 — 4th Exhibition San Francisco Art Association.
1873 — Snow & Roos, San Francisco.

14. "Looking toward Saddle Mountain from Baker Bay"*
Watercolor   9-1/4x17-3/4   Signed: Cleveland Rockwell   (1868)
Owner:Mr. and Mrs. E. H. Carruthers
Warrenton, Oregon
Exhibited: 1972 — OHS, Portland.

15. "Tongue Point"
Watercolor   11x16   Signed: Cleveland Rockwell   1869
Owner:David S. Edwards, Capt. USN (Ret.)
Bolinas, California
Provenance: U.S. Coast Survey Assistant William S. Edwards and
Assistant Louis Sengteller
Exhibited:
1965 — California Historical Society, San Francisco.
1972 — OHS, Portland.

16. "Entrance to the Columbia" — a variation on this subject.
Oil (1870)
Owner:William T. Shanahan (in 1883)
Published:
The West Shore. Vol. IX. July 1883. p. 158.
The West Shore. Vol. XVII. March 28, 1891. p. 207.
The Overland Monthly. Vol. XXIII. Second Series. February
1894. p. 186.
The Pacific Monthly. Vol. XIX. June, 1908, p. 659.

17. "The Forest Trail near Cathlamet"
Oil   24x16   Signed: Cleveland Rockwell   (1871)
Owner:Collection of Dr. and Mrs. Franz Stenzel
Portland, Oregon
Exhibited: 1972 — OHS, Portland.

18. "Lassen's Butte and Big Meadows"*
Oil   10-1/2x19-1/2   Signed: Cleveland Rockwell   (1873)
Owner:Edward Eberstadt & Sons
New York, N.Y.

19. "The Big Meadows" (1874)
Exhibited: 1874 — 6th Exhibition San Francisco Art Association.

20. "Morro Rock"
Watercolor   (1875)
Published: *The West Shore.* Vol. VII. No. 7 (July 1881) p. 196.

21. "Mt. Shasta" (1875)
    Exhibited: 1880 — 10th Annual Portland Mechanics Fair.

22. "Ship at Sea"
    Watercolor   12x21-1/4   Signed: Cleveland Rockwell   1875
    Owner:Mrs. Charles S. Tinney
              Santa Cruz, California
    Exhibited: 1972 — OHS, Portland.

23. "Mt. Tamalpais"
    Oil   16x24   Signed: Cleveland Rockwell   (1876)
    Owner:Edward Eberstadt & Sons
              New York, N.Y.

24. "Big Mountains, Plumas County"
    Oil   (1877)
    Exhibited: 1877 — San Francisco Art Association.

25. "Foggy Morning — sunrise"
    Watercolor   (1877)
    Exhibited: 1877 — San Francisco Art Association.

26. "It looks like clearing up"
    Watercolor   (1877)
    Exhibited: 1877 — San Francisco Art Association.

27. "California — Mount Shasta, from Strawberry Valley"
    Oil   17-1/2x33-1/2   Signed: Cleveland Rockwell   1879
    Owner:Seattle Collector (Anonymous)
    Exhibited: 1972 — OHS, Portland.
    Note: Two other versions of this painting are known. One appears
          under the title "California — Mount Shasta, from Strawberry
          Valley" as a double page spread in the *West Shore,* No. 242,
          January 24, 1891, pp. 58-59. It is not signed or dated. The other
          is the painting which Rockwell sent to his superintendent,
          Carlile P. Patterson in 1875, as noted in the Art section of this
          book. The latter was an oil, size unknown. It was sketched in
          1873. It is not known whether the painting was signed.

28. "Mt. St. Helens from the Columbia River"
    Oil   9-3/4x20   Signed: Cleveland Rockwell   1879
    Owner:Collection of Dr. and Mrs. Franz Stenzel
              Portland, Oregon
        Provenance:Ashford's Fine Arts, Portland.
    Exhibited: 1972 — OHS, Portland.

29. "Columbia River" (1879)
    Owner: John Muir (in 1885)
    Exhibited: 1885 — Annual Portland Mechanics Fair.

30. "Mt. St. Helen's" (1879)
    Owner: W.T. Shanahan (in 1885)
    Exhibited: 1885 — Annual Portland Mechanics Fair.

31. "Old Barn on the Slough of Sauvie's Island" (1880)
    Exhibited: 1880 — 10th Annual Portland Mechanics Fair.

32. "Clatsop Beach" (1880)
    Owner:Miss Henrietta Failing (in 1885)
    Exhibited:
          1883 — Annual Portland Mechanics Fair.
          1885 — Annual Portland Mechanics Fair.

33. "Marine" (1880)
    Exhibited: 1880 — 10th Annual Portland Mechanics Fair.

34. "The Swans"
    Watercolor   (1880)
    Exhibited: 1880 — 10th Annual Portland Mechanics Fair.

35. "Yosemite Valley"
    Oil   23x14-1/2   Signed: Cleveland Rockwell   1880
    Owner:The Oakland Art Museum — Art Division
              Oakland, California
    Exhibited: 1972 — OHS, Portland.

36. "Mt. Hood"
    Oil 11-1/2x19-1/2 Signed: Cleveland Rockwell 1881
    Owner:Kennedy Galleries
          New York, New York
    Exhibited: 1972 — OHS, Portland.

37. "Mouth of the Willamette River" (1881)
    Published: *The West Shore.* Vol. IX. No. 11 (November 1883) p.
       278.

38. "Mt. Hood from near the mouth of the Willamette"*
    Watercolor 14x21 Signed: Cleveland Rockwell (1881)
    Owner:Collection of Dr. and Mrs. Franz Stenzel
          Portland, Oregon
    Exhibited: 1972 — OHS, Portland.

39. "Multnomah Falls" (1882)
    Exhibited: 1883 — Annual Portland Mechanics Fair.

40. "Mount Hood and the Columbia River Bottom"
    Pen & ink (1882)
    Published: *Harper's New Monthly Magazine.* Vol. 66 No. 391
       (December, 1882) p. 8.

41. "Castle Rock"
    Pen and ink Signed: CR (1882)
    Published: *Harper's New Monthly Magazine.* Vol. 66. No. 391
       (December, 1882) p. 4.

42. "Basaltic Cliffs above Cathlamet, on the Columbia River"
    Watercolor Signed: CR (1882)
    Published: *Harper's New Monthly Magazine.* Vo. 66. No. 391
       (December 1882) p. 5.

43. "The Columbia Bar"
    Oil 1882
    Owner: Clatsop County Historical Society, Inc.
          Astoria, Oregon.

This is the first evidence of the painting of which a number of similar versions were painted.
March 21, 1907 *Evening Telegram* (Portland, Oregon) stated the first painting was purchased by Captain George Flavel, Astoria, Oregon, painted in 1882.
    Exhibited or published: 1883 — San Francisco Art Association.

44. "Wire-rope Ferry on Snake River"
    Watercolor Signed:CR (1882)
    Published: *Harper's New Monthly Magazine.* Vol. 66.
       No. 391 (December 1882) p. 9.

45. "Multnomah Falls"
    Pen & Ink Signed: Cleveland Rockwell (1882)
    Published: *Harper's New Monthly Magazine.* Vol. 66. No. 391
       (December 1882) p. 10.

46. "Highlands of the Columbia" (near Rooster Rock)
    Watercolor (1882)
    Published: *Harper's New Monthly Magazine.* Vol. 66. No. 391
       (December 1882) p. 11.

47. "Salmon Fishing on the Columbia" (Cape Hancock in the back-
       ground)
    Watercolor Signed:CR (1882)
    Published: *Harper's New Monthly Magazine.* Vol. 66.
       No. 391 (December 1882) p. 12.

48. "Cape Horn" (on the Columbia River)
    Watercolor Signed: CR (1882)
    Published: *Harper's New Monthly Magazine.* Vol. 66. No. 391
       (December 1882) p. 13.

49. "Cape Disappointment and Baker's Bay"
    Watercolor (1882)
    Published: *Harper's New Monthly Magazine.* Vol. 66.
       No. 391 (December 1882) p. 14.

50. "Indian Canoes on the Columbia River"
    Oil 27-1/2x47-1/2   Signed: Cleveland Rockwell   1883
    Owner: Rockwell Gallery,
            Corning, New York
    Exhibited: 1972 — OHS, Portland.

51. "Early Morning View of Tongue Point from Astoria Waterfront"*
    Watercolor 14x20   Signed: Cleveland Rockwell   (1883)
    Owner:Columbia River Maritime Museum
          Astoria, Oregon
       Provenance: Collection of George E. Kaboth,
                   Santa Barbara, California
    Exhibited: 1972 — OHS, Portland

52. "Cape Hancock Lighthouse"
    Oil   33x26-1/2   Signed: Cleveland Rockwell   1883
    Owner: Mr. and Mrs. Thomas Binford
           Portland, Oregon
    Exhibited: 1972 — OHS, Portland.

53. "Salmon Fishing Grounds — Mouth of the Columbia"*
    Oil   16x21   (1883)
    Owner: Collection of Dr. and Mrs. Franz Stenzel
           Portland, Oregon
    Provenance: Ashford's Fine Arts, Portland, Oregon
    Exhibited:
        1959 — University of Oregon, Eugene, Oregon
        1959 — Portland Art Museum, Portland, Oregon
        1963 — Washington Historical Society, Tacoma, Washington
        1963 — Eastern Washington State Historical Society, Spokane

        1963 — Montana Historical Society, Helena, Montana
        1972 — Oregon Historical Society, Portland, Oregon
    Published:
        An Art Perspective of the Historic Pacific Northwest. From the
        Collection of Dr. and Mrs. Franz R. Stenzel, Portland, Oregon.
        Exhibited at Montana Historical Society, August, 1963, and Eas-
        tern Washington State Historical Society, September 1963. p. 20.
        Illustration No. 45.

Northwest History in Art 1778-1963. Washington State Historical Society, Tacoma. Pacific Northwest Historical Pamphlet No.
3. Published April, 1963. Illustration No. 43.

54. "Seine Fishing, Tongue Point"
    Oil   10x20   Signed: Cleveland Rockwell   (1883)
    Owner: Collection of Dr. and Mrs. Franz Stenzel
           Portland, Oregon
    Exhibited: 1972 — OHS, Portland.

55. "Mount Hood from the Mouth of the Willamette River"
    Oil   15x23-1/2   Signed: Cleveland Rockwell   (1884)
    Owner: Cheney Cowles Memorial Museum of the
           Eastern Washington State Historical Society
           Spokane, Washington
    Exhibited: 1972 — OHS, Portland.

56. "Smoky Sunset on the Columbia River"
    Oil   33-1/2x27   Signed: Cleveland Rockwell   1884
    Owner: Mr. and Mrs. E. H. Carruthers
           Warrenton, Oregon
    Exhibited: 1972 — OHS, Portland.

57. "Whipping the Trask — Self Portrait"*
    Watercolor   10-1/2x12   Signed: Cleveland Rockwell   1884
    Owner: Collection of Dr. and Mrs. Franz Stenzel
           Portland, Oregon
    Exhibited: 1972 — OHS, Portland.

58. "Near Cathlamet"
    Watercolor   13-1/2x20-1/2 Signed: Cleveland Rockwell   (1884)
    Owner: Mr. and Mr. Ross T. Pierce
           Portland, Oregon
    Exhibited: 1972 — OHS, Portland.

59. "Bluffs above Cathlamet, Wash."
    Watercolor   Signed: Cleveland Rockwell   (1884)
    Published: *Pacific Monthly.* Vol. VII. No. 3 (March 1902) p. 101.

60. "Crossing the Columbia Bar"*
    (The *Joseph Pulitzer,* bar pilot, leading a three masted American
        sailing ship outward across the bar. A tug stands by.)
    Oil 29-1/2x49-1/2 Signed: Cleveland Rockwell (1884)
    Owner: Collection of Dr. and Mrs. Franz Stenzel
                Portland, Oregon
    Exhibited:
        1886 — Commercial National Bank, Portland, Oregon
        1963 — Eastern Washington State Historical Society, Spokane,
        Washington
        1963 — Montana Historical Society, Helena, Montana
        1972 — Oregon Historical Society, Portland, Oregon
    Published:
        Frontispiece for *The Canoe and the Saddle, or Klalam and Klicki-
        tat.* Edited by John H. Williams. Tacoma. 1913.
        An Art Perspective of the Historic Pacific Northwest. From the
        Collection of Dr. and Mrs. Franz R. Stenzel. p. 21, Illustration
        No. 44.

61. "Off the Straits of Fuca"
    Oil (1884)
    Exhibited: September-October, 1889 — 1st North Pacific Industrial
        Exposition, Portland.

62. "Looking Down the Inlet Near Juneau"
    Watercolor 13-1/2x19-1/2 Signed: Cleveland Rockwell (1884)
    Owner: Glenbow-Alberta Institute
                Calgary, Alberta
    Exhibited: 1972 — OHS, Portland.

63. "Sitka, Alaska" (1884)
    Published: Schwatka, Frederick. *A Summer in Alaska.* p. 29.

64. "Sitka, Alaska" (1884)
        Owner:J. C. Ainsworth,
                Oakland, California (in 1885)
        Published: Schwatka, Frederick. *Along Alaska's Great River.* p. 28.
            This is not the same "Sitka" painting that appears in Frederick
            Schwatka's *A Summer in Alaska.*)

65. "Davidson Glacier, Alaska"
    Watercolor Signed: Cleveland Rockwell (1884)
    Published: *Fine Arts Journal.* Vol. XV. No. 12 (December 1904) p.
        424.

66. "Alaskan Scenes"
    The entire page is entitled "Alaskan Scenes" and the larger one of
        "Sitka" is signed C. Rockwell; there are three overlapping
        paintings which are unsigned.
    Watercolor (1884)
    Published: *The West Shore.* Vol. XI. No. 6 (June 1885) p. 174.

67. "Grenville Channel, B. C. — Alaskan Waters"
    Watercolor 13-1/2x19-1/2 Signed: Cleveland Rockwell (1884)
    Owner: Glenbow-Alberta Institute
                Calgary, Alberta
    Exhibited: 1972 — OHS, Portland

68. "The Inland Passage, British Columbia"
    Watercolor 13-1/4x19-1/4 Signed: CR (1884)
    Owner: Glenbow-Alberta Institute
                Calgary, Alberta
    Exhibited: 1972 — OHS, Portland.

69. "Glacier on Frederick Sound, Alaska" (Indian camp in foreground)
    Watercolor 12-1/2x18-1/2 Signed: CR (1884)
    Owner: Glenbow-Alberta Institute
                Calgary, Alberta
    Exhibited: 1972 — OHS, Portland.

70. "Glacier on Frederick Sound, Alaska" (Passengers from sailing
     ship going ashore).
    Watercolor 13x19-1/4 Signed: CR (1884)
    Owner: Glenbow-Alberta Institute
                Calgary, Alberta
    Exhibited: 1972 — OHS, Portland.

71. "Golden Gate"
   Oil   16x23   Signed: Cleveland Rockwell   1884
   Owner: Edward Eberstadt & Sons
         New York, N. Y.

72. "A Scene in the Grand Coulee"
   Watercolor   (1885)
   Published: *The Pacific Monthly.* Vol. II. No. 3 (July, 1899) p. 102.

73. "The Columbia River from Government Island"
   Watercolor   10-1/2x17   Signed: Cleveland Rockwell   1885
   Owner: Mrs. Elinor Cushman
         Los Gatos, California
   Exhibited: 1972 — OHS, Portland.

74. "Vancouver Barracks"
   Oil   10x16-1/2   Signed: Cleveland Rockwell   1885
   Owner: Edward Eberstadt & Sons,
         New York, N. Y.

75. "Steamboat Rock"
   Pen & Ink   Signed: Cleveland Rockwell   (1885)
      Published: *The Pacific Monthly.* Vol. II. No. 3 (July, 1899) p.
      105.

76. "The Mouth of the Columbia River"
   Oil   (1886)
   Published: *Pacific Monthly.* Vol. VII. No. 3 (March 1902) p. 98.

77. "Ship on the Bar — Mouth of the Columbia River"
   Oil   17-1/2x29-1/2   Signed: Cleveland Rockwell   1886
   Owner: Arlington Club
         Portland, Oregon
   Exhibited: 1972 — OHS, Portland.

78. Untitled ("Cape Lookout" based on sketch page 39, Sketchbook 2)
   Pen & Ink   Signed: Cleveland Rockwell   (1887)
      Published: *Fine Arts Journal.* Vol. XV. No. 12 (December 1904) p.
      422.

79. "Beach and Tillamook Head"
   Oil   20x42   Signed: Cleveland Rockwell   1887
   Owner: Collection of Dr. and Mrs. Franz Stenzel
         Portland, Oregon
   Exhibited:
      1959 — University of Oregon, Eugene
      1963 — Eastern Washington State Historical Society, Spokane
      1963 — Montana Historical Society, Helena
      1972 — Oregon Historical Society, Portland
   Published: *An Art Perspective of the Historic Pacific Northwest.* From
      the Collection of Dr. and Mrs. Franz R. Stenzel. Exhibited at
      Montana Historical Society, August, 1963, and Eastern Washing-
      ton State Historical Society, September, 1963. p. 20. Illustration
      No. 48.

80. "Beach near Cape Falcon"
   Watercolor   10-1/2x17   Signed: Cleveland Rockwell   (1887)
   Owner: Collection of Dr. and Mrs. Franz Stenzel
         Portland, Oregon

   Exhibited:
      1959 — University of Oregon, Eugene
      1959 — Portland Art Museum, Portland
      1972 — OHS, Portland

81. "Haystack Rock"
   Oil   15-1/2x24   (1887)
   Owner: Collection of Dr. and Mrs. Franz Stenzel
         Portland, Oregon
   Provenance: Ashford's Fine Arts, Portland
   Exhibited:
      1959 — University of Oregon, Eugene
      1972 — OHS, Portland

82. "Scene on Sauvie Island"
   Watercolor   14x9-1/2   Signed: Cleveland Rockwell   1888
   Owner: Collection of Dr. and Mrs. Franz Stenzel
         Portland, Oregon
   Exhibited: 1972 — OHS, Portland.

83. "A Misty Day on Nestucca Beach"
    Watercolor   15x21   Signed: Cleveland Rockwell   (1888)
    Owner: Collection of Dr. and Mrs. Franz Stenzel
            Portland, Oregon
    Provenance: Kennedy Galleries, New York
    Exhibited: 1972 — OHS, Portland.

84. "Train near Mt. Sir Donald, British Columbia"
    Watercolor   15x11   Signed: Cleveland Rockwell   (1888)
    Owner: Collection of Dr. and Mrs. Franz Stenzel
            Portland, Oregon
    Exhibited: 1972 — OHS, Portland.

85. "Glacier House, Glacier Park, British Columbia"*
    Watercolor   14x19-1/2   Signed: Cleveland Rockwell   1888
    Owner: Collection of Dr. and Mrs. Franz Stenzel
            Portland, Oregon
    Exhibited: 1972 — OHS, Portland.

86. "40 Mile Cr. near Banff, Alberta"
    Watercolor   13-1/2x19-1/2   Signed: Cleveland Rockwell   (1888)
    Owner: Dr. and Mrs. Gene T. McCallum
            Salem, Oregon
    Exhibited: 1972 — OHS, Portland.

87. "Finn Town, Astoria, Oregon"*
    Watercolor   13-1/2x9-1/2   Signed: Cleveland Rockwell   (1868)
    Owner: Lt. Col. and Mrs. Alexander W. Chilton, Jr.
            Portland, Oregon
    Exhibited: 1972 — OHS, Portland.

88. "Big Meadows, Plumas Co., California" (1890)
    Exhibited: 1896 — 1st Annual Exhibition Oregon Art Association,
            Portland.

89. "Washington — Palisades of the Columbia River, Cape Horn"
    Oil   (1890)
    Published: *The West Shore.* No. 242. January 24, 1891. Cover.

90. "Mt. Rainier"*
    Watercolor   12x19   Signed: Cleveland Rockwell   1891
    Owner: Mrs. Robert Jacroux
            Seattle, Washington
    Exhibited: 1972 — OHS, Portland.

91. "Snow Scene" (1891)
    Owner: Miss Durham
    Exhibited: 1891 — 3rd Annual Portland Industrial Exposition,
            Oregon.

92. "Cape Foulweather, Coast of Oregon"
    Watercolor   14x20   Signed: Cleveland Rockwell   1891
    Owner: Collection of Dr. and Mrs. Franz Stenzel
            Portland, Oregon
    Provenance: Kennedy Galleries, New York
    Exhibited: 1972 — OHS, Portland.

93. "Gill Netters near Rooster Rock"*
    Watercolor   14-1/2x18-1/2   Signed: Cleveland Rockwell   (1891)
    Owner: Oregon Historical Society
    Provenance: Frederick V. Holman
    Exhibited: 1972 — OHS, Portland.

94. "Rooster Rock"
    Oil   10x19-1/2   Signed: Cleveland Rockwell   (1891)
    Owner: Department of Medicine
            University of Oregon Medical School
            Portland, Oregon
    Provenance: George Long, M. D.
                    In memory of Nell Spaulding Long
    Exhibited: 1972 — OHS, Portland.

95. "Beacon Rock, Columbia River"
    Watercolor   14x21   Signed: Cleveland Rockwell   (1891)
    Owner: Mrs. Gregg M. Paterson
            Portland, Oregon
    Exhibited: 1972 — OHS, Portland.

96. "Coffin Rock"
  Watercolor 12x19 Signed: Cleveland Rockwell 1891
  Owner:Collection of Dr. and Mrs. Franz Stenzel
       Portland, Oregon
  Exhibited: 1972 — OHS, Portland.

97. "Salmon Canneries, One Floating and One on Land"
  Watercolor 14x19-1/2 Signed: Cleveland Rockwell (1891)
  Owner:Collection of Dr. and Mrs. Franz Stenzel
       Portland, Oregon
  Exhibited:
       1963 — Eastern Washington State Historical Society, Spokane
       1963 — Montana Historical Society, Helena
       1972 — OHS, Portland
  Published: *An Art Perspective of the Historic Pacific Northwest.* From
       the Collection of Dr. and Mrs. Franz R. Stenzel. Exhibited at
       Montana Historical Society, August, 1963, and Eastern
       Washington State Historical Society, September, 1963. p. 20 —
       illustration No. 46.

98. "Rooster Rock on the Columbia"
  Oil 12x20 Signed: Cleveland Rockwell (1891)
  Owner:Edward Eberstadt & Sons
       New York, N. Y.

99. "Mt. Hood and the Columbia"
  Watercolor 11x22-1/2 Signed: Cleveland Rockwell (1892)
  Owner:Edward Eberstadt & Sons
       New York, N. Y.

100. "Scene on the Columbia River" (Sailboat and Sternwheeler passing
       Coffin Rock, Washington)*
  Watercolor 12-1/2x19-1/4 Signed: Cleveland Rockwell 1892
  Owner:Mr. and Mrs. Lloyd O. Graves
       Seattle, Washington
  Exhibited:
       1963 — Washington State Historical Society, Tacoma
       1972 — OHS, Portland

101. "Ships near the Mouth of the Columbia"
  Watercolor 12-1/2x19-1/2 Signed: Cleveland Rockwell 1892
  Owner:Mrs. Earl A. Marshall
       Portland, Oregon
  Exhibited: 1972 — OHS, Portland.

102. "Harrison Lake, British Columbia" (Passenger launch at dock)
  Watercolor 13-1/2x19-1/2 Signed: Cleveland Rockwell (1892)
  Owner:Glenbow-Alberta Institute
       Calgary, Alberta
  Exhibited: 1972 — OHS, Portland.

103. "In the Rocky Mountains" (Canada)
  Oil 33-1/2x59-1/2 Signed: Cleveland Rockwell 1892
  Owner:Collection of Dr. and Mrs. Franz Stenzel
       Portland, Oregon
  Exhibited: 1972 — OHS, Portland.

104. "Farm with Hop Drying Sheds in British Columbia"
  Oil 14x20 Signed: Cleveland Rockwell (1892)
  Owner:Collection of Dr. and Mrs. Franz Stenzel
       Portland, Oregon
    Provenance:Mr. and Mrs. O. K. DeWitt
  Exhibited: 1972 — OHS, Portland.

105. "Alaska Beach"
  Watercolor 14x20-1/4 Signed: Cleveland Rockwell (1892)
  Owner:Collection of Dr. and Mrs. Franz Stenzel
       Portland, Oregon
    Provenance:Kennedy Galleries, New York
  Exhibited: 1972 — OHS, Portland.

106. "Alaska, Rocks and Sea"
  Watercolor 19-1/2x13 Signed: Cleveland Rockwell 1892
  Owner:Collection of Dr. and Mrs. Franz Stenzel
       Portland, Oregon
    Provenance:Kennedy Galleries, New York
  Exhibited: 1972 — OHS, Portland.

107. "Mt. Hood from Fisher's Landing"*
Pen and Ink   3-1/2x7-1/2   Signed: Cleveland Rockwell   1894
Owner: Collection of Dr. and Mrs. Franz Stenzel
        Portland, Oregon
Exhibited: 1972 — OHS, Portland.

108. "Mt. Hood from Fisher's Landing"
Oil   16x24   Signed: Cleveland Rockwell   (1894)
Owner: Edward Eberstadt & Sons
        New York, N. Y.

109. "British Bark picking up Pilot on the Columbia River Bar"*
Watercolor   14-1/2x20-3/4   Signed: Cleveland Rockwell   1895
Owner: Mr. and Mrs. Edmund Hayes
        Portland, Oregon
Exhibited: 1972 — OHS, Portland.

110. "Fishermen Driven Ashore before a Storm" (Below the Mouth of
        the Columbia)
Oil   33-1/2x60   Signed: Cleveland Rockwell   1896
Owner: Collection of Dr. and Mrs. Franz Stenzel
        Portland, Oregon
Exhibited:
    1959 — University of Oregon, Eugene
    1959 — Portland Art Museum
    1961 — Fine Arts Museum, Santa Fe, New Mexico
    1962 — C. M. Russell-Trigg Museum, Great Falls, Montana
    1962 — Montana Historical Society, Helena
    1972 — OHS, Portland
Published:
    Early Days in The Northwest. Prints — Paintings. Drawings by
    James G. Swan. From the Collection of Dr. and Mrs. Franz
    Stenzel. September 23-October 25, 1959. Portland Art Museum.
    p. 26 illustration.
    Junior Historical Journal. Vol. V. No. 3. January 1945. p. 107
    illustration.

111. "Looking down the Columbia from near Wallula"
Watercolor   Signed: CR   (1900)
Published: *Pacific Monthly.* Vol. VII. No. 3 (March 1902) p. 133.

112. "Bunkers at Tunnel, Newport Mine, Oregon"
Pen & Ink   Signed: CR, del.   (1901)
Published: *The Engineering and Mining Journal.* February 15, 1902.
    p. 239.

113. "Seascape" (Clatsop Beach)*
Watercolor   14-1/2x20-1/2   Signed: Cleveland Rockwell   1901
Owner: Dr. D. W. E. Baird
        Portland, Oregon
Exhibited: 1972 — OHS, Portland.

114. "Sailing Ship at Sea"
Watercolor   8-1/2x11-1/2   Signed: Cleveland Rockwell   1901
Owner: Collection of Dr. and Mrs. Franz Stenzel
        Portland, Oregon
Exhibited: 1972 — OHS, Portland.

115. "Ocean Surf"
Oil   6x12   Signed: Cleveland Rockwell   1901
Owner: Mrs. Earl A. Marshall
        Portland, Oregon
Exhibited: 1972 — OHS, Portland.

116. "Mt. Hood from the banks of the Columbia"
Watercolor   9x11-1/2   Signed: Cleveland Rockwell   1901
Owner: Collection of Dr. and Mrs. Franz Stenzel
        Portland, Oregon
Exhibited: 1972 — OHS, Portland.

117. "Columbia River, East of Portland, showing Moffitt's Landing and
        Mt. Hood"
Watercolor   14x20   Signed: Cleveland Rockwell   1902
Owner: Collection of Dr. and Mrs. Franz Stenzel
        Portland, Oregon

Exhibited:
> 1963 — Eastern Washington State Historical Society, Spokane
> 1963 — Montana Historical Society, Helena
> 1972 — OHS, Portland

Published: *An Art Perspective of the Historic Pacific Northwest.* From the Collection of Dr. and Mrs. Franz R. Stenzel. Exhibited at Montana Historical Society, August, 1963, and Eastern Washington State Historical Society, September 1963. p. 20 Illustration No. 47.

118. "Mount St. Helens, from Portland Heights"
Watercolor (1902)
Published: *Fine Arts Journal.* Vol. XV. No. 12 (December, 1904) p. 424.

119. "On The Oregon Coast"
Watercolor (1902)
Published: *Fine Arts Journal.* Vol. XV. No. 12 (December 1904) p. 425.

120. "Columbia River, looking up"
Watercolor 15x21 Signed: Cleveland Rockwell 1904
Owner: Collection of Dr. and Mrs. Franz Stenzel
Portland, Oregon
Provenance: Kennedy Galleries, New York
Exhibited: 1972 — OHS, Portland.

121. "Cape Foulweather"
Watercolor 8-1/2x11-1/2 Signed: Cleveland Rockwell 1904
Owner: Dr. and Mrs. Howard P. Lewis
Portland, Oregon
Exhibited: 1972 — OHS, Portland.

122. Untitled. ("Cape Foulweather" based on sketch page 46, Sketchbook No. 2)
Pen and Ink Signed: Cleveland Rockwell (1904)
Published: *Fine Arts Journal.* Vol. XV. No. 12 (December 1904) p. 422.

123. "Salmon Fishing Fleet on Columbia River Running Free Before the Wind"
Watercolor Signed: Cleveland Rockwell (1904)
Published: *Pacific Monthly.* Vol. XV. No. 2 (February 1906) p. 166.

124. "A Fair Wind"
Watercolor Signed: Cleveland Rockwell (1904)
Published: *Pacific Monthly.* Vol. XV. No. 2 (February, 1906) p. 161.

125. "Seascape"
Watercolor 13-1/2x20 Signed: Cleveland Rockwell 1904
Owner: Oregon Historical Society
Portland
Exhibited: 1972 — OHS, Portland.

126. "Mount St. Helens and Spirit Lake"*
Watercolor 15x21 Signed: Cleveland Rockwell 1904
Owner: Mr. and Mrs. Harold K. Steen
Santa Cruz, California
Exhibited: 1972 — OHS, Portland.
Published: *The Pacific Monthly.* Vol. XV. No. 2 (February 1906) p. 164 illustration.

127. "Banff Springs Hotel in 1904"
Watercolor 14-1/2x20-1/2 Signed: Cleveland Rockwell 1904
Owner: Glenbow-Alberta Institute
Calgary, Alberta
Exhibited: 1972 — OHS, Portland.

128. "Mt. Edith, Canadian Rockies"
Watercolor 14-1/2x20 Signed: Cleveland Rockwell 1904
Owner: Mrs. Elizabeth Howe Rogers
El Paso, Texas
Provenance: Mrs. R. D. Delehanty
Mesilla Park, New Mexico
Exhibited: 1972 — OHS, Portland.

129. "Mt. Hood from the head of White River in Eastern Oregon"
    Watercolor   15x21   (1905)
    Owner:Collection of Dr. and Mrs. Franz Stenzel
            Portland, Oregon
        Provenance:Kennedy Galleries, New York
    Exhibited: 1972 — OHS, Portland.
    Published: *Pacific Monthly.* Vol. XV. No. 2 (February 1906) p. 165.

130. "Fishing Boat on Columbia River Bar"
    Watercolor   Signed: Cleveland Rockwell   1905
    Published: *The Pacific Monthly.* Vol. XV. No. 2 (February 1906) p.
        163.

131. "Otter Rock, on the Coast of Oregon, near Cape Foulweather"
    Watercolor   Signed: Cleveland Rockwell   1905
    Published: *The Pacific Monthly.* Vol. XV. No. 2 (Febrary 1906) p.
        162.

132. "Alaska, Rocks, Sea and Ships"
    Watercolor   21x15   Signed: Cleveland Rockwell   1906
    Owner:Collection of Dr. and Mrs. Franz Stenzel
            Portland, Oregon
        Provenance:Kennedy Galleries, New York
    Exhibited: 1972 — OHS, Portland.

133. "'Oregon Coast"
    Watercolor   6-1/2x10-1/2   Signed: Cleveland Rockwell   1907
    Owner:Collection of Dr. and Mrs. Franz Stenzel
            Portland, Oregon
    Exhibited: 1972 — OHS, Portland.

134. "Fly Fishing"
    Watercolor   13-1/2x6-1/2   Signed: Cleveland Rockwell   No date
    Owner:Mrs. John DeFrance
            Portland, Oregon
    Exhibited: 1972 — OHS, Portland.

Sketchbook #1

"Cleveland Rockwell
U.S. Coast Survey
New York, 1862
A. D. Bache, Supt."

Page	Portion of page	Complete or Incomplete	Title	Year
1*	Full	Complete	"Lake George from Fort William Henry Hotel" Sidewheeler at pier, guests waving goodbye to those ashore. Pencil.	(1862)
2 a.	1/2	Incomplete	"Lake George from the White Rock". Pencil.	(1862)
b.	1/2	Incomplete	"Fort William Henry Hotel from near White Rock". Pencil.	(1862)
3	Full	Incomplete	"Lake George from near White Rock" Hotel and wider vista of lake. Pencil.	(1862)
4 a.	1/2	Incomplete	"View on Lake George". Pencil.	(1862)
b.	1/2	Incomplete	"View on Lake George". Pencil.	(1862)
5	1/2	Complete	"View on Lake George — Roger's Slide & Anthony's Nose" signed "Cleve Rockwell 1862". Pencil.	1862
6 a.	1/2	Complete	"View on Lake George. Anthony's Nose from down the Lake". Pencil.	(1862)
b.	1/2	Incomplete	"Ruins at Fort Ticonderoga". Fragmentary sketch. Pencil.	(1862)
7	Full	Complete	"Mt. Desert and Iron Bound Island (Maine) from Deep Cove" signed "Cleve Rockwell 1862". Pencil.	1862

Page	Portion of page	Complete or Incomplete	Title	Year
8	Full	Complete	"Mt. Desert and Winter Harbor" signed "C. Rockwell 1862". Pencil.	1862
9	Full	Complete	"Mt. Desert from Ironbound Island" signed "Cleve Rockwell, Winter Harbor, 1862". Rockwell with crew surveying. Pencil.	1862
unnumb.	Full	Complete	"Mt. Desert and Frenchmans Bay from Jones Cove" signed "Cleve Rockwell, September 1862". Pencil.	1862
10	Full	Incomplete	"View on Lake Champlain". Pencil.	(1862)
11 a.	1/2	Incomplete	"View on Lake Champlain". Pencil.	(1862)
b.	1/2	Incomplete	"View on the Saugenay". Pencil.	(1862)
12	Full	Complete	"Quay and Market at Montreal, Canada" (Quebec, Canada). Pencil.	(1862-1904)
13 a.	1/2	Incomplete	"Citadel, Quebec from Steamboat Landing" (Quebec, Canada). Pencil.	(1862)
b.	1/2	Incomplete	"View on the St. Lawrence. Capour Mountains" (Quebec, Canada). Pencil.	(1862)
14 a.	1/3	Complete	"View of Murray Bay, St. Lawrence River" signed "CR 1862". Pencil.	1862
b.	1/3	Complete	"Pilgrim Islands. St. Lawrence River" signed "Cleve Rockwell." Pencil.	(1862)
c.	1/3	Incomplete	Untitled fragmentary sketch. Pencil.	(1862)

Page	Portion of page	Complete or Incomplete	Title	Year
unnumb.	1/2	Complete	"Old Catholic Church at Ha! Ha! Bay" (Quebec, Canada) signed "CR 1862". Pencil.	1862
15	Full	Incomplete	"Ha! Ha! Bay looking toward the mouth of the Saguenay" (Quebec, Canada). Pencil.	(1862)
16	Full	Incomplete	"Ha! Ha! Bay" (Quebec, Canada). Pencil.	(1862)
17 a.	1/3	Incomplete	"St. Alphonse from the Steamer" (Quebec, Canada). Fragmentary. Pencil.	(1862)
b.	1/4	Complete	"Cape Trinity. Saguenay River" (Quebec, Can.). Pencil.	(1862)
18 a.	1/2	Incomplete	"Cape Eternity and Trinity. Saguenay River" (Quebec, Canada). Pencil.	(1862)
b.	1/2	Incomplete	"St. Louis Isld. Saguenay River" (Que., Can.). Pencil.	(1862)
19 a.	1/2	Incomplete	"Saguenay River, Canada. Aug. 1862" signed "Aug. 1862" (Quebec, Canada). Pencil.	1862
b.	1/2	Incomplete	"Saguenay River, Canada. Aug. 1862" (Quebec, Canada). Pencil.	1862
20 a.	1/4	Incomplete	"R. Montmorency Bridge" (Quebec, Canada). Pencil	(1862)
b.	1/4	Incomplete	"Falls Montmorency" (Quebec, Canada). Pencil	(1862)
c.	1/2	Complete	"River Montmorency from below Falls" (Que.). Pencil	(1862)
21 a.	1/4	Incomplete	"Natural Steps, River Montmorency" (Quebec). Pencil	(1862)
b.	1/2	Incomplete	Untitled — fragmentary sketch. Pencil.	(1862)

Page	Portion of page	Complete or Incomplete	Title	Year
22	Full	Incomplete	Untitled. Partially completed pen and ink drawing. Probably near Mt. Desert, Maine.	(1862)
23*	Full	Complete	"Mt. Desert from the North" (Maine). Pencil and wash drawing. Rockwell and surveying crew, signed "C. Rockwell 1862".	1862
24	Full	Complete	"Mt. Desert from Sea — Maine" signed "Rockwell". Black and white wash drawing.	(1862)
25	Full	Complete	Untitled. (Winter Harbor, Maine?) Pen and ink drawing signed "CR 1863".	1863
26	1/2	Incomplete	"Alcatraz Island". Pencil.	(1867)
27	Full	Complete	Untitled. (Tropical scene — Magdalena River?) Black & white wash.	(1866)

Sketchbook #2

Page	Portion of page	Complete or Incomplete	Title	Year
28	Full	Incomplete	Untitled. Pencil, pen & some tinted wash.	(1887)
29	Full	Incomplete	"Cape Foulweather, Ogn". Pencil sketch.	(1887)
30	Full	Incomplete	"Cape Foulweather, Ogn". Pencil sketch.	(1887)
31	Full	Incomplete	"Cascade Head from Cape Foulweather." Pencil sketch.	(July 1887)
32	Full	Complete	"Cape Lookout and Haystack Rock from end of beach at Cascade Head. Sunday, July 3rd. 1887." Pencil sketch.	1887

Page	Portion of page	Complete or Incomplete	Title	Year
33	Full	Incomplete	"North end of Cascade Head. 1887". Pencil with some grey wash. 4 people shown.	1887
34	Full	Complete	"North end of Cascade Head from Slab Cr." Pencil sketch.	(1887)
35	Full	Complete	"Sand Cape and Haystack Rock" Pencil sketch.	(1887)
36	Full	Complete	"Sand Cape and Haystack Rock" Pencil and colored watercolor wash.	(1887)
37	Full	Complete	"Cape Lookout, Ogn." Pencil sketch	(1887)
38	Full	Complete	"Rock at base of Cape Lookout" Pencil sketch	(1887)
39	Full	Incomplete	"Cape Lookout." Pencil sketch — beginning of ink over drawing.	(1887)
40	Full	Incomplete	"Cape Lookout" Pencil sketch	(1887)
41	Full	Complete	"Cape Lookout, Ogn." Pencil sketch.	(1887)
42	Full	Complete	"Cape Lookout". Pencil and black & white wash.	(1887)
43	Full	Incomplete	"Cape Lookout" Black & white wash.	(1887)
44	Full	Incomplete	"Cascade Head and Arch Rocks, Ogn. 1887" Pencil sketch.	1887
45	Full	Incomplete	"Point below Salmon River, Ogn" Colored wash	(1887)
46	Full	Incomplete	"Cape Foulweather. Oregon Coast" Colored wash	(1887)
47	Full	Incomplete	"Near Salmon River. Oregon Coast" Colored wash	(1887)
48	Full	Complete	"Rocky Point below Salmon River" grey and blue wash.	(1887)
49	Full	Complete	"Mouth of Salmon River, Oregon Coast." grey and blue wash.	(1887)
50*	Full	Complete	"Haystack Rock. Cascade Head and Sand Cape" Watercolor. Exhibited	(1887)
51*	Full	Complete	"Cape Lookout from the South." signed "CR" watercolor. Exhibited	(1887)
52	Full	Complete	"North side — Cape Meares." pencil sketch	(1887)
53	Full	Incomplete	"Cape Meares — North face" pencil & grey wash	(1887)
54	Full	Complete	"Cape Meares — South side." Grey wash.	(1887)
55	Full	Complete	"Three Arch Rocks." "Copied." signed "Cleveland Rockwell." Grey wash.	(1887)
56	Full	Incomplete	"Cape Foulweather from Yaquina Pt." Pencil sketch.	(1887)
57	Full	Incomplete	"Cape Cascade Head from Cape Foulweather" Pencil sketch.	(1887)
58	Full	Incomplete	"Cascade Head and Haystack Rock from Cape Lookout." Pencil sketch.	(1887)

Page	Portion of page	Complete or Incomplete	Title	Year
59 a.	1/3	Incomplete	"Cape Meares & 3 Arch Rocks from end of Cape Lookout." Pencil & grey wash.	(1887)
b.	1/3	Incomplete	"Mt. Rainier — Summit — Lost in haze." "P.M. 2h 30m Sept. 18". Grey wash.	(1887)
60	Full	Complete	"Mt. Rainier and the Tacoma or Puyallup flats." Pencil sketch.	(1887)
61	Full	Complete	"Mt. Rainier in haze. Commencement Bay." "Copied." grey wash.	(1887)
62	Full	Complete	"Columbia River Bottom near Golden Selkirk Range." Black & white wash.	(1887)
63	Full	Complete	"Bow River from Banff, Alberta" (Canada) Black & white wash.	(1887)
64*	Full	Complete	"Hotel Banff & Twin Peaks. Alberta." Black & white wash.	(1887)
65	Full	Complete	"Spray River near Banff, Alberta" Black & white wash.	(1888)
66	Full	Complete	"Bow River Falls, Banff, Alberta" Black & white wash	(1888)
67	Full	Complete	"Valley of Bow River. Banff, Alberta" signed "Cleveland Rockwell" colored watercolor.	(1888)
68	Full	Complete	"Twin Peaks & Bow river near Banff, Alberta" Black & white watercolor.	(1888)
69	Full	Complete	"40 Mile Cr. Near Banff, Alberta" "Copied S T" Black & white watercolor.	
70	Full	Complete	"Revelstoke — Columbia River" (British Columbia, Canada). Black & white wash	(1888)
71	Full	Complete	"Burrard Inlet — Coal Harbor" (Vancouver, British Col., Canada). Black & white wash "1888"	1888
72	Full	Complete	"Burrard Inlet, B.C. Vancouver" Black & white wash	(1888)
73	Full	Complete	"Pacific Valley, Monterey Co. Cal." "Copied. Colored watercolor. May	1890
74	Full	Complete	"Tongue Point. Columbia River" "Copied" Black & white watercolor	(1889)
75	Full	Complete	"Pacific Valley. Monterey Co. Cal." (Point Lobos?	(May 1890)
76	Full	Complete	"A bit near Astoria" "Copied." Black & white wash	(1889)
77	Full	Incomplete	"Lake Washington 1892" Pencil sketch, some color was added.	1892
78	Full	Complete	"Lake Washington. Sisters" Colored watercolor	(1892)
79	Full	Complete	Untitled. (Sinking ship in British Columbia) Colored watercolor.	(1892)
80-81	Full	Incomplete	"Beacon Hill Point near Victoria 1892" Colored watercolor.	1892
82	Full	Incomplete	Untitled. Colored watercolor.	(1892)

Page	Portion of page	Complete or Incomplete	Title	Year
83	Full	Incomplete	Untitled. Signed "Cleveland Rockwell 1892" Beach scene. Colored watercolor.	1892
84	Full	Incomplete	Untitled. Signed "Cleveland Rockwell 1892" Beach scene, penciled figures, colored water-color.	1892
85	Full	Complete	Untitled. Pencil study of girl (Sketch club?)	( )
86	Full	Complete	Untitled. Pencil study. Bust portrait of #85 (sketch club?)	( )
87	Full	Complete	Untitled. Pencil sketch.	( )
88	Full	Incomplete	Untitled. Pencil sketch. 2 girls wading out from shore. Two sailboats	( )
89	Full	Complete	Untitled. (Yaquina Bay?) signed "Cleveland Rockwell 1892." Colored water color.	1892
90	Full	Complete	"Yaquina Bay. Aug. 10th 1892" signed "Cleveland Rockwell"	1892
91	Full	Complete	Untitled. Study of rocks & foliage. Colored watercolor	( )
92	Full	Complete	Untitled. Study of Rocks & foliage. Colored watercolor	( )
93	Full	Incomplete	Untitled. Pencil study of rocks & foliage	( )
94 a.	1/2	Complete	Pencil drawing details of small sail boat	( )
b.	1/2	Complete	Pencil drawing 3 masted sailing vessel	( )

Page	Portion of page	Complete or Incomplete	Title	Year
95 a.	1/2	Complete	Pencil and wash drawing of sail boat	(1892)
b.	1/2	Complete	Pencil and wash drawing of row boat	(1892)
96 a.	1/2	Complete	Pencil and wash drawing of Indian girl	(1892)
b.	1/2	Complete	Pencil and wash drawing of row boat on shore	(1892)
97-98	2 pages	Complete	Untitled. "Copied. S" Black & white wash drawing. (Salmon Canneries, One floating and One on land)	(1892)

Sketchbook #3

Page	Portion of page	Complete or Incomplete	Title	Year
99	Full	Complete	"Wreck of Viscata" signed "March 28, 1868 C.R." Pencil study	(1868)
100	Full	Incomplete	"Wreck of Viscata" Pencil.	(1868)
101	Full	Complete	"Wrecked Boats" Pencil.	(1868)
102	Full	Incomplete	"Helmet rock — San Francisco Bay" Pencil.	(1868)
103	Full	Complete	"Trout Brook" Pencil.	(1868)
104	Full	Complete	"Trout Brook" Colored water-color.	(1868)

Page	Portion of page	Complete or Incomplete	Title	Year
105*	Full	Complete	"Solon" Pencil. (full length study of possibly George Davidson).	(1868)
106	Full	Incomplete	"Fir tree" Pencil.	(1868)
107	Full	Complete	"Prairie Schooner". Pencil study.	(1868)
108	Full	Complete	"Botanical drawing." Pencil.	(1868)
109	Full	Incomplete	"Davenport Canon. Popes Valley. Cal." Pencil.	(1868)
110	Full	Complete	"Saw Mill in Popes Valley. Napa Co. Cal." Pencil.	(1868)
111	Full	Complete	"Tongue Pt. & Columbia River, Oregon" Pencil.	(1868)
unnumb.	2 page	Incomplete	"Cape Disappointment from Baker's Bay — Washington Terr."	(1868)
112	Full	Incomplete	"Mouth of Columbia river from Saddle Mt." Pencil.	(1868)
113	Full	Complete	"Mts. St. Helens, Adams & Hood from Summit of Saddle Mt. Oregon" Pencil.	(1868)
114	Full	Complete	"Mt. Rainier, St. Helens & Adams from Saddle Mt. Oregon" Pencil.	(1868)
114a*	Full	Complete	"Chinook Canoe & Indians — Oregon" colored watercolor. Exhibited	(1868)
115	Full	Complete	"Youngs river falls — Aug. 10th, 1868 — Oregon". Pencil. 3 men around campfire.	1868
116	Full	Complete	"Surf & waves". Pencil study.	(1868)
117	Full	Complete	"Moores Creek" Pencil	(1868)
118-119	2 pgs.	Complete	"Tillamook Head from the north, Oregon" Pencil.	(1868)
120-121	2 pgs.	Incomplete	"View from beach on Clatsop Plains looking towards Tillamook Head-Oregon" Pencil.	( )
122-123	2 pgs.	Incomplete	"Clatsop Plains, Oregon. looking south" Pencil.	( )
124-25	2 pgs.	Complete	"Roadstead of Santa Barbara looking south. Cal." Pencil.	( )
126-27	2 pgs.	Complete	"Roadstead of Santa Barbara looking south. Cal." Pencil.	( )
128-29	2 pgs.	Complete	"View looking up the Valley of Santa Barbara, Cal." Pencil.	( )
130	Full	Complete	"Landing at El Coxo. Cal." Pencil.	( )
131-32	2 pgs.	Complete	Untitled. (Pt. Bonita) Pencil.	( )
133-34	2 pgs.	Complete	Untitled. Pencil drawing.	( )
135	Full	Incomplete	Untitled drawing. Pencil.	( )
137-38*	2 pgs.	Complete	Untitled. (Santa Barbara Mission)	( )
139-40	2 pgs.	Complete	Untitled drawing. Pencil.	( )
141-42	2 pgs.	Complete	Untitled drawing. Pencil.	( )
143*	Full	Complete	Untitled drawing. Pencil. (Fort Canby)	( )
144	1/3	Complete	Untitled. Watercolor, colored. Sailing vessel.	( )

Page	Portion of page	Complete or Incomplete	Title	Year
145	Full	Complete	Study of 2 barges. colored watercolor.	( )
146	Full	Complete	Untitled. Study of man. (Possibly George Davidson)	( )
150	Full	Complete	Untitled. Pencil drawing.	( )
151	Full	Complete	Untitled. Pencil drawing.	( )
152	Full	Complete	Untitled drawing. Pencil.	( )
153	Full	Complete	Untitled drawing. Crayon.	( )
154	Full	Complete	Untitled. Ink and bl. & wh. wash.	( )
156	Full	Complete	Untitled. (California Mission) Pencil.	( )
157	Full	Complete	Untitled. (California Mission) Pencil.	( )
158	Full	Complete	Untitled. (Duck hunting) Pencil.	( )
159	3/4	Complete	Untitled. (Similar to "Whipping the Trask") Pencil.	( )

Sketchbook #4

Page	Portion of page	Complete or Incomplete	Title	Year
167	Full	Complete	"Upper Gold Bluffs. Cal. Aug. 8th, 1877" Black and white watercolor.	1877
168	Full	Complete	Untitled. (Columbia River near Crown Point) Pencil.	(1877)
169	Full	Complete	"Upper Gold Bluffs. Cal. Aug. 8th, 1877" Black and white water color.	1877

Page	Portion of page	Complete or Incomplete	Title	Year
170	Full	Complete	Untitled. (Oregon Coast) Black and white watercolor.	( )
171	Full	Complete	Untitled. (Oregon Coast) Pencil.	( )
172	Full	Complete	Untitled. Pencil.	( )
173 a.	1/2	Complete	Untitled. Colored watercolor studies.	( )
b.	1/2	Complete	Untitled. Colored watercolor studies.	( )
174	Full	Incomplete	Untitled. Colored watercolor drawing.	( )
175	1/3	Incomplete	Fragmentary	( )
176-77	2 pg.	Incomplete	Untitled. Black & white wash.	( )
178	Full	Incomplete	"Maxwells Landing. Aug. 6, 1904. CR" Black & white wash, pen & ink added.	(1904)
179	Full	Incomplete	Untitled. (Mt. Hood?) colored watercolor.	(1904)
180	Full	Incomplete	Titled but illegible. colored watercolor.	(1904)
181	Full	Complete	"Near Collins Springs. Oct. 1904" Pencil.	1904
182	Full	Complete	Study of rocks. Pencil.	(1904)
183	Full	Complete	Study of Girl Knitting. Pencil.	( )
192	Full	Complete	"Almota from below looking up. May 3, 1880" (a landing on Snake River). Pencil.	1880
194	1/2	Complete	Untitled. (Rains Block house — Columbia River). Pencil.	(1890)

Page	Portion of page	Complete or Incomplete	Title	Year
195	Full	Complete	"Looking down from Almota — Snake River. May 1, 1880" Pencil.	1880
196	Full	Complete	"View from Celilo. Looking down. May 5, 1880" Pencil.	1880
197	Full	Incomplete	Untitled. Pencil.	( )
198-99	2 pg.	Complete	Untitled. Pencil.	( )
200	Full	Complete	Untitled. (Indian camp upper Columbia) Pencil.	( )
201	Full	Complete	Untitled. (Upper Columbia)	( )
202	Full	Incomplete	Untitled. Pen & ink.	( )
203-4	Full	Incomplete	Fragments.	( )
205-6	Full	Incomplete	Studies	( )
207 a	1/2	Incomplete	Untitled. (Officers row-Vancouver Barracks) Pencil.	(1880)
b	1/2	Complete	"Near Wallula — April 29, 1880" Pencil.	1880
208-9		Complete	Studies	
210	Full	Complete	Untitled. (Vancouver Barracks). Pencil.	(1880)

Sketchbook #5

Page	Portion of page	Complete or Incomplete	Title	Year
211-247	Full	Complete	Floral drawings. Mendocino County, Del Norte County, Klamath River, Blue Mountain, Ogn.	( )
242*	Full	Complete	Untitled. (Surveyors' camp). Black and White watercolor.	( )

Sketchbook #6

In some of the sketchbooks erasures of dates are apparent. In this sketchbook covering an Alaskan trip which is otherwise undocumented, it is critical. Probably the daughters Neely and Gertrude are the culprits. Their portrait sketches have been covered with paper and then this was partially torn out.

From the use of raking rays of light and by examination in ultra violet light, in several instances the partially erased date of 1884 is disclosed. In five instances, the eradicated dates have been penciled in and the paper pasted over the girls' portraits has been removed.

The above circumstance explains how Rockwell's illustration could have been used in Frederick Schwatka's *Along Alaska's Great River,* published in 1885. Until the above discovery, Rockwell's 1884 trip was not known.

Page	Portion of page	Complete or Incomplete	Title	Year
248	Full	Complete	"North Head and Cape Disappointment" Pencil and black and white wash.	(1884)
249	Full	Complete	Untitled. (Bakers Bay). Pen and black and white wash.	(1884)
250	Full	Complete	Untitled. Pencil and black & white wash.	(1884)
251	Full	Complete	"New Tacoma" (Loading docks). Pencil.	(1884)
252	Full	Complete	Untitled. (Mt. St. Helens). Pencil.	(1884)
253	Full	Complete	"Old Tacoma, March 20, 1884". Pencil and black & white wash.	1884
254	Full	Complete	"New Dungeness. The Olympic Range. April 9th, 1884 — a fair day". Pencil.	1884

Page	Portion of page	Complete or Incomplete	Title	Year
255	Full	Complete	"Near Bachelor's Island. Columbia River". Signed "C.R." Pencil and black & white wash.	(1884)
256	Full	Complete	"Mt. Baker from Port Townsend — a fine day" Pencil and black & white wash.	(1884)
257	1/2	Incomplete	Untitled. (Tree and field). Pencil.	
258	Full	Complete	"Ship 'Benmore' San Francisco, February 25, 1888". Signed "Cleveland Rockwell" Pencil and black and white wash.	1888
258 a	Full	Incomplete	Untitled (Small steam vessel). Pencil.	( )
258 b	Full	Details	"Whaler. San Francisco. Foggy & calm" Pencil and some black & white wash.	( )
259	Full	Complete	"The Cascade Mts. & wharf at Port Townsend — April 1884. A beautiful fair day". Pencil	1884
260	Full	Complete	"Willamette River, Ogn. Dec. 11, '83" (Two sailing ships at anchor). Pen sketch.	1883
261	Full	Complete	"Olympic Range from Port Townsend. April 1884 — a fair day". Pencil and black & white wash.	1884
262	Full	Complete	"Olympic Range from Victoria outer harbor April — 1884 a.m. a fine day". Pencil and black & white wash.	1884
263	Full	Complete	"Departure Bay, Vancouver I. (Island), B.C.". Pen and black & white wash.	(1884)

Page	Portion of page	Complete or Incomplete	Title	Year
264	Full	Complete	"Hie-pish Narrow. Grenville passage. Sansero Reach looking south. Morning." Pencil & black & white wash.	(1884)
265	Full	Complete	"Grenville passage looking North, sunrise". Pencil and black and white wash	(1884)
266	Full	Complete	"Grenville passage looking north. Cool, clear. Fraser's reach". Pencil and black and white wash.	(1884)
267	Full	Complete	"Frasers reach between Work I. & Pt. King canal". Pencil and black & white wash.	(1884)
268	Full	Complete	"McKays reach. Trevitt Pt. & Pilot Pt. looking down North East". Pencil and black & white wash.	(1884)
269	Full	Complete	"Grenville Channel. looking down". Pencil and black & white wash.	(1884)
270	Full	Complete	"Ne-ah Bay — off Duke of Clarence Sound Saturday 1884". Pencil and black and white wash.	1884
271	Full	Complete	"Caasan or Carlin Bay. Prince of Wales Island May 1st, 1884. looking West. Mod. Calm". Pencil and black & white wash.	1884
272	Full	Complete	"Caasan Beach looking toward Prince of Wales I., Alaska". Pencil and black and white wash.	(1884)

Page	Portion of page	Complete or Incomplete	Title	Year
273	Full	Complete	"Fort Wrangel harbor. Sitka". Pencil and black and white wash.	(1884)
274*	Full	Complete	"Street in Fort Wrangel, Alaska". Pencil and black & white wash.	(1884)
275	Full	Complete	"Fort Wrangel from the distance". Pencil	(1884)
276	Full	Complete	"Wrangel narrows, Alaska. Sunday". Pencil and black & white wash.	(1884)
277	Full	Complete	"Wrangell [sic] Narrows. Alaska. Sunday May." Signed "Cleveland Rockwell 1884". Pencil and black & white wash.	1884
278	Full	Complete	"The Devils Thumb from Entrance to Prince Frederick Sound. Wrangel narrows North end. Clear. Cool. sun at my back." Pencil and black & white wash.	(1884)
279	Full	Complete	"From near Harrisburg 1884". Pencil and black & white wash.	1884
280	Full	Complete	"The Davidson glacier. Chilcat inlet Alaska front view". Pencil and black and white wash.	(1884)
281	Full	Complete	"View on Chilcat inlet opposite Pyramid Harbor. A fair and windy day." Pencil and black and white wash.	(1884)
282	Full	Complete	"Pyramid harbor. Chilcat inlet, Alaska. Tuesday May 13, 1884". Pencil and black & white wash.	1884

Page	Portion of page	Complete or Incomplete	Title	Year
283*	Full	Complete	"The Davidson Glacier. Chilcat Inlet, Alaska. 6 miles wide, 150 long". Pencil and black and white wash.	(1884)
284	Full	Complete	"The Davidson Glacier Chilcat Inlet, Alaska 84". Pen, pencil and black and white wash.	1884
285	1/2	Incomplete	Untitled.	
285	Full	Complete	"Mouth of Endicott river. Chatham Straits". Pencil and black & white wash.	(1884)
287	Full	Complete	"Eagle glacier. Lynn Canal". Pencil and black & white wash.	(1884)
288	Full	Incomplete	Untitled.	(1884)
289	Full	Incomplete	"Olga Bay, Whitestone narrows and pivot Straits". Pencil and black & white wash.	(1884)
290	Full	Complete	Untitled. (Same location as previous sketch). Pencil and black & white wash.	(1884)
291	Full	Complete	"Mt. Verstova from Whitestone narrows Alaska". Pencil and black & white wash.	(1884)
292	Full	Complete	"Seacoast below Sitka harbor, Alaska". Pencil and black and white wash.	(1884)
293	Full	Complete	Untitled. Pencil and black & white wash.	(1884)
294*	Full	Complete	"Adams, Mt. Edgcombe. Sitka Harbor — Alaska". Pencil and black & white wash.	(1884)

Page	Portion of page	Complete or Incomplete	Title	Year
295	Full	Complete	"Murders [sic] Cove. Admiralty island. Alaska." Pencil and black & white wash.	(1884)
296	Full	Complete	"Murderers Cove. Admiralty I. Baronoff Is. in the distance. Friday, April 18, 1884". Pencil and black & white wash.	1884
297	Full	Complete	Untitled. (Glacier). Pencil and black and white wash.	(1884)
298	Full	Complete	"Suchoi Channel near Prince Frederick Sound" Pencil and black & white wash.	(1884)
299	Full	Complete	Untitled. Pencil and black & white wash.	(1884)
300	Full	Complete	"Red Bay. Prince of Wales I." Pencil and black & white wash.	(1884)
301	Full	Complete	"Mt. Stevens from the Weynton [?] passage" Pencil and black & white wash.	(1884)
302	1/2	Complete	"High Glacier on Chilcat inlet – Near Davidson glacier. April 15, 1884". Pencil and black & white wash.	1884
303	1/2	Incomplete	Untitled (Fishing nets drying). Pencil and partial black & white wash.	(1884)
	1/2	Complete	Untitled. (Details of row boat). Pencil.	(1884)
304	1/2	Complete	"Glacier – east side of Prince Frederick sound looking north. Patterson glacier." Pencil sketch.	(1884)
	1/2	Incomplete	"Prince Frederick Sound, Alaska. Looking east. Luchoi channel". Pencil and partial black and white wash.	(1884)
305*	Full	Sketches	In pencil. (teams of horses, details of masts and rigging — pencil and black and white wash of two girl heads (N(eely) and G(ertrude). These were obscured with paper pasted as over the third figure.	(1884)
306	Full	Incomplete	"Pt. between Whale Passage and Douglas Inlet." Pencil and incomplete black & white wash.	(1884)
307	Full	Incomplete	"Entrance to Douglas Inlet opposite Whale passage". Pencil and incomplete black and white wash.	(1884)
308	Full	Incomplete	"Scarborough Head, Columbia River, fair day" Pencil.	(1884)

Sketchbook #7

Page	Portion of page	Complete or Incomplete	Title	Year
309	Full	Complete	"Old barn in Pacific Valley" signed "Cleveland Rockwell, May 18, 1890". Pencil.	1890
310	1/2	Complete	"Camp on Summit of Mt. above Pacific Valley" signed "C.R. May 26th, 1890." Pen and ink.	1890
	1/2	Complete	"Camp on Summit of Mt. above Pacific Valley" signed "May 26th, 1890" (both show gnarled trees) Pen and Ink.	1890
311	1/2	Complete	"Summit of Mt. – Camp above Pacific Valley" signed "C.R. May 26th, 1890" Pen and Ink.	1890

Page	Portion of page	Complete or Incomplete	Title	Year
	1/2	Complete	"Summit of Mt. — Camp above Pacific Valley" signed "C.R. May 26th, 1890." Pen and Ink. (both are gnarled trees and rocks)	1890
312	Full	Complete	"Coast Range above Pacific Valley" dated "May 26th, 1890"	1890
313	1/2	Incomplete	Untitled. (A survey camp). Pencil and partly inked.	(1890)
	1/2	Incomplete	Untitled. (Study of rocks) Pencil.	(1890)
314	Full	Complete	Untitled. (California coast from high above.) Pencil.	(1890)
315	Full	Complete	"Pacific Valley from Camp" signed "C.R." Pencil.	(1890)
316	Full	Incomplete	Untitled. (Study of rocks and trees) Pencil.	(1890)
317	Full	Complete	"On the Columbia opposite Vancouver" signed "Cl.S.R." Pencil.	(1890)
318	Full	Incomplete	"Mt. Hood from the Garrison, Vancouver" Signed "Cleveland Rockwell 1890". Pencil and incomplete wash.	1890
319	Full	Complete	Untitled. (Mt. Hood from near Government Island) signed "Cleveland Rockwell 1891" Black and white wash.	1891
320	Full	Complete	Untitled. (Mt. Hood from Columbia River near Washougal) Pencil and black and white wash.	(1891)
321	Full	Complete	"Harrison Lake, B.C." signed "Cleveland Rockwell, 1892". Colored watercolor.	1892
322	Full	Complete	Untitled. (Another view of Harrison Lake) Colored watercolor.	(1892)
323	Full	Complete	"Harrison Hot Springs, July 1892" Colored watercolor.	1892
324	Full	Complete	"China town at Harrison Springs" signed "Cleveland Rockwell, 1892". Colored watercolor.	1892
325	Full	Complete	Untitled. (Another view of Harrison Lake) signed "Cleveland Rockwell, 1892". Colored watercolor.	1892
326	Full	Complete	Untitled. (Farm with hop drying sheds in British Columbia). Signed "Cleveland Rockwell, 1892". Colored watercolor.	1892
327	Full	Complete	Untitled. Harrison Lake, British Columbia, passenger launch at dock). Pencil.	(1892)
328	Full	Complete	"Jolon, Cal. 1890". Pencil.	1890
329	Full	Complete	"Mansfield Cove. Pacific Valley" "May 16, 1890". Pencil.	1890
330	Full	Complete	"Hotel Banff and Bow River". Colored watercolor.	(1892)
331	Full	Complete	"Mt. Sir Donald and the Illiciliwack Creek". Pencil.	(1892)
332	Full	Complete	Untitled. (Beach on Oregon Coast — 3 females sitting on log) signed "Cleveland Rockwell, 1892" colored watercolor.	1892

Page	Portion of page	Complete or Incomplete	Title	Year
333	Full	Complete	Untitled (Agate Beach, Oregon with Yaquina Head Lighthouse) signed "Cleveland Rockwell, 1892". Colored watercolor.	1892
334	Full	Incomplete	Untitled. Pencil.	(1892)
335 & 36	2 page	Complete	Untitled. (beach scene) colored watercolor.	(1892)
337	Full	Complete	Untitled. (Home and commercial building) Pencil.	(1892)
338	Full	Complete	Untitled. (Wooden foot bridge across a stream). Signed "Cleveland Rockwell 1892" Colored watercolor.	1892
339	Full	Complete	Untitled. (Steps and walk from bluff down to beach). Signed "Cleveland Rockwell, 1892". Colored watercolor.	1892
340	Full	Incomplete	Untitled. (Portrait of a man) Pencil with some colored wash.	(1892)
341	Full	Incomplete	Untitled. (Portrait of a man) Pencil with some colored wash.	(1892)
342	Full	Incomplete	Untitled. (Portrait of a woman). Pencil.	(1892)
343	Full	Complete	Untitled. (portrait of a woman). Pencil.	(1892)
344	Full	Complete	Untitled. (Portrait of a woman). Pencil.	(1892)
345	Full	Complete	Untitled. (Unidentified portrait of a young male). Pencil.	(1892)

Page	Portion of page	Complete or Incomplete	Title	Year
346	Full	Complete	Untitled. (Unidentified portrait of a young female). Pencil and colored wash.	(1892)
347	Full	Complete	Untitled. (Unidentified portrait of a young man — same as 345?) Pencil.	(1892)
348	Full	Incomplete	Untitled. (Unidentified portrait of a young woman). Pencil and colored wash is partially applied.	(1892)
349	Full	Complete	Untitled. (Unidentified portrait of middle aged male). Pencil.	(1892)
350	Full	Complete	Untitled. (Unidentified portrait of middle aged male, apparently same as 349). Pencil with flesh tones added.	(1892)
351	Full	Complete	Untitled. (A head, waist length and full length portrait, all three of same adolescent male). Pencil, flesh tones added.	(1892)
352	Full	Complete	Untitled. (Unidentified male, young). Pencil with flesh tones added.	(1892)
353	Full	Complete	Untitled. (Unidentified female, undetermined age). Pencil.	(1892)
354	Full	Complete	"Yaquina. 1892" signed "Cleveland Rockwell" Pencil and colored watercolor.	1892
356	Full	Complete	Untitled. (Probably Yaquina) Signed "Cleveland Rockwell". Pencil and colored wash. "1892"	1892

Page	Portion of page	Complete or Incomplete	Title	Year
357	Full	Complete	Untitled. (Unidentified house). Pencil.	(1892)
358	Full	Complete	Untitled. (Unidentified, probably Yaquina) Signed "Cleveland Rockwell. 1892". Colored Watercolor.	1892
359	Full	Complete	"Jim Crow and Tongue Point". Signed "C.R. April 24, 1889". Pencil.	1889
360	Full	Complete?	Untitled. (Unidentified scene). Pencil.	( )
361	Full	Complete	"Kicking Horse pass and Mt. Stephens" (Banff National Park) Pencil	(1892)
362	Full	Complete	"Mount Sir Donald" (shows railroad track) Pencil.	(1892)

Page	Portion of page	Complete or Incomplete	Title	Year
363	Full	Complete	"Great Glacier". Pencil.	(1892)
364	Full	Complete	"The toe of the great Glacier". Pencil.	(1892)
365	Full	Complete	"The Great Glacier". Pencil.	(1892)
366	Full	Complete	"Hermit Range & Rogers Pass". Pencil.	(1892)
367	Full	Complete	"Ross Peak & Glaciers" (Canada). Pencil.	(1892)
368	Full	Complete	Untitled. (Another view of Ross Peak?) Pencil.	(1892)
369	Full	Complete	"Glacier House". Pencil.	(1892)
370	Full	Complete	"Great Glacier". Pencil.	(1892)

PUBLISHED ARTICLES BY ROCKWELL

"Morro Rock." *The West Shore.* Vol. VII. No. 7. July 1881. p 196.
Illustration "Morro Rock."
   Description of the physical geography of the region, the extremely dangerous entrance to the bay and the safety for vessels once they have passed the entrance and are behind the rock.
   Note: Neither illustration nor article are credited to Cleveland Rockwell by *The West Shore,* though he is the obvious author and artist.

Rockwell, Cleveland. "Entrance to the Columbia." *The West Shore.* Vol. XVII. March 28, 1891. p. 207.
   Illustrated by Cleveland Rockwell painting: p. 207 "Entrance to the Columbia River."
   Relates importance of the Columbia River to the Pacific Northwest commerce, the historical background of the river and its tributaries.
   Cleveland Rockwell is not given credit for the article or the painting. The same painting was used in *The West Shore* eight years prior to this issue — Vol. IX. No. 7. July 1883. p. 158. (No article — one painting by Rockwell and other illustrations photographic.)

Rockwell, Cleveland. "Mount Shasta." *The West Shore.* No. 242. January 24, 1891. pp. 59-60-61.
   Illustrated by two Rockwell paintings:
   On the Cover: "Washington — Palisades of the Columbia River, Cape Horn" pp. 59-60 — double fold illustration: "California — Mount Shasta, from Strawberry Valley."
   A description of the topography, climate, beauty, rigors, trail to the summit, summer hotels at the base and derivation of the name "Shasta."
   Cleveland Rockwell is not given credit for the two illustrations or the article.

Rockwell, Cleveland. "The Columbia River." *Harper's New Monthly Magazine.* Vol. 66. No. 391. December 1882. pp. 3-14.
   Illustrations by Rockwell are:
   "Castle Rock"
   "Basaltic Cliffs above Cathlamet, on the Columbia River"
   "Mount Hood and the Columbia River Bottom"
   "Wire-rope Ferry on Snake River"
   "Multnomah Fall" [sic]
   "Highlands of the Columbia"
   "Salmon Fishing on the Columbia"
   "Cape Horn"
   "Cape Disappointment and Baker's Bay"
   A scenic description of Rockwell's boat trip up the Upper Columbia and Snake rivers and down the lower Columbia ending at Cape Hancock.

Rockwell, Capt. Cleveland, Late of U.S. Coast and Geodetic Survey. "Physical Characteristics of the Northwest." *The Pacific Monthly.* Vol. I. No. I. October 1898. pp. 3-12.
   No illustrations. A discussion of scenery, climate, soil, as well as mountain peaks, ranges and ocean floors.

Rockwell, Capt. Cleveland. Late of U.S. Coast and Geodetic Survey. "Digging the Gold." *The Pacific Monthly.* Vol. I. No. 3. December 1899. p. 85.
   No paintings. Photographic illustrations. The text concerns modern methods of mining on the Pacific Coast, including Nevada, Montana and Alaska. There is no specific description of mining in the Northwest.

Rockwell, Captain Cleveland. "The Musical Woodpecker of Burnt River." *The Pacific Monthly.* Vol. II. No. 5. September 1899. pp. 211-12.
   No illustrations. An article about the bird and its habitat in "Three Cent Gulch" near Sumpter, Oregon.

Rockwell, Captain Cleveland. "The Grand Coulee." *The Pacific Monthly*. Vol. II. No. 3. July, 1899. pp. 103-108.
Illustrated by two Rockwell paintings:
   p. 102. "A Scene in the Grand Coulee" — watercolor credited to Capt. Cleveland Rockwell.
   p. 105 "Steamboat Rock" — a pen and ink sketch signed by Cleveland Rockwell.
   p. 108. A photographic portrait of Rockwell.
A geological explanation of the Grand Coulee and its plateaus. Rockwell weighs the question as to whether the Coulee bed had ever held the Columbia River and arrives at a negative conclusion.

Rockwell, Cleveland. "A Mediaeval Medallion." *The Pacific Monthly*. Vol. V. No. 6. May 1901. pp. 291-92.
No illustrations. A short Shakespearian-like trilogy. Francisco and Lady Sylvia, young lovers, are betrothed. Francisco gave her a jeweled poignard to protect herself. Francisco later finds the evil Duke Pietro bending over the beautiful Sylvia. She tells her betrothed she has used the poignard to save her honor from the Duke. She dies but not before Francisco has dispatched the Duke with his own dagger.

Rockwell, Captain Cleveland. "The Great Columbia River Basin." *The Pacific Monthly*. Vol. VII. No. 3. March 1902. pp. 97-134. *Special Columbia River Edition*.
Contains largely photographic illustrations.

Three paintings by Captain Rockwell are:
p. 98 "The Mouth of the Columbia River" — oil
p. 101 "Bluffs above Cathlamet, Wash." — watercolor
p. 133 "Looking down the Columbia from near Wallula" — watercolor
In the same issue on p. 140 under heading "Men and Women" is a scant biographical sketch with no significant details and a portrait of "Capt. Cleveland Rockwell."
A description of the Columbia River Basin considering boundaries of its watershed, its resources, beauty and potential for development.

Rockwell, Cleveland. "The Coos Bay Coal Fields.-1." *The Engineering and Mining Journal*. 73: Part I, February 15, 1902. pp. 238-40. Part II, February 22, 1902. pp. 270-71.
A scientific discussion of certain coal fields in Oregon. Illustrated by a map of "Coos Bay Coal Fields, Oregon" and a sketch "Bunkers at Tunnel, Newport Mine, Oregon," both drawn by Rockwell.

Rockwell, Captain Cleveland, formerly of the United States Coast and Geodetic Survey. "The First Columbia River Salmon Ever Caught with a Fly." *The Pacific Monthly*. Vol. X. No. 4. October 1903. pp. 202-203.
No paintings. Photographic illustrations.
A whimsical account by Rockwell of his catching a salmon in the lower Columbia River on a fly.

PUBLISHED REFERENCES ABOUT ROCKWELL

Schwatka, Frederick, *Along Alaska's Great River.* New York. Cassell & Co., Ltd.. 1885. 345 pp. Illustrated. Folding map.
p 28. "Sitka, Alaska"
"From a painting by Captain Cleveland Rockwell in the possession of J. C. Ainsworth, Esq., Oakland, Cal. (with the kind permission of artist and owner)."
The painting of Sitka is distant and the settlement looks smaller then in Frederick Schwatka's *A Summer in Alaska.*
Frederick Schwatka, American born 1849. Graduate of U.S. Military Academy 1871. Admitted to the bar in Nebraska. Received Medical degree at Bellevue Hospital Medical College, New York City. Veteran of at least three Alaskan exploring expeditions. Member several Geological Societies. Author of five books.

The West Shore. Portland, Oregon. Published by L. Samuel. Vol. XI. No. 6. June 1885.
p. 174. "Sitka" signed C. Rockwell. This reproduction has 3 unsigned small paintings overlapping the edges. The entire page is entitled "Alaskan Scenes". These relate to article on Sitka, p. 183, not titled or signed.

History of Portland, Oregon with illustrations and biographical sketches of Prominent Citizens and Pioneers. Edited by Harvey Whitefield Scott. D. Mason & Co. Syracuse, N.Y. 1890. pp. 409, 411, 412.

Harvey Scott was the editor of the *Oregonian* from 1865 to 1910 (except 1870-76 when he was United States Collector of Customs).
The book briefly details the history of banks in Portland up to 1890. Cleveland Rockwell, at that time, served on the board of directors of three Portland banks, The Portland Savings Bank, The Commercial National Bank and The Portland Trust Company.

The West Shore. Vol. XVII. No. 7. March 7, 1891. pp. 158-62. "A Day with Ducks" by George L. Curry.
No illustrations.
The story of duck hunting on the Columbia River. The hunting boats transported 100 or more hunters and their dogs to the duck blinds, the boat leaving around midnight. This was a weekly affair and Rockwell is mentioned on p. 159 as being one of those who has made the largest killings of ducks.

The West Shore. Vol. XVII. April 18, 1891. p. 260. "Encampment of G.A.R."
No illustrations.
Report of a two day encampment of the G.A.R. at Astoria, Oregon. Election and installation of officers was held and Cleveland Rockwell was named on the Council of Administration.

Hines, Rev. Harvey Kimball. *An Illustrated History of the State of Oregon.* Lewis Publishing Company, Chicago. 1893. p. 598.

The Overland Monthly. San Francisco, California. Vol. XXIII. No. 134. Second Series. February 1894.
Article "Up the Columbia in 1857" by Fred M. Stocking. pp. 86-134.
Contains several photographic illustrations, one painting illustration, as follows:
p. 186 "Columbia River Bar" painting by Cleveland Rockwell.
A scenic description by Fred M. Stocking of a 24-hour journey aboard steamer *Columbia* to Portland in 1857. He relates the background of the settlers of Portland and Willamette Valley.
In 1859 Mr. Stocking describes his first trip to The Dalles aboard the steamer *Mountain Buck* with J.C. Ainsworth as Captain and Henry L. Hoyt, Pilot. He relates the history, mythology and business prospects of each stop along the way.
He details the very shallow bar at lower end of Swan Island indicating that it was passable only at high tide.

Schwatka, Frederick. *A Summer in Alaska.* St. Louis, Mo. J. W. Henry. 1894.
"A Popular Account of the Travels of an Alaska Exploring Expedition Along the Great Yukon River from its source to its mouth, in the British North-west Territory and in the Territory of Alaska."
p. 29 "Sitka, Alaska". Painted by Cleveland Rockwell.
This plate is credited to Cleveland Rockwell, according to the index. In being reduced in size and in preparation of the plate, any semblance of Rockwell's technique has disappeared.

A Record of the Republican Party in the State of Oregon. Compiled and Published with the approval of the Republican State Central Committee of 1894-1896, and the Executive Committee of the Republican League of Oregon for 1894-1896. Portland, Oregon: Register Publishing Co. 1896.
Fifth Ward Club of Portland, Joseph N. Dolph, David Dalgleish, M. C. George, W. H. Harris, B. P. Cardwell, Wallace McCamant, Cleveland Rockwell, Russell E. Sewell (R. G. Morrow, Proxy) George A. Steele, J. A. Strowbridge, Tyler Woodward, A. L. Maxwell, A. B. Croasman, A. W. Witherell, Clark Hay, William M. Ladd, John Ring, George E. Watkins, W. C. Noon, Buell Lamberson, E. H. Habighorst. p. 86.

White, Marian A. "Cleveland Rockwell Distinguished Painter of the Pacific Slope. " *Fine Arts Journal.* Vol. XV. No. 12. Chicago. December 1904. pp. 421-25.
Marian A. White, editor of *Fine Arts Journal,* lauds Rockwell's work as an artist. No significant facts or any details of his art training are included.
3 untitled and unsigned pen and ink sketches by Rockwell:
"Davidson Glacier, Alaska" dated 1884 — watercolor
"Mount St. Helens, from Portland Heights" — watercolor
"On the Oregon Coast" — watercolor

Rockwell, Cleveland. "Oregon Scenery." *The Pacific Monthly.* Vol. XV. No. 2. February 1906. p. 161.
No text accompanies the paintings reproduced from watercolors painted by and in the possession of Captain Rockwell, Portland, Oregon.
"A Fair Wind"
"Otter Rock, on the Coast of Oregon, Near Cape Foulweather"
"Fishing Boat on Columbia River Bar"
"Mount St. Helens from Spirit Lake"
"Salmon Fishing Fleet on Columbia River Running Free Before the Wind"
(Currently in the Collection of Dr. and Mrs. Franz Stenzel.)
"Mt. Hood from the head of White River in Eastern Oregon"

Chamberlain, George E., Governor of Oregon. "The National Importance of Oregon's Waterways." *The Pacific Monthly.* Vol. XIX. No. 6. June 1908. p. 659.
Painting by Cleveland Rockwell, "The Columbia River Bar," is used on the top half of the page above the title of the article. Another version of a sailing ship. The illustration is only vaguely related to the article by Oregon's governor.

Gaston, Joseph. *The Centennial History of Oregon 1811-1912.* The S. J. Clarke Publishing Company, Chicago. 1912. Vol. III. pp. 368-69.

Winthrop, Theodore. *The Canoe and the Saddle, or Klalam and Klickatat.* Edited by John H. Williams. Tacoma 1913. Frontispiece by Cleveland Rockwell. (Original painting in Collection of Dr. and Mrs. Franz Stenzel.)

Rasmussen, Louise. *Art and Artists of Oregon 1500-1900.* Unpublished and undated manuscript at Oregon State Library. Salem, Oregon. (1930)
Cleveland Rockwell is listed.

A Catalogue *Art of the Oregon Territory.* Paintings from the Collection of Dr. and Mrs. Franz Stenzel, Oregon Centennial Festival of Art. Museum of Art, University of Oregon, Eugene, Oregon. 1959.
A brief biographical sketch of Cleveland Rockwell and a description of the paintings in the exhibition.

"Mt. St. Helens from the Columbia River"
"Salmon Fishing Grounds — Mouth of the Columbia"
"Haystack Rock"
"Beach near Cape Falcon"
"Fishermen Driven Ashore before a Storm (Below the Mouth of the Columbia)"
"Beach and Tillamook Head"

Early Days in the Northwest. Prints — Paintings. Drawings by James G. Swan. From the Collection of Dr. and Mrs. Franz Stenzel. September 23 — October 25, 1959. Portland Art Museum. Portland, Oregon.
A short account of Cleveland Rockwell's life and an explanation of the paintings exhibited.
p. 20 "Salmon Fishing Grounds — Mouth of the Columbia"
p. 21 "Beach near Cape Falcon"
p. 21 "Fishermen Driven Ashore before a Storm (Below the Mouth of the Columbia)"
p. 26. illustrated: "Fishermen Driven Ashore before a Storm (Below the Mouth of the Columbia)"

The Artist in the American West 1800-1900. October 8 through November 22, 1961. Fine Arts Museum of New Mexico. A unit of the Museum of New Mexico. Santa Fe, New Mexico. 1961.
The catalogue contains a biographical summary of Cleveland Rockwell and lists the Rockwell painting exhibited:
No. 69 Fishermen Driven Ashore before a Storm (Below the Mouth of the Columbia). Collection of Dr. and Mrs. Franz Stenzel.

Northwest History in Art 1778-1963. Washington State Historical Society, Tacoma. Pacific Northwest Historical Pamphlet No. 3. Published April, 1963.
A concise review of Rockwell's career, a notation of two paintings exhibited and an illustration of one of the two paintings.
No. 43 — "Salmon Fishing Grounds — Mouth of the Columbia." (illustrated) Collection of Dr. and Mrs. Franz Stenzel, Portland, Oregon.
No. 44 — "Scene on the Columbia River" (Sailboat and Stern-

wheeler passing Coffin Rock.) Mr. and Mrs. Lloyd O. Graves, Seattle.

An Art Perspective of the Historic Pacific Northwest. From the Collection of Dr. and Mrs. Franz R. Stenzel, Portland, Oregon. Exhibited at Montana Historical Society, August, 1963 and Eastern Washington State Historical Society, September 1963.
Biographical notes on Cleveland Rockwell, description and illustration of each of the five paintings exhibited.
p. 20 — No. 45. "Salmon Fishing Grounds — Mouth of the Columbia"
p. 20 — No. 46. "Salmon Canneries, One Floating and One on Land"
p. 20 — No. 47. "Columbia River, East of Portland, showing Moffitt's Landing and Mt. Hood"
p. 20 — No. 48. "Beach and Tillamook Head"
p. 21 — No. 44. "Crossing the Columbia Bar"

The Morning Oregonian, Friday February 14, 1936. "Files of Old Days — 50 Years Ago — February 14" (1886).
"Portland Art club holds picture exhibit showing 14 subjects, the artists being C. Rockwell, C. L. Smith, John Gill, A. Burr, C. C. Maring, G. T. Brown, H. Epting, J. Norman Biles, Clyde Cook, J. E. Stuart, E. W. Moore, Lou Goldsmith, Edward Espey and James Pickett."

Truchot, Theresa, "Cleveland Rockwell, Marine Artist". *Junior Historical Journal.* Vol. V. No. 3. January 1945. pp. 106-107.
A two-page article illustated by the writer with a pencil portrait of Rockwell taken from a photograph, and reproducing "Fishermen coming in before a Storm," a Rockwell painting.
(Referred to in *Oregon Historical Quarterly,* 46:80.)

Burrell, O. K. *Gold in the Woodpile* an Informal History of Banking in Oregon. (Eugene, Oregon: University of Oregon, 1967.)
For Cleveland Rockwell's involvement in the 1893 Portland bank closings, see "Trouble in July." pp. 129-67.

INDEX

Common names —	— Indian names (Tillamook language)
Cape Meares	Nascowitzen.
Netarts Bay	Nataats
Cape Lookout	Nasitseltz
Sand lake	Nawoka
Haystack rock	Tadalsallo
Nestucca Bay	Nestuck
Slab Creek	Nascowen
Cascade Head	Nastucco
Salmon river	Nachesne
Devils lake	Na-ahso
Siletz Bay	Nachicolcho

U.S Coast and Geodetic Survey

F.M.Thorn, Superintendent

Sketch.

showing progress of the Topographical Reconnaissance

of the

Coast of Oregon.

from

Yaquina Head to Tillamook Bay

by

Cleveland Rockwell, Assistant

1887.

Scale $\frac{1}{200.000}$

Statute miles

Cleveland Rockwell

Assistant